LONDON MIDLAND & SCOTTISH

A Railway in Retrospect

ENGINES AT PERTH GENERAL, SEPTEMBER 1926

Left to right: Highland Ben, Fowler compound, Caledonian Dunalastair IV

Painting by the author, by courtesy of the Locomotive and Allied Manufacturers Association

LONDON MIDLAND & SCOTTISH

A Railway in Retrospect

HAMILTON ELLIS AIMechE FRSA

LONDON

IAN ALLAN

First published 1970

SBN 7110 0048 4

£3·00

5058610
385.'0941

Published by Ian Allan Ltd, Shepperton, Surrey and printed in the United Kingdom by The Press at Coombelands Ltd, Addlestone, Weybridge, Surrey

Contents

	Introduction	*page*	7
1	Constituents and Subsidiaries		9
2	The New Company		31
3	Mechanical Development to 1930		57
4	The Viziership of Ernest Lemon		96
5	Stanier's Time		132
6	The Vortex, 1939-1945		169
7	Götterdämmerung		193

APPENDICES

A	The Irish Enclave	205
B	Locomotive Shed Indications	213
C	Summary of Named Stanier Locomotives	216
	Index	220

Introduction

To WRITE a history of a great undertaking, less than a quarter-century after it has ceased to exist as a company, is not impossible, but it is rash. I was required to do so, and even started with that in mind. But now it is better to call the result a *retrospect*. History ought to be written at long range, to be at once impartial and accurate. The obituaries of kings, presidents, general-party-secretaries and such other potentates are often biased, even sycophantic; unless, on the other hand, they are savagely abusive owing to some revolution that must be immediately glorified.

Throughout, I have most punctiliously left half-a-century's Minutes alone. Mind you, I have dodged them once or twice! Without hearing Sir John Elliot talk of the line he inherited as Chief Regional Officer (and of many things before that), without the inestimable help of Major R. M. L. Lemon who was sired by that alarming Vice-President, Sir Ernest; without hearing John Shearman talk about the earlier rivalries of road and railway; without hearing T. W. Royle gently yarning after a good dinner (Sir Hugh Jackson was host); some of what one considers the more important parts of the following book had never been written. Much of the rest of my account had been written already, in other ways. For instance, if one would know what really went-on in LMS works and drawing offices during the 'thirties and 'forties, E. S. Cox's *Locomotive Panorama* contains the lot, or at any rate as much as is likely to be published. Presently one can make only a summary of mechanical history. That is as much as I have pretended to do in this work, which so bravely began as an intended history, but at best has ended as a series of essays. Nor can I pretend that it is without prejudice. There are some parties in high places who seem to the author simply obnoxious; admirable men, too! As admirable as Sir Richard Moon, Mr. Francis Webb – or for that matter Bishop (*Soapy Sam*) Wilberforce, Oliver Cromwell, and some others.

So, then, let it be a retrospect, and from outside at that. Perhaps better so! My generation was that which saw the beginning and the end of the four British main-line railway companies constituted under the Railways Act, 1921. I knew many of their constituents, quite intelligently, I hope, before 1923; I watched the gradual welding of old practices and old loyalties into new ones. How they worked out, I have tried to show. One can surmise, but surmise is not the stuff that history is made of. That may be spoken some day. In the meantime I have endeavoured to show something of what that remarkable institution, the LMS, was like to those who looked across its frontier, and, at one time and another, were its customers.

C.H.E.

Edinburgh Princes Street, Hogmanay 1947

CHAPTER ONE

Constituents and Subsidiaries

IF THE earnest student of social, technical and economic history were suddenly to be set down at Euston Station, London, in the middle of 1923, to make a journey by the London Midland & Scottish Railway to anywhere from Watford and points south to Georgemas Junction and points north, he would be surrounded by a scene almost exactly the same as he might have beheld ten years before, in 1913. No matter that in that decade there had been one of the most gory and hazardous turning-points in history! The scene would be practically the same. There would be that ancient, interesting, and most inconvenient railway station which Queen Victoria had known. Timetables, handbills and advertisements would inform him of a corporation known as the London Midland & Scottish Railway Company, already wearing easily the initials LMS, but the station, and the trains within it, would be London & North Western, and would bear the initials thereof. At the head of the supposed Scotch Express would be a Prince of Wales, or a Claughton, or possibly both if the train were nearly twice as heavy as a corresponding Midland one also with two engines. The uniformed staff would have looked the same. The male passengers would have looked the same, in spite of an intermediate baptism of blood, mud and other horrors. The female passengers would have looked the same except that skirts were flared instead of hobbled and hats had somewhat altered. The language was the same except for such odd expressions as war spawns. LMS? It was all still very London & North Western, from the air of shabby pride about the station to the white-panelled carriages and the din of safety-valves blowing off. And on that same day, it would all be very Midland over at St. Pancras, and very Caledonian at Glasgow Central, and very Highland at Inverness. In the 'twenties, a line did not change its face in a day, as lines were fated to do in the 'sixties by being closed overnight.

Still, on that hypothetical day in 1923, the LMS was there. It had come into being on January 1, of that year, and very shortly would be under the influence, and impending Chair of that wily old lawyer Sir William Guy Granet, sometime Dictator of the Midland. To be sure, amalgamation was not absolutely complete with the Caledonian and the North Stafford; these things took time. On the other hand, the amalgamation of the old London & North Western with the old Lancashire & Yorkshire had already taken place on January 1, 1922. That had been an easy conclusion;

the LNWR and the L&Y had long worked together and agreed very well on the whole. As an accomplished fact, the London Midland & Scottish Railway faced the world as the largest joint-stock company for the operation of land transport in that world.

Now that last statement might, and even in the 1920s did, call forth cries of protest. Certainly, in 1923, the new undertaking possessed the largest privately-owned railway system in Europe. By route, it was 780 miles longer than the Paris, Lyons and Mediterranean, then the largest company-owned railway in Continental Europe, for the Deutsche Reichs-bahn Gesellschaft, the German State Railway Company, was not yet formed. But the LMS was less extensive, geographically and by route mileage, than several railways in the United States, themselves larger than the New York Central, which styled itself for years The Standard Railroad of the World (a sort of American Premier-Linemanship!). The LMS was the world's largest railway company, in terms of paid-up capital. Its traffic and equipment exceeded those of any other company-owned railway, indeed of any railway under a single authority, for the Russian lines at that time were in a bad way, though officially under a single authority called, with unintended irony, the People's Commissariat of Ways and Communications.

Enough, anyway, of foreign instances! Origins of the London Midland & Scottish Railway, as of its contemporary companies from 1923 to 1947, were in Parliamentary legislation, as in the Railways Act, 1921. In the days when railway companies had a monopoly of heavy land transport throughout the country, some of them were rather rich, and these were not necessarily giants. The Isle of Man Railway could describe its own financial situation as *very satisfactory*. But others, working important lines, were poor, living on a long but tenuous shoestring. Some tottered on the brink of bankruptcy, and even fell over, as the London, Chatham and Dover had done right back in mid-Victorian years. The war years, 1914–1918, demonstrated many new things apart from their more bloody paradoxes. They resulted in a mighty advance of the heavy motor. They demonstrated the possibilities of long-distance flight, though as yet this was not of much commercial significance. Gustav Hamel had flown the first official air-mail from Hendon to Windsor in 1911; in 1919 one could fly to Paris for fifteen guineas, but these things were still regarded as *larks*, and as was noted in 1919 about the Paris flights (Handley-Page or de Havilland): "The journey cannot be guaranteed every day, owing to the bad climate, and at present engine failure cannot be entirely eliminated and forced landings and delay may occur." But the challengers were there, and growing in strength. Already the tatlers were saying that railways were finished. The author can remember being told that the five years 1925–1930 would see the end of them, and when, in 1923, Barbot flew the

Channel on a 15hp engine, it occurred to some of the more lunatic commentators that the motor car was finished too.

Reverting to serious history; wartime Government control of British railways, far more than the well-established examples of countries like Belgium and Italy, had shown Government that there were indeed desirable possibilities in the central authority and consolidated economy of railways, even though the country did not go as far as universal State ownership with, at most, divisional operation.

Great Britain's first Minister of Transport, Sir Eric Geddes, was an old North Eastern man, and those who liked him least darkly suggested that the whole idea behind the obligatory amalgamation of the country's railways into grouped companies had sprung from old North Eastern ambitions to control all the East Coast traffic between the Metropolis, the North East, and Scotland, with some of the North West thrown in too. Perhaps a myth? Perhaps history? Be it remembered that some myths are more probably true than some accepted history. Today, on purely scientific evidence, Noah's flood, or something like it, seems to be well supported, while the Wicked Uncle's murder of the Princes in the Tower is held in question.

On both the Left and the Right side of politics, there was strong favour for this grouping of railways. To Radical thought, this was a real step towards State ownership. In the Conservative mind, it was pure business, a very reasonable consolidation. The only apparent problem was, how to carry it out, and a politician, of whatever colour, often had but the foggiest notion. Harsh things were often said about Sir Eric Geddes, that his was a case of Administrative Megalomania with a lovely new big Ministry, a very airship among Government Departments, to inflate. But Geddes was at least a railwayman; he knew a great deal about his portfolio, not by cramming but by experience. There had been the question of how many groups to be formed. One plan envisaged relatively little amalgamation on a grand scale. Another purposed a single railway company to run all lines north of the Border, which may have been approved of for reasons of Scottish national prestige but, even then, might have meant a very shaky financial edifice, not at all to the liking of a people famous for the shrewd transaction of business. As we know, the final decision was for four groups, each belonging to amalgamations of constituent companies and absorption of smaller, subsidiary companies. The railways were still in a somewhat run-down state as a result of more than four years of war. Some were better, some worse, but they were in a much better state altogether than those of many foreign countries. The end of wartime Government control came on August 15, 1921. Four days later, on August 19, the Railways Act received the Royal Assent. On December 20, amalgamation of the old allies, the London & North Western and the

Lancashire & Yorkshire Railway, was confirmed. As remarked, it took effect on January 1, 1922, the combined undertaking having the title of the former company.

During that following year of 1922, the ultimate fusion of what had been called the "North Western, Midland, and West Scottish Group" was being carefully prepared, though there were some bumps, as there were bound to be. The suggestion of "London Midland & Northern Railway" for a title implied, to the justifiably sensitive Scots, that Scotland was a province somewhere in the North of England, and was, besides, most clumsy as a name. "London Midland & Scottish", though it were a mouthful, and had none of the sonority of "Midland", "Caledonian" or even plain "North Western", was accurately descriptive, and its abbreviation "LMS" was immediately and quite happily accepted. Obstacles less apparent to the public, but none the less formidable in their way, were conflicting loyalties.

Directors, officers and all other grades, might wrangle, having rows and hates and strikes within their midst, but in every railway there was what could only be called a regimental feeling, which even the bitterest industrial dispute could not entirely break. Thirty years before, in the notorious *Scotch Strike*, the Highland Railway had successfully kept its men at work while the Caledonian men were out and even scuffling with evicting officers, constabulary and soldiers, not to mention breaking all the glass in Motherwell Station. But that the London & North Western should become one with the Midland was obnoxious to many people under both companies, who in extreme cases hated each other as cordially as did rival nations remembering a recent war between them. Further, the constituent companies had operating methods and mechanical traditions which were much apart. It was hard to imagine two big railways more different than the London & North Western and the Midland, though both served many of the same cities in what once had been the kingdoms of Mercia and Strathclyde. But the presence of a London & North Western train at Derby, or a Midland one at Crewe, one imagines, might have caused a riot. Yet these two were to be the largest constituents in the new LMS. It is not suprising that officers in each decided in advance that *they* were going to run this outfit.

In Scotland, conflicting loyalties caused less difficulty, for the two biggest Scottish railways, the Caledonian and the North British, had gone into separate camps under the Act, though there may have been some heartburnings in Glasgow and South Western quarters. The Highland Railway had ever accepted whatever Providence, the Caledonian and the North British had offered it at Perth, and, after a rough time in the war, its fusion was honourable. One imagines that it had far sooner become part of an English railway than amalgamate with the Great North of

Scotland, and it was spared that! Of course, nobody in his sober senses called the LMS an English railway, unless he were of some ignorant crowd like the Germans or the Americans. It was a *British* railway, and it contained, as remarked, a blessed national adjective in its title, which was more than the neighbouring London & North Eastern was to do. An old Edinburgh engineman once told your then youthful author that this (the LNER) should have been called the London and North British! On the other side, London Midland & Scottish would do, like beer in a pub with no spirits licence.

So let us survey its constituents as they were in 1922. First, the London & North Western: 1846 had seen its formation by amalgamation of the London & Birmingham, Grand Junction, and Manchester & Birmingham Railways. Thus when it began, it was itself an anticipation of the London Midland & Scottish 77 years after, at first a loosely united set of company-owned railways which had their own methods and young but jealously-guarded traditions. Also, in their history, there had been already a lot of amalgamation. The London & Birmingham had been the first great main line out of London, yet the Grand Junction was senior to it, for it had taken in the Bolton & Leigh Railway, dating from 1828, and the Liverpool & Manchester of 1830, and it was in respect of the latter that the London & North Western claimed, with some prevarication, to be *the oldest established firm in the railway passenger business*. At least the Liverpool & Manchester had been the first public railway as later generations were to understand the term, taking passengers from city to city, with decent stations, on up and down roads, with mechanical traction.

The Grand Junction proper, a Locke line, had been opened throughout from Birmingham to Warrington, with connections thence to Liverpool and Manchester, on July 4, 1837. The London & Birmingham, opened in stages, had been completed and opened throughout on September 20, 1838. Of other important London & North Western constituents, the Lancaster and Carlisle had reached the Border city in 1846. Though worked by the London & North Western over many years, it was not taken into that company until 1879.

In between, the North Union, based on Preston, had been joint with the Lancashire & Yorkshire since 1846, though the joint arrangement between LNWR and L&Y which was in force until the amalgamation of 1922 was one concluded more recently, in 1888. The Lancaster & Preston (1840) became part of the North Western in 1859. Down in the Midlands, the Trent Valley line dated from 1847, in which year the joint station of Carlisle Citadel was also opened. As for the Irish Mail route, the Chester and Holyhead Railway had been completed, with the Britannia Bridge over the Menai Strait, in 1850, and taken into the London & North Western in 1858. The Central Wales line had taken the company into the rich country of the Valleys in 1865. In Ireland, the company owned Dublin North Wall, and nearly all the stock of the Dundalk, Newry and Greenore Railway. It had always been a close neighbour, and more and more by degrees a supporter, of the North London Railway. This was administered by London & North Western officers from the end of 1908, though it continued to be worked more or less as a separate system, the steam trains being North London stock while London & North Western electric trains handled the Richmond traffic. In its latter years, the North London Railway had the most archaic rolling stock to be seen on any British main line. In itself it was a very small system, but during independence it covered considerable distance by running powers.

At the end of 1921, the London & North Western Railway had a total route mileage, including all lines leased and worked, or jointly owned, leased or worked, of 2,066 miles 12 chains. Lines directly owned accounted for 1,806 miles 55 chains; share of joint lines, 207 miles 10 chains; lines leased or worked, 47 miles 35 chains; share of lines jointly leased or worked, 4 miles 72 chains. Apart from its sometimes rambling and antiquated stations, and even after those war years just past, the London & North Western Railway had a good presence. Its permanent way was superb. In the public view, it was still admired for the comfort and cleanliness of its rolling stock – the pull-and-push train between Harrow and Stanmore had a greater elegance than the Highland Railway's North Mail from Inverness to Wick – but that rolling stock (like the Highland's) included some astonishing antiques. Equipment was highly stylised. Its style in respect of rolling stock had not changed since the 1870s, unlike that of the Great Western, which had had the Churchward Revolution.

Like the London & North Western, the Lancashire & Yorkshire Railway was a product of amalgamation. Its title had been assumed in 1850 by the Manchester & Leeds Railway, which had been opened by stages from 1839 to 1841, the completing link in the Pennines having been between Littleborough and Summit. In 1846 the Manchester & Bolton, and the Liverpool & Bury Railway were both amalgamated with the Manchester & Leeds, to which was transferred, under its own Act, the West Riding Union Railway. A later constituent was the East Lancashire Railway, occupying those valleys which its name suggested: (it had been incorporated in 1844 as the Manchester, Bury & Rossendale Railway).

The L&Y – never did initials become more truly a title – was as essentially a provincial railway as the London & North Western was, in the true sense of the term, a metropolitan railway. It carried an enormous traffic, both passenger and goods: it ultimately found a Continental outlet by way of the Humber, and although it was grossly mismanaged in mid-Victorian years, it never embarked on fool-schemes to have yet another competitive main line to the capital, as did its near neighbour the

Manchester, Sheffield & Lincolnshire Railway. Hence its cordial relations with the London & North Western company, which went so far as to get the latter into trouble with the Majesty of Law in the 1870s, when it exceeded its statutory rights by building locomotives at Crewe for its neighbour.

When one reads between the lines of Normington's unofficial history of the L & Y – he having been a disgruntled superintendent thereof – one can understand the nature of mismanagement already remarked, or at any rate the appalling stagnation which distinguished the railway in its middle years, for of such was that mismanagement. No wonder Normington never became General Manager and retired with a grievance, for he was a principal human unit in the stagnant part. One needs only to read him, without needing to chuckle at the disinterested funny stories of E. L. Ahrons. The company's great man undoubtedly was Sir John Aspinall, sometime in charge of its mechanical engineering and later General Manager. From the Aspinall Era, the L & Y went forward to its ultimate, and very reasonable, amalgamation with the London & North Western. Really, it was a very good railway, though the Spartan appearance of its coaching stock sometimes put-off travelling Sybarites accustomed to such plushy trains as those of the Midland.

Before it amalgamated with the London & North Western at the end of 1921, the Lancashire & Yorkshire Railway had 533 miles of route owned, 68 miles 28 chains share of joint lines, making a total route of 601 miles 28 chains. Rolling-stock statistics for both constituents were thus: London & North Western Railway: 3,336 locomotives, 7 steam rail-motors, 73 electric motor coaches, 112 electric trailer cars, 9,551 steam coaching vehicles, 76,674 goods vehicles and 7,057 service vehicles; Lancashire & Yorkshire Railway: 1,650 locomotives, 18 steam rail-motors, 119 electric motor coaches, 122 electric trailer coaches, 4,310 steam coaching vehicles, 34,676 goods vehicles, 2,716 service vehicles. Dreary things are bald statistics, but there are some curiosities about these. The London & North Western, by route, was nearly three-and-a-half times the size of the Lancashire & Yorkshire, but it had only just over twice the number of locomotives and a slightly higher ratio of goods vehicles, those wagons on whose ton-miles both railways chiefly lived. The L & Y, having two distinct suburban electric systems extending from Liverpool Exchange and Manchester Victoria respectively, had over 50 more electric-train vehicles than the London & North Western, which worked its own from Euston and Broad Street in London.

At the time of this preliminary amalgamation, the Chairman of the original London & North Western was the Hon. Charles Napier Lawrence, who had been appointed Deputy Chairman, with Sir Gilbert Claughton, in 1909. Claughton became Chairman in 1911, and was created a Baronet in the following year. He held the Chair until 1921, and has gone down to history as a wise and able governor of the company's fortunes. Not least were his powers of diplomacy with sympathy. *His word was his bond*, wrote George Alcock, one of the great lights of organised railway labour, and author of *The History of Trade Unionism, 1666–1921*; scarcely the sort of man to fawn upon chairmen of companies. Lawrence was to become the first Chairman of the London Midland & Scottish Railway.

At Headquarters, the way to amalgamation was already being made easier by the appointment of a joint General Manager as early as the beginning of 1921, before the passing of the Railways Act. The London & North Western Railway's General Manager from 1919 to the end of 1920 had been Sir Thomas Williams, who had been Acting General Manager, in the absence of Sir Guy Calthrop as Coal Controller in Government. Williams had been with the London & North Western Railway since 1876. Briefly in 1920 there was an instance, believed unique, of father and son both being railway general managers, for in that year Howard Williams took on the Central Argentine Railway. The family name later became Howard-Williams.

Up in the North, Arthur Watson had become General Manager of the Lancashire & Yorkshire Railway in January 1919, when Sir John Aspinall had retired. Watson had been articled to the Chief Engineer of the L&Y in 1890 and had thus risen on the Engineering, as opposed to the Commercial side in Williams' case. In 1911 he had become Superintendent of the Line and in 1918, additionally, Assistant General Manager pending Aspinall's retirement. As from January 1, 1921, he was General Manager of both the Lancashire & Yorkshire and the London & North Western companies. The two had a pool of certain traffics as far back as 1863, so their long delayed amalgamation might seem surprising. It should be noted that there was great public distrust of big company mergers, through antagonism towards monopoly, and the London & North Western, not without reason, was suspect as an acquisitive giant, wickedly wise in power politics.

But its stocks were a blessing to the widow and the orphan on whose behalf investments had been wisely made and tied-up. This is not the sort of string on which a Victorian Radical would have harped. Readers of your author's generation, and older, will recall a book by Conan Doyle called *The Poison Belt*, in which two highly antagonistic professors, the wife of one of them, an aristocratic big-game hunter, and a reporter from The Street, find themselves apparently the sole survivors of mankind, owing to skilfully-sealed doors and windows, and several cylinders of oxygen, while the planet is passing through a noxious drift of ether. Motoring later to London, they find in an attic of the dead city one old woman, an asthmatic with a supply of oxygen, who, with the shrewdness of elderly female recluses, had taken similar steps, and she immediately assails them with an anxious inquiry as to whether the calamity will have an adverse effect on her little shares in the London & North Western Railway.

To revert to the constituent companies of the London Midland & Scottish: Williams and Watson had both been members of the Railway Executive during the war years, the latter on behalf of Sir John Aspinall whom, in 1914, German authority had caught on holiday and immediately interned. He had remained on the REC when Aspinall was fairly quickly repatriated (presumably as an Englishman above military age; an example of that curious stupidity which sometimes offset German diligence and ingenuity).

Fixing the point between Northern and Southern Divisions at Crewe equalised the system in a way that would not have been done by making the former Lancashire & Yorkshire system a division in itself. R. C. Irwin was the obvious choice as Secretary, he coming from the L&Y, as J. Bishop, the previous LNWR Secretary, was due in any case to retire. The two Superintendents of the Line, L. W. Horne of the LNWR and Ashton Davies of the L&Y, became Divisional Superintendents, Southern and Northern respectively, and though the former might, had he been a jealous man, have felt that he had lost something of his former vice-royalty, they were equally responsible to Watson.

More ticklish, one imagines, had been the office of Chief Mechanical Engineer. Crewe was Crewe, and had been a law unto itself under the formidable Francis Webb right back in the awesome days when Sir Richard Moon was Chairman; as he was for 30 years, with Cawkwell and Findlay as his successive General Managers. What Crewe revealed constituted the True Faith among all London & North Western locomotive men, and all else was heresy and false doctrine. At the time of this first amalgamation, Hewitt P. M. Beames was Chief Mechanical Engineer at Crewe, having succeeded the late Bowen Cooke in 1920. But at Horwich on the L&Y was the revered veteran George Hughes, who had been in office since 1909 and was in no mind to retire yet. So Hughes became CME of the enlarged railway, while Beames became Divisional Mechanical Engineer, Crewe, and subject to him. For a man to have commanded Crewe, however briefly, and then to become "Divisional" was without precedent, but seniority was seniority. Some Crewe men may have comforted themselves with the reflection that Hughes was one himself, in so far as he had been a Crewe Premium Apprentice under Webb from 1882 to 1887, though immediately after that, he had gone out into the wilderness on the flanks of the bare Pennines.

Ernest F. C. Trench, a wise and witty Irishman from County Kerry, was the obvious choice for Chief Engineer. He had served his time on the

London & North Western. In 1899 he had gone to the Midland as Resident Engineer, to superintend certain important widenings then being made. From 1903 to 1906 he was Chief Engineer of the North London Railway, then going back to the London & North Western, he had become its Chief Engineer in 1909. He knew most of the important lines that were to become part of London Midland & Scottish Railway in 1923, when indeed he became Chief Engineer of that in its turn. One remembers with singular pleasure a spry old man with a pointed white beard and an alert, birdlike eye, on the occasion of the Britannia Bridge Centenary as recently as 1950, drawing one aside without warning, in true Irish fashion, to share a sudden funny recollection. It seemed as if he had known Robert Stephenson, and that the memory still tickled.

As noted, he had been in his time a Midland man, and such switches between North Western and Midland, not to mention a switch back, were very unusual. For indeed, the Midland was a very different railway. With the public it was liked because of the very high quality of its passenger carriages, naturally an endearing thing with both regular and unused travellers, though to be sure it had seemed, in the pre-war years, rather prone to burn those beautiful coaches, passengers included, in the course of some terrific smashes. This is not meant spitefully; public opinion of the time is the thing concerned. The Midland gave good service for both passengers and goods, and whatever the respective architectural merits of Euston and St. Pancras in London, the standard of stations on the Midland was higher than that of the North Western. Some of them, both great and small, were really beautiful buildings, notably Francis Thompson's in Derbyshire.

As for its bare statistics, at the end of 1922 it had 2,169 miles 20 chains of route, whereof 1,793 miles 6 chains were fully owned. Share of joint lines, which included the Cheshire Lines, the Somerset and Dorset, and the Midland and Great Northern, accounted for 278 miles 17 chains; lines leased or worked came to only 16 miles 49 chains, while the Midland share of lines jointly leased or worked came to 80 miles, 28 chains. When it came to formation of the LMS, there was no change in the Midland's share of the three joint railways mentioned. (It was the London & North Eastern that secured a two-thirds share of the Cheshire Lines from the amalgamation of the Great Central and the Great Northern.) There were 3,019 locomotives, which probably had the highest average age of any main-line railway stock in the country; 48 electric motor coaches with 49 trailers, and 20 electric tramcars. Steam stock comprised 6,019 coaching vehicles, 107,617 goods, and 8,098 service vehicles. The trams belonged to the Burton & Ashby Light Railway; the electric railway vehicles were those of the experimental Lancaster, Morecambe and Heysham scheme.

In Ireland, as we have seen, the London & North Western had a bridgehead at North Wall, Dublin, and an absolute controlling interest in the Dundalk, Newry & Greenore, but the Midland, playing on this same Irish chessboard like the god Midir against King Eochaidh, had acquired the entire Belfast & Northern Counties Railway as far back as 1903. Whether this move benefited the Midland Midir as much as did the legendary one (the god carried off Queen Etain) one simply wonders. Your author, remembering the reporting of LMS meetings, years ago, also recalls a curiously apologetic note in the Chairman's speech when he referred to "our Northern Counties Railway", and in later years the Northern Irish Government seemed simply to regard it as a pawn in the game of killing the admirable Great Northern Railway (Ireland).

Still, the Irish venture was truly in the Midland tradition of amalgamation, and a reminder that this, like the Lancashire & Yorkshire, was a provincial railway, whose heart was ever at Derby and whose branches led to London and Carlisle: (the main line was from Leeds to Bristol). Ulster was another province, whereas to the London & North Western, Greenore and North Wall were outposts of empire. Clearly the fusion of North Western and Midland would present a problem or two, which had been scarcely more than negligible in the case of North Western, and L&Y. Still, so it had to be.

Once again, in the Midland, we had a great railway system, the third-largest in Great Britain, which had been built up on a series of amalgamations. It had begun in 1844, as a company comprising the former Midland Counties (1839–40), North Midland (1840) and Birmingham and Derby Junction (1839). The Birmingham & Gloucester Railway was completed in 1840 and the Bristol & Gloucester in 1844, and both came into Midland ownership, the Bristol with an unwelcome dowry in the form of Brunel's broad gauge, which had to be put down at the Midland company's earliest convenience. Those were the stout old bones of the Midland Railway, which was to grow a much more complex skeleton in the course of the years. Its traffic reached London, by running powers over the Great Northern, in 1858, but not over Midland track throughout until 1868. Later still, in 1876, it reached Carlisle from Settle. The Dore and Chinley line, including the second-longest tunnel in the country (Totley) did not come until 1893. The last, and least probable, of Midland acquisitions had been the London, Tilbury and Southend, an obvious Great Eastern appendage, in 1912.

One of the most interesting things about the Midland in its latter years had been its centralised traffic control, in which the moving spirit was J. H. Follows, then a promising younger officer with Cecil Paget, General Superintendent. Beginning with an experimental control at Masborough in the year 1907, control spread all over the Midland Railway after it had proved its worth in the most congested areas. In this, the Midland led the country, thanks to Paget and Follows. Sir Guy Granet had been its General Manager from 1906 to 1918. Like Sir George Gibb, sometime of the North Eastern Railway, Granet was a lawyer and a clever one. He it was who had twitched the little Tilbury railway out of the groping hands of the Great Eastern into the huge Midland landing-net. He was to be the last Chairman of the Midland Railway and the second of the London Midland & Scottish.

As to visible peculiarities of the Midland, many people remarked what was called its "small engine policy", which certainly distinguished it from all the other major British lines. Long before it became an LMS component, Richard Deeley, as Locomotive Superintendent at Derby, had powered it with its heaviest express engines, the famous Midland compound 4–4–0, designed with his improved version of W. M. Smith's system which S. W. Johnson had essayed back at the beginning of the century. He had designed bigger engines – an ambitious 2–4–4–2 tank locomotive and a handsome 4–6–0 compound express, but apparently never was allowed to go farther than the drawings. That there was harsh friction between Deeley and his management has been several times stated. Mr. E. M. Deeley has vehemently denied that there was any between his uncle and Paget, who had been his assistant at Derby, a thing I conveyed some time back in *The Midland Railway*. But friction there certainly was somewhere. Let me not rake up again the old yarns about Deeley and Paget's experimental locomotive, but instead tell one, a new one, about the "small engine" policy; new, that is, to me.

Paget and Follows were one day sitting in the official saloon. Maybe they had been discussing the possibility of larger Midland locomotives, maybe not. But quite near was one of the big four-cylinder 4–6–0 engines of the London & North Western's Sir Gilbert Claughton class, and she was starting up one of those heavy trains which the North Western cheerfully assigned to one engine only. Whether the sand were wet or the rails oily, one knows not, but the Claughton slipped vehemently, and went on slipping with thunderous din. One can imagine the augurs nodding, if not winking. (Follows, assuredly, was not the winking sort of man.) But the Midland Railway went on to the end of its separate existence with only one big engine in regular service, the great ten-coupled used for banking on the Lickey Incline. This was well after Deeley had quitted Derby Works without even looking back in anger. On the North Western in 1922 one saw a George or a Prince rampaging along with an enormous West Coast express, while over on the Midland a somewhat lighter train, also bound from London to Glasgow or Edinburgh, would be headed by two compounds, or maybe a compound and a Class 3. The North Western train with its one engine would be indeed the noisier of the two: the North Western was ever a noisy line. A little 0–6–2 Coal

Tank seemed capable of more din than the Lickey Banker. Relative merits of the two company's methods in those days will probably be debated, even with heat, for as long as men survive to cherish loving memories of steam express trains.

A little thing, yet in its way characteristic of the two companies: London & North Western having coined the magnificent title of *Premier Line* – a masterpiece of expressed commercial pride – the Midland styled itself *The Best Way*, but perhaps not with quite the same superbly arrogant assurance. Then the North Western used "Bestotel" as a telegraphic address for its stately caravanserais, and the Midland had to make-do with "Midotel". Yet, to some, that "Bestotel" seemed rather specious. The North Western hotels seemed the more pompous, and the Midland ones the more gilded; perhaps reflections of the characters and tastes of the long-dead Sir Richard Moon and Sir James Allport. But one could think of all sorts of claims to have *the best hotel*. Out of the past came a memory of a prospectus beginning with the words: "This Hotel which is the Best in Italy is most splendid commode . . ." One thought that perhaps it might not be so, after all.

Third-largest of LMS constituents, and the second-largest railway in Scotland, was the Caledonian, and although amalgamations and absorptions had figured in its history, it was an original company incorporated in 1845. Its main line had been opened from Carlisle to Beattock in 1847, and to Glasgow in 1848, with branches to Edinburgh and to a junction with the Scottish Central Railway at Greenhill. Before its initial opening, it had already purchased one of the oldest railways in Scotland, the Glasgow, Garnkirk and Coatbridge, which had begun as the Garnkirk and Glasgow in 1831. It was taken over in 1846. Of Caledonian constituents, the Scottish Central from Greenhill to Stirling and Perth dated from 1848. The route from Perth to Aberdeen was completed by 1850, under the Scottish North Eastern Railway, itself an amalgamation of the Scottish Midland Junction and the Aberdeen Railway. The Scottish Central had taken over the Dundee, Perth and Aberdeen Junction and the ancient Dundee and Newtyle Railway before it merged with the Caledonian. One long branch worked by the Caledonian was the Callander and Oban Railway, through the mountains to the West Coast. It retained its independence to the end of Caledonian days, however.

Although its permanent way was of a rougher order than that of the London & North Western or the Midland, and its passenger carriages on ordinary services were of more Spartan sort, the Caledonian made very fine vehicles for its Aberdeen and Oban services, and also as a contribution to the West Coast Route, though most of the West Coast Joint stock was of London & North Western design, including all the sleeping and dining cars. Caledonian locomotive design had long been of a very high order, and its timetables in pre-war days had shown very sprightly work indeed, notably on the mile-a-minute timing over a relatively short stretch between Forfar and Perth. The Caledonian shared with the London & North Western in the running of the West Coast Special Travelling Post Office, supreme mail train of the world. Down the years that world has contained such prodigies as the Indian Mail between Calais and Brindisi (which carried passengers in Wagons-Lits), and those two all-Post-Office trains The Fast Mail on the New York Central and the Limited Mail on the Pennsylvania which once tried nightly to do each other down between New York and Chicago. They came and they went.

Compared with the other constituents, the Caledonian had not completed final negotiations for amalgamation by the end of 1922, when none had been elected from the Caledonian to the LMS Board, though most of the necessary reorganisation of senior staff had been done. William Pickersgill, the Caledonian CME, became Mechanical Engineer at St. Rollox, with David Urie (son of Robert Urie of the London & South Western, sometime Works Manager at St. Rollox) as Assistant Mechanical Engineer. Pickersgill was a veteran, who previously had commanded Inverurie on the Great North of Scotland Railway. Robert Killin, who had been the Caledonian Superintendent of the Line since 1916, was to become General Superintendent (Midland Division) of the LMS during 1923, and General Superintendent (Northern Division) later in the same year. Three Caledonian directors were elected to the LMS Board when negotiations had been completed. Names of the full Board will be given later, with their origins.

In contradistinction from the Midland, and even compared with the London & North Western, the Caledonian had long been a "big-engine line". Right back in the 1860s, Benjamin Conner's 8ft. single-drivers had been among the heaviest and most powerful express engines in Great Britain, a massive Scottish version of what France, with unusual deference to an Englishman's name, called *Le Buddicom*. Dugald Drummond's engines, still giving useful service in 1922, need no introduction, though it is worth recalling that their designer had experimented with 200lb. pressure, in his time an almost fearsome figure. John McIntosh had taken the Drummond engine to its logical conclusion, culminating in the superb Cardean class 4–6–0. Pickersgill's two-cylinder 4–6–0 express engines of 1922 formed a design briefly augmented by the LMS, as did McIntosh's 0–4–4 tank engines. Admitting the probability of controversy, the most handsome locomotive stock to be taken over by the new company was that of the Caledonian Railway, and the elaborate blue livery had not everything to do with this.

Though the track was indifferent – and thus noticeable after the North Western's – Caledonian stations were often of a high order, like those of the Midland, and in the country places the art of gardening, long highly developed among Scotsmen, improved their aspect, though some of the most ornate performance in this direction was to be found on the independent Callander and Oban Railway, at such places as Strathyre and Loch Awe, where the situation helped.

For convenience, though we have not done with all the English and Scottish constituent companies, the Highland Railway may be mentioned here, for it gave the road to the London Midland & Scottish Railway's *Ultima Thule*, the remote earldom of Caithness, where railways were at their farthest north in the British Isles.

Geographically the Highland Railway had formed an *omnium gatherum* for traffic from and to the more southerly companies. Every summer afternoon in the years before 1914 a train would pull out of Inverness with coaches and sleeping cars for London via three different routes, West Coast, East Coast and Midland. Early next morning, a corresponding train would head northwards from Perth. A German would have said, inaccurately but not altogether unreasonably: "*Ach Gott!* That could only in England happen!" An American no doubt would have applauded such fine free enterprise. A Frenchman might have understood, on the premise that shrewd Scots profited by English madness.

The Highland was a poor company, so naturally it was glad that both the West Coast and the East Coast offered it traffic at Perth. The North British Railway was in something of the same position, having rival English allies in the North Eastern and Great Northern one side, and the Midland in the middle.

Taking a long view back, rather like, at this stage, peering through the wrong end of a glass, one feels that the Highland ought long ago to have been amalgamated with the Great North of Scotland Railway. (For many years the two companies had sordidly squabbled over the traffic they shared between Inverness and Aberdeen.) Had that been so, the Great North probably would have become part of the LMS, for the northern Caledonian terminus was at Aberdeen and, after the amalgamation of 1923, the Great North had become an isolated part of the London & North Eastern Railway, attainable only by running powers over what had been part of the Caledonian. But Perth General, though a joint station like that at Aberdeen, was on the Caledonian main line. The North British reached it only by the branch through Glenfarg, and the Highland company by running powers south of Stanley Junction. It was therefore reasonable to treat the Highland as a part of the London Midland & Scottish, *vice* the Caledonian, and Albert Pullar, of the famous commercial family in Perth, and Deputy Chairman of the Highland Railway, went into the LMS Board.

Basic statistics of both railways were as follows: Caledonian Railway:

Total route mileage, 1,114 miles 47 chains, including 152 miles 70 chains leased or worked, 60 miles 78 chains share of joint lines, 4 miles 21 chains share of lines leased or worked jointly. It had 1,070 locomotives, 3,040 coaching vehicles, 32,136 goods vehicles and 1,786 service vehicles. The Highland Railway had 505 miles 79 chains of route, including 21 miles 15 chains worked but not owned. There were 173 Highland locomotives, 799 coaching vehicles including two sleepers, 2,718 goods vehicles and 112 service vehicles.

The Highland's history had begun with the quite isolated Inverness and Nairn Railway in 1855. The Perth and Dunkeld Railway was opened in the following year. The line from Nairn to Keith was opened in 1858 and amalgamated with the Inverness and Nairn, as the Inverness and Aberdeen Junction Railway, in 1861. The Inverness & Perth Junction Railway, diverging from the I and AJR at Forres and striking south over the mountains to Dunkeld, followed in 1863. All these went to form the Highland Railway, constituted in 1865. North of Inverness there was some of that sort of development which was rare in the go-getting provinces of England and Lowland Scotland; building railways for the general benefit of the community, such as it was. In the earlier years of last century, the popular reputation of the ducal family of Sutherland had been most unsavoury – pitiless evictions of a depressed peasantry, roofs set on fire over bedridden old women (as in Strath Naver) and so forth – but the third Duke built much railway mileage in the Far North out of his own pocket, by way of an improvement far removed from the "improvements" in the shape of population clearances carried out under the Countess Elizabeth[1]. The Duke of Sutherland's Railway from Golspie to Helmsdale (1871) was at once a benefaction and an act of restitution, rather late in the historical day. The Highland Railway system, owned or worked, was completed to Wick and Thurso by 1874. The Dingwall & Skye Railway, quite separate but likewise worked by the Highland, dated back to 1870, and was extended from Strome Ferry to the Kyle of Lochalsh in 1897.

Even in the days of railway monopoly, the Highland Railway could be scarcely regarded as a very profitable investment. But for the Railways Act of 1921, it would have either perished or, possibly, become the first British State, or State-subsidised, main-line railway. From 1913 your author recalls a senior kinsman racing the train from Inverness to Aviemore with his massive Wolseley motor car. The thing was to get a good lead before Slochd, on the Carr Bridge line opened in 1898.

On the eve of amalgamation, the Highland company's locomotive stock was in unexpectedly good condition; unexpected because during the

---

[1] This infamous woman held the sometime Earldom of Sutherland for 72½ years, 1766–1839. She married Viscount Trentham, afterwards Marquis of Stafford and first Duke of Sutherland, hence recurrence of the names of both Stafford and Sutherland in the naming of London & North Western and Highland Railway locomotives in later years.

way years it had been nearly worn out and the railway had had to borrow some twenty engines from other companies. There had been much emergency rebuilding and general overhaul by various firms, including Hawthorn Leslie at Newcastle and Andrew Barclay at Kilmarnock, which gave new life to the old engines while Christopher Cumming at Inverness designed some handsome modern ones, which Hawthorn Leslie also undertook. The rolling-stock was decidedly old-fashioned on the whole, with a deplorable paucity of lavatory-access even for the long rides through remote country, very few corridor coaches, and, north of Aviemore, a complete dependence on station refreshment rooms and the baskets they purveyed. South of Aviemore there were Pullman dining cars based on the Caledonian Railway in Glasgow. It was a very difficult line to run, especially in the brief summer peak when successive heavy trains had to be worked over a main line consisting largely of single track and it was to the company's credit that many of the delays could be traced to late arrivals at Perth, where it took over.

Of LMS constituents, and back in England, there was the North Staffordshire Railway, another which had its roots in amalgamation, though this had been initial (1847), a consolidation of the Potteries, Churnet Valley, and Harecastle and Sandbach lines, which had been authorised in the previous year. The Potteries Loop Line (Hanley to Kidsgrove) was opened at the end of 1875, and various other lines were added by amalgamation in the ensuring years.

The North Stafford was geographically a small railway, with 220 miles 45 chains of total route mileage which included 5 miles 79 chains share of joint lines and 8 miles 21 chains leased or worked. In the Potteries, its traffic was extremely heavy, but its running powers and through workings were widespread, *eg* to North Wales and to Manchester London Road. Certain of the London & North Western expresses between the cities ran via Stoke, with North Stafford motive power for part of the way.

The North Stafford was unusual among LMS constituents in that it included a narrow-gauge section, the 2ft 6in gauge Leek and Manifold line which had been independently started, with opening in the summer of 1904. Manifold equipment was closely akin to that of the Barsi Light Railway in India, and certainly the carriage stock was very superior to those of the Lynton and Barnstaple and the Vale of Rheidol lines, which were narrow-gauge railways within the compass of Southern and Great Western respectively. Mechanically the North Stafford company was well equipped. One of the celebrated Adams family, J. H. Adams, had commanded the Locomotive Department from 1902 to his sudden death in 1915. Son of William Adams of the South Western, his designs were markedly Adams-Pettigrew, with good proportions and adequate bearing surfaces. W. F. Pettigrew, who had been the elder Adams' No. 1 on the

LSWR, went to the Furness Railway. J. H. Adams' successor at Stoke, J. A. Hookham, is chiefly remembered for his practical experiments with four-cylinder eight-impulse propulsion, in a single engine (No. 23), o–6–o tank, and intended for short distance passenger haulage in the Potteries. Amalgamation stopped the possible production of further examples of this interesting design. No. 23, under the LMS, had her tanks taken off and a tender added (with the necessary surgery at the back).

To describe the shape of the North Stafford – so auspiciously nick-named "Knotty" – is scarcely easy, for it wandered about an enclosed space rather like an unusually imaginative lion varying the pacing of his enforced habitation in a zoo, making loops and counter-turns. In terms of actual route owned, it extended from Colwich and Norton Bridge on the North Western, and Market Drayton on the Great Western, in the south-western quarter, and connections in the Burton and Derby area in the south-eastern area to the Midland and the Great Northern, to Crewe and Macclesfield (both with the London & North Western) with Congle-ton in between. As already remarked, its running powers were extensive, ranging to Manchester, North Wales, Warrington, Buxton and Notting-ham, and southwards as far as Wellington, Wolverhampton and Birming-ham, and even as far south as Rugby.

Last of the English constituents of the LMS was the Furness Railway, a very old undertaking dating back to incorporation in 1844, first opened from Barrow-in-Furness to Dalton and Kirkby, chiefly for mineral traffic, in 1846. In our own time it was most notable in being an ally with both the London & North Western and the Midland companies, on entirely cordial terms. In the meantime it had engaged, very lucratively, in the traffic with the then rich mining enterprises of Cumberland, and, a little later, took travellers full of Wordsworth to the Lake Country which he had laid before them in verse (an ironic twist, for he had been horrified at the advent of the steam railway to his holy land!). For many years it had been to some considerable extent a family property of the Ramsdens, one of whom was its Chairman to the end. The main line extended from Carnforth on the London & North Western (with a joint line shared by the Midland to Wennington Junction) to Whitehaven, east and north of which were important lines jointly owned with the LNWR. It owned a fleet of steamers on both Windermere Lake (six) and Coniston Water (two).

There were 158 miles 21 chains of route including 23 miles 62 chains share of joint lines, and 19 miles 37 chains leased or worked. There were 136 Furness locomotives, 361 units of coaching stock, 7,365 goods vehicles and 373 service vehicles. As on the North Stafford, Adams influence was strong through the work of Pettigrew, who in 1918 had been succeeded by David Rutherford, a Scot from the North British who already had been Engineer to the company since 1909.

The Furness Railway, though a smaller constituent, was an important owner of docks, with 278 acres of water space at Barrow, including a 21-acre timber dock, with 2¼ miles of quays. An excellent lease had been that of the 146½-acre Cavendish Dock to Vickers Ltd.

North of the Border again; the Glasgow and South Western Railway occupied a large portion of Carrick and Galloway, and its components included the old Kilmarnock and Troon Railway dating back to 1811, which had seen Scotland's first, and not very successful, essay at steam traction in 1817. The company had been formed by amalgamation of the Glasgow, Paisley, Kilmarnock and Ayr Railway (1840) and the Glasgow, Dumfries and Carlisle Railway in 1850, in which year the latter had been completed by the opening of the sections Auchinleck–New Cumnock and New Cumnock–Closeburn. It was not until 1876, however, that completion of the Midland Railway's Settle and Carlisle line along the western escarpment of the Pennines made of the Glasgow and South Western Railway a main line to England. South of Dalry, indeed, it had two main lines, both somewhat mountainous, for there was that from the old Ayr and Troon line southwards to Girvan and thence to Galloway where it joined the Portpatrick and Wigtownshire Joint Railway running east to west between Castle Douglas and Stranraer, with a picturesque but disappointing branch to Portpatrick which looked over to Ireland.

In terms of route mileage, the Glasgow and South Western was very slightly less than the Highland, but, in spite of the expanse of railwayless, mountainous country in the middle of its terrain, it was a much more concentrated system, with heavy industrial traffic in and from the area south and west of Glasgow. Total route mileage was 493 miles 36 chains, including 44 miles 36 chains share of joint lines and a minute share – 24 chains – of lines leased or worked jointly. There were 528 locomotives, 1,604 coaching vehicles, 19,252 goods vehicles and 1,349 service vehicles; all very much larger stocks than those of the Highland Railway. Robert Whitelegg, previously of the London, Tilbury and Southend Railway, commanded the Locomotive Department, with works at Kilmarnock. His predecessors had been a long line of Scots locomotive men; both the famous Stirling brothers, Hugh Smellie, James Manson and Peter Drummond.

Locomotives and vehicles were of rather high standard, though some of the former, dating back to James Stirling's days, were very old. There was more elegance and comfort about the passenger carriages than might be found on larger Scottish Railways, and not merely in those held jointly with the Midland Railway for south traffic. The "Sou' West" liked sumptuous dining cars, and it carried a considerable and quite exacting user on its lines to and from the Clyde Coast towns, whence it ran its own steamship services. The most important joint railway in Scotland was the already-mentioned Portpatrick and Wigtownshire with its Castle Douglas-Stranraer line and Portpatrick branch dating from 1861 and 1862 respectively, having been opened by the old Portpatrick Railway. The Wigtownshire Railway, once leased and worked as a family business by Thomas Wheatley, dated from 1875–77. In 1885 the Portpatrick and Wigtownshire lines were jointly acquired by the London & North Western, Midland, Caledonian, and Glasgow and South Western Railways, whereof the two Scottish companies provided motive power. There were locomotive repair shops at Stranraer. The Caledonian Railway's standards were used for the permanent way. Passenger and goods vehicles were hired from the owning companies, on a mileage basis. The P & WJR owned a four-fifths share of the steamer fleet on the Stranraer–Larne run, the remainder being vested in the Midland Northern Counties Committee. Both the railway and the steamship line (worked in 1922 by a pair of turbine steamers) became an outright component of the London Midland & Scottish Railway on completion of amalgamation, unlike the three major English joint railways.

These were describable as railways in their own right, and as such had their separate histories, particularly as formation of the LMS made no important difference to their status.

Subsidiary companies of the LMS, at the time of its formation, included several which also had been railways in their own right, working their own traffic. The North London has been mentioned already, and as noted, although it had become part of the London & North Western from a business point of view, it had remained still a very different railway, with peculiarly distinctive locomotives and vehicles.

The Maryport and Carlisle Railway's Act of Incorporation dated back to 1837. To quote a *Railway Year Book* reference too good to miss: "Contrary to the usual experience, the revenue from the first opening of the line (a section on July 15, 1840, and throughout on February 10, 1845) almost equalled the estimate." It had been engineered by the Patriarch, George Stephenson, and had not been one of his more difficult jobs; hence, no doubt, the circumstance of desire not having outrun performance too far. Eighty years after, it still was quite unlike any of its more massive neighbours at Carlisle, unless one whiffed a faint odour of archaic Glasgow and South Western about the locomotives. It brought to the initial LMS stock 33 of these, with 71 carriages, 1,464 goods and 67 service vehicles. It had 42 miles 63 chains of route.

Down in the West Midlands, the Stratford-upon-Avon and Midland Junction Railway dated from an amalgamation, as recently as 1908, of the East and West Junction (1864), the Evesham, Redditch and Stratford-upon-Avon Junction (1873) and the Stratford-upon-Avon, Towcester and Midland Junction Railway (1879). The years are those of incorporation. Under an Act of 1910, it had acquired the Northampton and Banbury Railway (1863). Its prime object was in iron ore, though it worked a rather wayward passenger service and had thriftily and by-no-means unwisely invested in some old Midland coaches, still much better in their old age than the sort of thing one found on some major railways. A peculiarity of the SMJ was in the chord connections it made between several very important main lines; with the Midland at Ravenstone Wood and at Broom Junction, east and west respectively, the London & North Western at Blisworth and Cockley Brake, the Great Central at Woodford and Hinton, and the Great Western at both Stratford and Fenny Compton. Its modest route came to just over 67½ miles.

Up on Merseyside the Wirral Railway, having its origins in the Hoylake Railway (incorporated in 1863), dated as a company from 1883. Its title was perpetuated in amalgamations of 1891. Its user was of different sort compared with those of other smaller subsidiary railways. With an end-on connection to the underground Mersey Railway (which was outside the scope of the Railways Act) it carried both suburban business passengers and short-distance seaside traffic, which had steadily increased as the Birkenhead sprawl extended along the sandhills. Someone – possibly in the Wirral Railway's Advertising and Publicity Department, called West Kirby "The Mentone of the North" and, of course, there was New Brighton, whose charms one remembers being boldly advertised at the principal southern terminus of the London, Brighton and South Coast line. In 1922 the route totalled only 13 miles 56 chains, worked by 17 locomotives, 71 carriages, 80 goods and 17 service vehicles.

In Cumberland, the Cleator and Workington Junction Railway was purely a mineral and goods line, 30½ miles long, with 6 locomotives and 248 freight vehicles.

Long worked as an appendage of the North Stafford, the Leek and Manifold Valley Light Railway on its 2ft 6in gauge, already noted, was yet a subsidiary company when it came to the LMS Amalgamation. These completed the component lines owning their own rolling stock. As to outposts of empire, one should not forget the County Donegal Railways, serving beautiful, remote and unprofitable areas of Western Ireland, nearly all in the new Free State but working both the Letterkenny Railway and the NCC's Derry–Strabane line within the Six Counties. Of 3ft gauge, on which it used some quite imposing rolling stock, it had 24 locomotives, 59 coaching vehicles and 312 goods and miscellaneous wagons. Its route mileage came to 91 miles owned, plus 19 miles (Letterkenny) and 15 miles worked for the NCC. Its inclusion here owes to its becoming an LMS joint property. West of Strabane, the lines were joint between the Northern Counties Committee and the Great Northern Railway (Ireland). Unlike the NCC, which in later years looked very much a poor relation of the

Midland, the County Donegal resembled nothing but itself, save that Midland Railway pictures turned up in two or three of its first-class carriages. Fair enough, one supposes, seeing how the London & North Western had been fond of illustrating Great Southern and Western territory, especially, it seemed, in dining saloons, by virtue of Greenore and North Wall!

These, then, were the operating railways which went to form the London Midland & Scottish Empire. At worst, they might have been the ingredients for as shaky and divided a realm as any that ever was misgoverned by one of the less creditable Roman Emperors, but the future was not as black as some feared it would be.

CHAPTER TWO

The New Company

EXCEPT, perhaps, for the Great Western, all the new main-line companies which came to serve Great Britain in 1923 had their pains. Birth pangs there were to be sure, but in the case of an undertaking as large as the London Midland & Scottish, the worst trouble was more nearly comparable to indigestion. The old doctor, Sir W. Guy Granet, had his combination of wisdom and skill, and later, Sir Josiah Stamp, as he then was, had a more ruthless but certainly effective surgical technique, though this, rough and ready though it were, was not of such a drastic sort as Dr. Richard – later Lord – Beeching was to apply some thirty years later, under circumstances of a more critical sort.

By no means everybody was satisfied at the treatment he and his were receiving under that formidable Railways Act, 1921. It was not until March 21, 1923, that the LMS absorbed one of the oldest railways in the kingdom, the Dundee and Newtyle, small though it might be. Of that Scottish giant the Caledonian, one heard a good deal. In April, 1923, final proceedings began on the exchange of Stock, and the question at issue concerned LMS Stock to be allocated in exchange for certain Caley Ordinary, which had been split. That a company such as the Caledonian should go down without a bonny fight was unthinkable, and all properly artistic students of railway history are still glad that there was at least some sort of a Battle of Mons Graupius.

The Caledonian had made reservations in regard to four-per-cent Guaranteed Annuities, as it ought, and four-per-cent Lanarkshire and Dumbartonshire Guaranteed Stock. In respect of Caledonian Deferred Ordinary Stock Nos. 1 and 2, the LMS claimed that it had no value and should be cancelled. Sir Alexander Kaye Butterworth made the point that the LMS offer did not sufficiently consider the position of this Deferred Ordinary. The fact that it had been split should have been faced, and its specific value considered. For the LMS Mr. Tomlin contended that Caledonian Deferred Ordinary had *no gambling value*. The great question to be decided was on Caledonian Preferred and Deferred Ordinary shares. The Tribunal decided on the following allocations: For each £100 Caledonian Preferred Ordinary, £50 LMS four-per-cent Preference and £13 6s 8d LMS Ordinary; for every £100 Caledonian Deferred Converted Ordinary, £10 LMS Amalgamated Ordinary. For each £100 Caledonian Unconverted Ordinary, £50 LMS 1923 four-per-cent Preference and

31

£23 6s 8d LMS Ordinary, and so in proportion for any part of £100.

Mr. MacMillan, KC, for the Caledonian, called it *cauld kail het again*, which might have been paraphrased by a South Country wife in respect of the husband she henpecked: "I warmed up his old cabbage".

The Tribunal declined to state a case for appeal on any point of law. The scheme was to be sealed on June 29, to come into operation on July 1, 1923. It confirmed the final fusion of the great and jealous Caledonian Railway with the greater London Midland & Scottish. LMS original capital amounted to £398,339,167 with power to raise an additional amount of £15,488,106 and further borrowing powers to the amount of £9,717,077. The North Stafford was irrevocably roped-in at the same time. It had long been a very close ally of the London & North Western. For every £100 of its three-per-cent Debenture Stock it received £75 LMS four-per-cent Debenture Stock. For each £100 of its five-per-cent Guaranteed (Canal Purchase) £20 shares it received £125 LMS four-per-cent Guaranteed Stock, plus £2 15s 0d for surrender of contingent rights; £100 North Stafford three-per-cent Preference Stock became £75 LMS Preference, and £100 North Stafford Ordinary was worth £74 LMS Ordinary. Considering all things, the "Knotty" had not done so badly, "but there can have been few of the staunch local supporters of the line who did not regret the bargain".[1] Arnold Bennett once wrote: "Though we return Radicals to Parliament, we are proud of a Railway."[2] Of other local authors, only H. G. Wells sneered, and he was an *emigré* from London, Chatham and Dover country, who had a destructive attitude towards most if not all of the old railway companies, even towards their method of transport once he had got a whiff of the late Mr. Brennan's monorail.[3]

LMS terms to the Wirral Railway, which, though small, carried many of those whom at that time only America called *Commuters*, amounted to £50 cash for every ten £10 shares of Wirral Ordinary. The Directors were paid off. Wirral Stockholders of four-per-cent and 4½-per-cent Preference got LMS four-per-cent Preference.

As to smaller undertakings, the LMS offer to the Garstang and Knott End Railway assured its proprietors a three-per-cent return, which was better than anything they had enjoyed hitherto. Considering past history of the Knott End company, they were lucky. Their equipment, which compared favourably with that of the East Kent, Weston Clevedon and Portishead, and other valiant undertakings which were outside the scope

[1] *The North Staffordshire Railway* by "Manifold" (J. R. Hollick, C. A. Moreton, G. N. Nowell-Gossling, F. M. Page and W. T. Stubbs).
[2] In *The Grim Smile of the Five Towns.*
[3] In *The War in the Air* and *In the Days of the Comet.* In *Mr. Britling Sees It Through* he betrayed a soft spot for the Great Eastern, which in those days served his home at Dunmow, but in *The Shape of Things to Come* he abolished railways altogether.

"Coronation Scot"; the nose, 1936.

Eric Treacy

ABOVE: Twilight of Crewe Practice;
reboilered Caprotti Claughton near
Wavertree, Liverpool.

Eric Treacy

BELOW: Indian Summer; decrepit
compound at Carlisle.

Eric Treacy

ABOVE: "Mid-day Scot" near Tring;
No. 6156. *The South Wales Borderer*.

BELOW: Turbine Locomotive No.6202,
near Wavertree.

Eric Treacy

Eric Treacy

scription with the remark: "What are you going to do about that silly gap?" The gap in the present case was the Caledonian company, whose intransigent attitude is mentioned already. When that gap was closed, Caledonian elections to the LMS Board were: J. Hamilton Houldsworth, James Whiteford Murray and Frederick Bower Sharp. With their advent, the London Midland & Scottish Railway truly became a settled corporation.

As suggested, there was at first very little visible change from pre-amalgamation days, though the decision to paint engines and carriages red, and goods vehicles lead-grey, came in that first year. A piece of rebuilding which involved a structure dating back to the very earliest days of the railway industry was that of the bridge over the Regent's Canal in Camden Town, London. The bridge dated back to 1837 and had a floor of cast-iron plates. Its abutments had been strengthened with concrete in 1890, and two years later steel cross-girders had been laid between the original cast-iron members. Even the London & North Western Railway was making its engines rather bigger about that time, with such giants as Webb's *Greater Britain* in the offing of impending mechanical history. The new LMS bridge has six steel plate main girders with steel cross-beams, and as the big West Coast and Irish expresses had been worked by Claughton class four-cylinder engines for some while past, it was perhaps high time.

Another interesting civil engineering work initiated at this time was the replacement of Chevet Tunnel, 702yd long with a maximum depth about 90ft. Through it passed the main-line traffic from Leeds to the south between Chevet Junction and Syndale Junction, Wakefield. Sir W. G. Armstrong, Whitworth and Company had the contract, and during the years 1923–25 the old tunnel was demolished and its site turned into a four-track cutting, one of the deepest in the country, through a mixture of hard rock and shale. Traffic was maintained throughout the conversion.

From constructive to destructive things: July 5, 1923, saw the newly constituted company's first big smash; though to be sure, considering the circumstances and effects, things might have been much more awful. At Diggle, the four roads through the old and new Standedge Tunnels through the Pennines – third-longest in the country after the Severn and Totley Tunnels and parallel to the ancient canal tunnel of pre-railway days – were divided into two going south via Friezland and two turning north by Greenfield (quadruple track being resumed at Stalybridge). At 10.6 am on that day a goods train by the up South line was stopped by flag. An up Leeds express, travelling on the Northern up line, was to be crossed to the southern line for Stalybridge via Friezland. This train consisted of ten carriages headed by Experiment class 4-6-0 engine No. 1406 *George Findlay* and piloted by 0-6-0 No. 1027 (a Cauliflower). The Diggle signalman accepted this train, and took in the flag with which he had halted the goods to avoid alarming and stopping the drivers of the express. Now the fireman of the goods did, as he ought, carry out Rule 55 and go to the box, but he did not ask how long his driver was likely to be kept waiting, nor did the signalman give any message that his driver was not to move. When this driver saw the flag taken in, his fireman having rejoined the engine, he moved forward, and immediately after the express came roaring out of the tunnel, striking his wagons on the crossover, and also coming in violent contact with the tender of his engine No. 1062. The pilot engine of the express was turned almost completely round by the shock, and very severely damaged. The train engine, *George Findlay*, came to rest leaning against the cutting side to the left and telescoping took place between the first two coaches which were of the ordinary London & North Western wooden-body type. All carriages were electrically lit except one, a Great Western composite, which was badly raked but fortunately not set on fire.

Four persons were killed; two passengers, Driver Walker of the goods, who had moved without proper authority, and the fireman of the unlucky Cauliflower which had been thus chucked all over the junction. It was, as may be imagined, a collision of the spectacular sort wherein one surveyed the battered and disordered locomotives and wondered where on earth *that* one (the 'Cauliflower') could have been before impact. Indeed, the fatalities were mild considering all other things. While the Diggle signalman was held at fault for not having properly informed the goods driver through his fireman, the signalling was faulted also. There should have been a fixed signal, an inner home, instead of that vague and fallible flag from the box. Colonel Sir John Pringle inquired and reported.

Of other early accidents on the LMS there were two, both worse than that at Diggle, in the following year. On April 26, 1924, a London-bound FA Cup Final special train from Coventry was halted in the tunnel just north of Euston, on the up slow line. Now a Scotch express had just gone in by the up fast line, and the singalman concerned immediately cleared this on his up slow instead of his up fast instrument. He then admitted an electric suburban train to the up slow. The electric train went full tilt into the rear of the Cup Final special. The steel frame of its leading motor coach cut viciously into the old wooden carriages of the special and five passengers were killed. Its motorman, though badly hurt and trapped for five hours, survived the impact.

It was impossible afterwards to lift any heavy rolling-stock inside the tunnel, and the damaged vehicles had to be pulled out in pieces. Fortunately people were careful about fire, for the tunnel was reeking with gas from the old, broken London & North Western carriages.

Thirdly, on November 3, 1924 a Liverpool–Blackpool train was derailed at Lytham, with the death of fifteen persons. For once in a while, it was a case of mechanical failure and not one of human fallibility. The train involved was the 4.40 pm from Liverpool Exchange to Manchester and Blackpool, and at the time of the accident consisted of the Blackpool portion only, having slipped the remainder. It was headed by L&Y 4–4–0 locomotive No. 1105, a 7ft 3in Aspinall type dating from 1891 but rebuilt in 1908 with a superheater and Walschaerts gear. This engine had come from Horwich only ten days before, following a general overhaul. Behind the tender were four ordinary L&Y non-corridor coaches, wooden and gaslit, built between 1899 and 1910, and full of passengers.

At 5.46 pm, between Moss Side and Lytham on the coast line, on a right-hand curve, the left hand leading bogie wheel tyre broke and went off into an adjacent field on a curve like that of a hockey stick. The engine-men were not immediately aware, and the engine ran for about 300 yards with the bogie derailed. The derailed wheels struck first the crossing of the Lytham Gasworks siding connection, and then the girders of the bridge over Main Dyke, which broke the other leading tyre, severed the bogie and flung it out to the left. The engine went over at high speed and finished up on her right side, separated from the tender and turned completely round so that both were headed back towards Moss Side.[1] The first two coaches overran the engine and tender, separated from the rest of the train by coupling breakage. The third and fourth carriages overturned against Warton Signalbox, which one of them demolished. The signalbox fire was scattered amongst the wreckage of one of these old gaslit coaches. Fortunately the passengers were extricated in time, and the signalman himself, though badly hurt, had a remarkable escape. The sheared-off engine bogie was found close beside the fourth coach. The driver and twelve passengers were killed and two more passengers died of their injuries. Rescue and clearance work were delayed by further adversity. Destruction of the signalbox had cut all communication – the accident was in open country – and the steam crane of the Preston breakdown train burst a boiler tube when it reached Kirkham South, two hours and twenty minutes after the initial derailment.

Colonel Sir John Pringle, who inquired into the accident, found that fracture of the critical tyre had resulted from an invisible flaw. The tyre dated from 1920 and had run 100,000 miles. It had been made with the single-ingot (beehive) system of casting steel, replaced at Horwich in 1923 by the long-ingot system. Thirty tyres of the former sort, still in service at the time of the accident, were then withdrawn. There were

[1] Another example of an overset express locomotive being turned completely round and then overtaken by the carriages was at Wellingborough on the Midland in 1898 (a Johnson 4–4–0).

some sharp remarks about the lighting of trains by oil gas, which had been generally used by the L&YR. None of the carriages involved were of that company's later "fireproof" sort. A photograph of the overturned engine shows the lights still on in one of the carriages which had overtaken it after derailment. This accident made some public sensation. The Liverpool–Blackpool business traffic was heavy and important; also this was the worst smash since formation of the London Midland & Scottish company. Mechanical failure is more likely than human error to make people uneasy.

There were of course the usual quaint letters in the newspapers from self-qualified experts, but one of these parties even put in an appearance at the Government Inquiry, said everybody else was wrong, and asserted that the tyre had broken because the train's brakes were in the wrong place. He fumed for some time and then Pringle shut him up. As for engine No. 1105, she was by then thirty-three years old, and sixteen-years-on from her only rebuilding, so this accident became her sad end. She was taken to pieces in Lytham yard and the mangled remains were then carried off by special train to Horwich for the final cutting up. It was very rare for a locomotive to become a total loss through accident, even in cases of violent collision. The famous London & North Western engine *Hardwicke*, when quite new, had survived the ordeal of falling off a bridge in Birmingham, into a yard below, after an argument with a Midland train. (May 27, 1892.) The Midland was apparently playing at *First into New Street*.

The London Midland & Scottish – indeed both Northern lines, had ill luck as to accidents in those early days of the new companies, the 1920s. Accidents were relatively few in the south and west of England, though France had a series of frightful smashes in these years, and from 1926 one personally recalls a collision of singular enormity in Munich, initiating a spell of troubles for the Germans. These things were sufficient for us to have a slightly holier-than-thou attitude about railway accidents for a little while; rather a dangerous sort of complacency. In 1928, the London & North Eastern had, at Darlington, the worst British collision since the sanguinary year of 1915, and in October the LMS was to have a holocaust at Charfield, of which more later.

For a brief while, in text, to more cheerful things! There were great managerial and even constitutional changes on the LMS at this time. In 1924 that shrewd, dome-headed Lancashire & Yorkshire man, Sir Arthur Watson, was succeeded as General Manager by the Rt. Hon. H. G. Burgess, who for a long time had managed the London & North Western company's business in Ireland, being for twenty years a member of the Dublin Port and Docks Board and for eighteen years a Commissioner for Carlingford Loch. (He was also for sixteen years a Director and for four years acted as Deputy Chairman of the Dublin and South Eastern Railway.) In 1919 he had entered Government (Ministry of Transport, Director of Irish Transport). In 1920 he became Principal Assistant to the General Manager of the London & North Western, and in November, 1923, he became Assistant General Manager. He succeeded Sir Arthur Watson in March, 1924, but his preferment was not, nor was intended to be, of very long duration. It was indeed recognised as a temporary position and his time for retirement was ripe. Sir Guy Granet himself, certainly growing no younger, was preparing what might have been called a palace-revolution. His company was still bedevilled by old rivalries which, the constituent companies having been as great and jealous as they were, could not be put down by making this or that interest a dominant one.

In May, 1925, the LMS Board announced the creation of a new office, that of President of the Executive. Executive control was to be invested in that President, with four Vice-Presidents to form an Executive Committee assisted by the Secretary and the Chief Legal Adviser of the company. There were some forebodings over this bold departure from old con-stitutional procedure. It is believed to have been the invention of Sir Josiah Stamp, an economic genius of whom Granet had got hold and who was destined to head the organisation.

Josiah Charles Stamp had been born on June 21, 1880. He was an eminent example of the Office-Boy-Who-Made-Good by intellectual gift which had been developed by industry and piety. Having joined the Civil Service in 1896; when he was of age, he was still simply an industrious clerk who never stopped working, conscientiously for his employers under Government who were those popularly dubbed the Income Tax Men. He never slackened on his own education for the sort of career he had chosen. He took a First Class in Economics and Political Science in 1911; he was Cobden Prizeman, 1912; DSc 1916, and Hutchinson Research Medallist of that year. Also in 1916 he was a Council Member of the Royal Statistical Society; he was its Joint Secretary, and Editor of its *Proceedings* during the years 1920–1930. Later, he was to be its President (1930–32) and Hon. Vice-President thereafter. In 1920, also, he had become a Council Member of the Royal Economic Society. His first official con-nection with transport had been as far back as 1898, when he had been briefly in the Marine Department at the Board of Trade. His entry into big business stemmed from his able administration of Excess Profits Duty during the 1914–18 war, which had brought him into contact with the great industrial undertakings. In March, 1919, he had left his office under Government to become Secretary and a Director of Nobel Industries, Limited. This firm was merged into the great new organization Imperial Chemical Industries in December, 1926. For American business organisa-tion, with which he had had experience in his dealings with the Du Pont de

Nemours Chemical Group, he had the greatest admiration, and he strongly influenced the nascent ICI, whose Board he joined in 1926.

Prior to his LMS appointment he had become CBE in 1918, KBE in 1920 and GBE in 1924. In the latter year he had been British Representative on the Reparations Commission's 1924 Committee on German currency and finance, which initiated the formation of the German State Railway Company, which was to continue under one form or another until the fall of the National Socialist Government in 1945. The Deutsche Reichsbahn, as it was known at home, was formed late in 1924 under the Dawes Plan, to be a commercial undertaking from whose net revenue and from transport tax there should come substantial contributions towards German war reparations.[1] It is interesting to recall that Stamp had that much to do with the formation of the Reichsbahn. In Germany, Julius Dorpmuller was a great general manager. It has been said that Granet introduced Stamp to transport, but whether the Reichsbahn connection was a result or a cause of this may be argued. Your author is not prepared to open the discussion *ex cathedra*.

Stamp took office in January, 1926. In October, the abolition of the old office of General Manager was made public. Burgess was to retire at the end of March, 1927. In those fourteen months, quite a lot was to happen. The four Vice-Presidents in 1926 were J. H. Follows, CBE, for the Railway Traffic Operating and Commercial Section; S. H. Hunt, CBE, for the same; J. Quirey, MInstT, for the Accounting and Service Departments; and R. W. Reid, MIMechE, who had been Carriage and Wagon Superintendent, for Works and Ancillary Undertakings. Follows had joined the Midland Railway at twenty, in 1890. He came to Derby as Traffic Inspector in 1901 and was given the Derby District, with that office, late in the same year. He became Superintendent of Freight Trains on the Midland in 1911, Divisional Superintendent in 1912, Superintendent of Operation in 1914, and Chief General Superintendent in 1917.

John Follows, whose father also had served the Midland Railway for forty years, was a man distinctly after Stamp's heart, single-minded, methodical, and austere in his personal life. Both men got themselves official saloons for moving about the country, but Follows' was the Spartan one of the two, made out of an old rail-motor body, I was told, though it looked more like a Lancaster–Morecambe electric trailer car, nearly all its windows with opaque bathroom glazing, so that neither could the mutable many impertinently gaze on him as he worked his way about the system, nor could he be distracted by their idle antics or by the inconsequent scenery. There were a bedroom and a bathroom;

[1] The Young Plan replaced the Dawes Plan in 1929, and broke down in the economic crisis of 1931. Reparations payments were suspended in the following year. Under the Nazi regime, the Reichsbahn became something of a boondoggle, doubtless under the advice of Dr. Schacht.

the second-named contained an enamelled-iron tub with a cold tap only. Stamp's carriage was of a more sumptuous sort, though all in the puritan manner, and had a London & North Western look about it, enhanced by a special departmental livery of maroon with cream-coloured upper panels. There was a kitchen, and one recalls a vision of the President of the Executive, dining in solitary state to the accompaniment of what looked like dry-ginger-ale, at the rear end of the "Royal Highlander" as it rolled through Harrow one summer evening.[1]

Stanley Hunt, at the time of his appointment as a Vice-President, had been the company's Chief Goods Manager, having been appointed to that office on the London & North Western at the beginning of 1919. He was a veteran, for he had joined the Railway Service at Liverpool Waterloo in the year of Stamp's birth. By 1898, he was Assistant District Traffic Superintendent, Lancaster. In 1903 he was Traffic Superintendent, Garston Docks, and in 1910, in London, he was Assistant to the General Manager, and Chief of the Buying and Sales Department. During the war he was with Sir Guy Calthrop in France and with Sir Francis Dent, General Manager of the South Eastern and Chatham, in the Near East (Salonika and Egypt). Calthrop died in Government service and so never returned to the London & North Western; he had previously run the Caledonian on lines so methodically Saxon that he considerably shook some of the Gaelic people thereon. Hunt's association with him entailed acquisition of a far-flung knowledge about what had become a single system, and he brought a West Coast leavening into an Executive which might have been Midland-dominated.

Midland in the bone, however obviously Scots his origins, was the fourth Vice-President, Robert Whyte Reid, who had become Works Assistant in the Carriage and Wagon Department, Derby, under David Bain in 1909. Bain, first on the North Eastern and then on the Midland, had been one of the most prominent makers of really comfortable and nicely-designed railway carriages, and Reid, succeeding him, carried on very much in his Chief's ways. Serving the LMS in the same capacity, he continued to make passanger vehicles in the Midland style, more comfortable than those of other lines but with a certain old fashion about them. (Of British freight stock at this time and for many years after, the less written the better! It was effetely antiquated, the rolling-laughing-stock of Europe, let alone America.)

Chief officers at this time (apart from the Locomotive Department which will be mentioned separately), included the following: C. R. Byrom, OBE, MInstT, was Chief General Superintendent. (How all the railway companies loved that title *Superintendent*! Apart from transport, one

---

[1] King Edward VIII, who intensely disliked his grandfather's royal train, liked Stamp's carriage, which the President was always willing to lend.

associated it with such variously good-working institutions as work-houses and Sunday schools. Stamp exemplified one of the latter sort.) Charles Reginald Byrom previously had been Assistant General Super-intendent of the LMS, having been the London & North Western's Superintendent (Southern) when LNWR and L&Y amalgamated in 1922. When the LMS was formed, he became Assistant General Super-intendent (Passenger and Commercial). He was of the solid Victorian-English professional class, born in a Cheshire rectory in 1878 and educated at Shrewsbury.

Three English Divisional Superintendents were G. N. Ford at Euston, E. D. Grasete at Derby, and T. W. Royle, MBE, MInstT in Manchester. Of Royle the author has pleasant personal memories, though from much later years, and a good deal of anecdote. Mrs. Royle, as a little girl, had been turned over and spanked after a tea party at the Chief Mechanical Engineer's house in Crewe, for innocently asking Francis Webb why his new engines (The Greater Britains) sometimes turned their four big wheels in opposing directions at starting. The General Superin-tendent (Passenger and Commercial) was Ashton Davies, MBE, MInstT, a very remarkable man who had joined the Lancashire & Yorkshire Railway in 1890, became one of the apostles of train control, and, when Watson succeeded Sir John Aspinall as L&Y General Manager in 1919, became his Superintendent of the Line. He became Northern Divisional General Manager when his company amalagamated with the London & North Western, and General Superintendent, LMS Northern Division, from January 1, 1924. In the same year he achieved the office initially mentioned.

Chief Civil Engineer was Alexander Newlands, CBE, a Highlandman of Moray who had joined the Highland Railway in 1892 after serving his time as an apprentice, and had been Resident Engineer on the Strome-Ferry Kyle of Lochalsh line, including the deep water pier at the Kyle, from 1893 to 1897. He was also Resident Engineer on the doubling of the Highland line over Druimuachdar Pass between Blair Atholl and Dalwhinnie (narrowed again, but with improvement in curvature, at the time of writing) and became Engineer in Chief of the Highland company, following the steps of such great eminences as Joseph Mitchell and Murdoch Paterson, in 1914. In 1923 the LMS made him its Divisional Engineer, Inverness, and in 1924 Divisional Engineer, Crewe. No more worthy man, with more experience of great railway engineering could have succeeded as Chief Engineer of so great a railway company. Further, he wrote an admirable pocket-history of Scottish railways. From a chance meeting in 1932 one recalls a genial character and a man of venerable port.

Apart from his official status with the Highland and the LMS, Newlands had surveyed, both on the mainlaind and in the isles of Scotland, those fascinating railways which never came into being, and, owing to the rise of, firstly and entirely properly, the commercial motor, and, secondly the availability of the mass-produced private motor to both the small-burgess and the proletarian classes of this over-crowded Realm, never will.

Upheavals of social history having been thus introduced, let us turn to that of the middle 1920s, concurrent with the reorganisation of the London Midland & Scottish company's own government. Social and industrial unrest had been brewing for some time, ever since David Lloyd George's Land Fit for Heroes to Live In had not quite come off. The Establishment of the period was still expecting to live in the grand Victorian manner, and on the surface there seemed to be no reason why it should not, whatever might be going on in Russia. On the map, the British Empire looked even vaster and more grandly scarlet than ever before, including not only the former German colonies but even the memorable city of Jerusalem and some other places. But things were bad in the coalfields, in those mines whence much of that Empire's wealth had been drawn. The miners had one of the more perilous and less well-paid of all important callings. They struck. Many others followed very important and relatively ill-paid callings; as in transport, heavy engineering and printing. Great Britain's first Socialist Government had come and gone. The Administration was in the hands of Stanley Baldwin, a West Midland steelmaster who, until recently a Conservative Back-bencher, had suddenly become Prime Minister because, apparently, some influential people had decided that Lord Curzon was far too dangerous a possibility. Aristocracy and burgess were almost solidly behind Baldwin. Labour loathed him and all he stood for. The crunch was imminent. The mining subsidy ended on April 30, with certain results.

In sympathy with the miners, a general strike of industry and transport, called by the Trades Union Congress, began on May 4, 1926. Everything that normally went, seemed to stop.[1] On the LMS 85 per cent of the wages staff and 41 per cent of the salaried staff came out. They numbered 197,001 and 18,633 persons respectively. It was a very great stoppage. The company enrolled 21,807 volunteers; people who liked railways and longed to help make a railway go for its own sake; gay – and in those days strictly Tory – undergraduates from the universities who were quite ready for a less futile lark than usual; sober retired railwaymen who thought the strike a calamity, and were not by any means sorry to become drivers and guards once again, if only, they hoped, for a little while. Of the volunteers enrolled, only 7,662 were actually engaged in railway work. Unlike the railway strike of 1924, this involved both the National Union of

---

[1] The author, then cramming in Munich, gathered even from the highly Conservative *München-Augsburger Abendzeitung* that the English Revolution had begun.

Railwaymen and the Associated Society of Locomotive Engineers and Firemen (only the later had been out in the previous strike). Most of the signalmen were out, and it was now that the great value of centralised control became apparent. The motor drivers were out. So were the dockers and quay staff, though not the sailors. The only steamship services suspended entirely were those between Heysham and Belfast, Holyhead and Greenore, and Liverpool–Drogheda. Two Clyde steamers plied between Wemyss Bay and Rothesay. The Goole–Continental services were much interrupted by stoppage in the docks.

On the line, the first thing to be done was the clearance of trains which had been abandoned. Food was an absolute priority, and milk traffic was almost normal from the beginning of the strike. On the first day, as to passenger services, the LMS ran a few Watford electric trains. (Naval stokers were put into the great power stations and took to their job very naturally.) On May 4 the LMS ran 163 passenger trains, but its vast goods and mineral traffic was completely still. On May 5 the company ran 423 passenger trains and 23 goods. In the second week of the strike, May 10 saw 1,132 passenger trains and 95 goods trains on the LMS and on May 14 there were 1,623 passenger and 242 goods trains.

Generally the strikers were very well-behaved: only on the London & North Eastern was there major sabotage, the "Flying Scotsman" being derailed (by colliers) near Cramlington. The situation was really much less *ugly* than it had been on the Caledonian in 1891. Most people abode strictly by Union Rules. Intransigent exceptions were not only dismissed but prosecuted. Terms of railway settlement were signed on May 14, but there was not universal reinstatement. The continued coal strike made things very difficult, and there were still 59,000 railwaymen not yet reinstated on May 20.[1] There were minor casualties in the system itself. The company's steam tramway from Wolverton to Stony Stratford and the line between Langley Mill and Ripley ceased work for good. The Deanside goods line, Renfrew, stopped at the beginning of October, and in the following year, on February 19, there was an end to the electric tramcars on the 3ft 6in gauge Burton and Ashby Light Railway, sometime a small but in its way useful and engaging appendage of the former Midland Railway.

The aspect of the LMS in these middle-twenties had not changed much from its constituents' days. From St. Pancras to Carlisle and from Leeds to Bristol, the Midland still looked almost exactly like the Midland. On what had been the London & North Western, red paint, patchily on the engines and rolling stock, and the advent of some new Midland compound

---

[1] Visiting England and Scotland in July, the author found things apparently normal on the railways, apart from the appalling soft coal – possibly Polish, or German and Belgian – being burnt by some of the engines, even of Scotch expresses.

locomotives, bespoke difference from former aspects, and so it was, too, in Scotland. Difference was most apparent on the Highland lines north of Perth–Stanley Junction, owing to an influx of corridor coaches and dining cars from other lines, all of more venerable vintages and many still in their old colours: London & North Western and Caledonian white uppers, Midland red, Furness blue, and of course the Lancashire & Yorkshire's two revolting shades of brown. But the immigrants included some good old carriages, and Highland travel had become noticeably less disagreeable.

The aspect of the railway at this time nevertheless was not good. The stations, best on the Caledonian and the Midland lines, were ancient, and getting shabby, and the same applied to much of the rolling stock. Of constituent systems, the Midland and the Glasgow and South Western looked best as to the trains, though the Highland locomotives were reputed to be in excellent condition, doubtless owing to a sort of mass-general-overhaul which the older ones had received owing to something near mechanical breakdown late in the war years. It was also becoming what seemed a critical time for railways generally. Not until 1929 did the Wall Street crash detonate the economic slump which was to wrap itself round the Western and Southern World (Russia was still struggling through the marginal mud of revolution and China was in the chaos made by contending war-lords.) But things were steadily becoming more uneasy, and though the General Strike had come and gone, the coal dispute dragged on through 1926. Further, the whole principle of railway transport was becoming unpopular.

With the best of intentions, the London & North Eastern had held those Stockton and Darlington Centenary celebrations in 1925, with royal patronage, but to many the event had suddenly rubbed in that railways were now over a hundred years old, and therefore *old-fashioned*. One could buy a T-Model Ford motor car new for £100, and jokes about that useful conveyance were already stale. Doctors ran Wolseleys. Minor civil servants were putting-on enormous side with bullet-nosed Morris cars; even the poor Vicar pensioned-off his old pony and started visiting the remoter sick in the funniest little motor car you ever saw, an Austin Seven. Motoring still could be pleasant; we had not an inkling of the nightmare to come, so if we could, we acquired motors and, human nature being what it is, some of us looked down our noses at people who walked two miles to the station, took a train for eight miles, and then walked on two miles more. The youthful rich, with more patrician vehicles than those mentioned, emphasised the heartiness of their caste[1] by driving

[1] It had its reflection in popular fiction of the period. Sapper's *Bulldog Drummond* became larger than life at the wheel of a Bentley; in a novel called *Hippy Buchan*, Ethel Boileau made her futile hero drive thus at terrific speed through the night, gratuitously adding that *Hippy detested trains*.

through the night to Scotland, even the best of sleepers being unthinkable. People used the early airliners and for months after kept talking about it, only skipping the part about vomiting into a paper-bag and the fact that after the holiday they had sneaked home by train and by a ship in which one could more decently be sick.

The train was no longer fashionable. All the same, nearly everybody continued to use it for ordinary journeys over any distance. Road hauliers certainly made some inroads on freight, and then there came the motor coach, joint offspring of the touring motor *char-a-banc* and the motor bus This, however, did not become stylish. Persons of the landed and professional classes, though already great users of the private motor, would not have been seen dead in one of those things! The lower middle classes, however, received the motor coach with enthusiasm; their more Radical members called it "the poor man's limousine" and there was a sort of slogan: "First-class comfort at less than third-class fares" which was something of a prevarication as to the comfort part. Working-class user flocked to the motor coach, which, with its meretricious gaudiness, lifted vast crowds from the scruffy Lancashire and Yorkshire horse-hair seats whereon they had been wont to make pilgrimage to Blackpool.

In 1930 there was yet another large-scale Railway Centenary celebration, this time commemorating the Liverpool and Manchester opening, with an outdoor exhibition in Wavertree Park, Liverpool. Perhaps it would not have been such a damp squib had not the rain come down in torrents on the first day (as indeed it had done at the original opening in 1830). But it had none of the triumphant pride that there had been in the Darlington one, even though it had a wonderful thing in the shape of an oval track whereon the ancient locomotive *Lion*, recently rescued and rehabilitated, gave people rides in a beautiful set of replica carriages. An enormous pageant in costume, with mock-up locomotives powered by spluttering motor engines, was a sad thing, especially for the poor girls who had to look jolly and picturesque in gay bonnets, great skirts and frilly trouserines that became saturated. Some of the mud was memorable.

The LMS had been striving for some time to create an image of itself, which should command public respect; to make in fact a new Premier Line which was not the London & North Western warmed-up, a new Best Way which was not the Midland hashed. The sort of resistance it had to meet has just been described; in the 'twenties only the Great Western had any sort of social status among British railway companies, and that was because it preserved a much older image with no visible change, as if it were a Saxon Godwin, or a Norman Gresley among a lot of jumped-up nobodies whose peerages had been created by the House of Hanover.

One of the LMS company's earlier and most successful efforts, an admirable thing indeed, had been the commissioning of eminent artists to paint posters illustrating both its territory and its activities. In the past, railway pictorial posters had been generally eye-catching, and sometimes picturesque in a vernacular way, though many were of singular vulgarity. With some affection – it was just the sort of thing to appeal to the eye of a child – one recalls the London & North Western Railway's *Put Your Works Here*! It showed a huge single-block factory about to descend like an Unidentified Flying Object upon an oblong meadow beside the line, to which the company had already laid on a siding with the inevitable Webb coal engine awaiting custom. As to passenger business, what nobody then called *sex-appeal* was widely used and was exemplified by an incredibly overdressed, overhatted, overcorseted young female person against a panoramic background, such as Coniston Water. Goodness only knew how she had got up the the mountain with all those things on!

Much better was the Caledonian's famous *Golfing Girl* at Gleneagles, whom the LMS took up with pleasure. She had been variously driving-off, or using her No. 7 in a bunker, since well before the '14 war, and her neat tweeds changed with the years and the vagaries of fashion. Plenty of children were depicted at the seaside; some of them were horrible little fat-cheeked brats, but others were really charming.

But for years, the London & North Western had commissioned work from a very eminent painter, Norman Wilkinson, who specialised in marine subjects. In his struggling youth, when professional models came dear, his nice sister obliged him, and a poster of the ship-to-train transfer at Holyhead showed Miss Wilkinson sailing up the platform like a clipper before the South East Trades. In 1923, Norman Wilkinson persuaded the new company to produce pictorial posters on a new and at the same time patrician scale. He wrote at the time: "There is an idea very generally entertained that a poster is a particular form of art, and must be handled on certain conventional lines. This to me is a fallacy. A poster – I am speaking now of pictorial posters – is something that will attract and arrest the attention of the public. It therefore follows that if the bulk of the posters now displayed are on certain lines, one is likely to achieve greater success with something that is not essentially on those lines."

Just before Christmas, 1923, the London Midland & Scottish company announced the commissioning of Royal Academicians for the production of its new posters. There was to be no lettering on the pictures (a horrid custom of the past!) and very little on the borders. Had Stephen Potter reached maturity in those days, he might have remarked that the LMS had achieved a masterly piece of one-upmanship on the lofty old Great Western and some others. (The London & North Eastern, however, was quick off the mark. Brangwyn produced for it a glorious *Royal Border Bridge*.) To the LMS the several distinguished painters variously responded.

Sir D. Y. Cameron (an alarming man in some ways) painted simply *The Scottish Highlands*, rather in the manner of his famous *Shadows of Glencoe*; a very fine picture of mountains in those rich after-storm colours which lovers of Western Scotland have known for so long with such delight. Then Sir William Orpen, eminent painter of eminent personages' portraits, contributed a picture of enginemen in the cab, on a night express, but, one feels with less success. One would not dare to criticise Orpen's figures of the driver and fireman, and his drawing of the engine cab (indubitably London & North Western) was technically correct, but one suspected that he was not really at home with a locomotive. The glare of the open firedoor suggested that someone had dropped a fuzee into a box of fireworks, and the slobby stuff in front of the panel-plate suggested anything but the flying vapours of a locomotive at full speed in the night. Norman Wilkinson, of course, painted an Irish Sea packet under a sky of vast mounting cumulus. Stanhope Forbes painted *Platelayers*, a very agreeable picture of men lifting a rail into chairs and marred only by the pose of the lookout man who had turned to look round instead of having both eyes on the Up Fast and his warning horn at the ready.

There were various others; some good and one or two ineffably bad. Specially finished and mounted colour lithographs went to decorate the Great Hall at Euston, and by many who paused to look at them were thought to be the originals.

In 1926 came a rather different sort of poster, devoted in a matey sort of way to the working of the railways itself. Arthur Watts drew *The Driver*, *The Signalman*, *The Porter* and *The Guard*, and E. V. Knox (Evoe of *Punch*) furnished verses underneath.

The company's Advertising and Publicity Department owed much to the London & North Western company, which had been one of the very first to realise the popular appeal not only of the places and scenes the railway served but of the railway itself. One believes that Sir Frank Ree had had something to do with this. G. H. Loftus Allen became LMS Advertising and Publicity Officer in 1927, having joined the London & North Western service in 1913. In 1915 he had gone to France as an RTO, subsequently becoming Deputy Assistant Director of Railway Transport. Back in company's service, he had held office as Runner in various districts, being Superintendent of the Line's Runner, Birmingham, during the year 1922–23. He had six months in the United States under an LMS scheme. In the 1930s, one of his young men was Derek Barrie, journalist-turned-railwayman, who years after was to command the North Eastern and Eastern Regions of British Railways.

During those 'twenties, there was more image-creation by the official naming of certain trains. The title "Irish Mail", of course, went back to the beginning of main-line railways, but none of the West Coast expresses had official names. True, an old London & North Western picture post-card described something headed by an "Experiment" as being the "Flying Scotchman" (*sic*) on Bushey Troughs. Then a poster advertising the West Coast services of the LMS was decorated by a picture of a blackcock (one remembers the bird as looking more like a stout pigeon) and the legend "The Cock o' the North". But this name eventually went to the other side of the country, to be bestowed on a London & North Eastern locomotive. The ten-o'clock day train from Euston to Glasgow and Edinburgh became the "Royal Scot". The sometime "Corridor" became the "Midday Scot". The night train to Inverness became the "Royal Highlander" and the Midland route acquired for its day trains the less sonorous titles of "Thames–Forth Express" and "Thames–Clyde Express"; (on both the Scottish lines Carlisle to Edinburgh Waverley and Carlisle to Glasgow St. Enoch, people went on calling them "Pullmans").

In 1928 there brewed up a little lark, recalling the West Coast/East Coast rivalry of the 1880s and 1890s, though there was as yet no hell-for-leather running with the latest-possible locomotives hauling the lightest-possible trains. The London & North Western had long prided itself on occasional very long non-stop runs, usually with the royal train. But for years, too, the Great Western had been running, in summer, non-stop from London to Plymouth, the longest stretch in the world. Now that fact may have *niggled* some people in the North for just as long. (One recalls a most nice and friendly citizen of Leeds saying quietly over glasses: "Oh yes, we hate Lancashire people like poison! But mind you, we're in it together if we're up against you Southerners!") This observation was in no way offensively meant. It was a statement of fact, as of Bolivians hating Paraguayans but concurring when it came to *Gringos* of any sort; Munich hating Berlin except when it came to common ground on Leipzig, and so forth. What right had those folk in the South to be so stuck-up about some unimportant holiday train out of a terminus where nobody had ever heard of Blackpool? What Cornish? What Riviera?

There *must* be non-stop running between the capitals of England and Scotland, and the fact that this would in no way favour any cities in the North of England was immaterial. At both Euston and Kings Cross, the heart was Northern, or at least a great part of it was. Their respective railways were Northern, just as Bolivia and Paraguay were Spanish-American, more or less.

Now Edinburgh was the natural destination of East Coast expresses and Glasgow was that of West Coast expresses. So it was not unexpected that the London & North Eastern should propose running from Kings Cross[1] to Waverley, holing-out in one. Quietly and without fuss, the LMS

[1] LNER Headquarters, however, was at Marylebone.

divided its Royal Scot on April 27, 1928, so that the Edinburgh portion made quite a light train behind standard compound engine No. 1054. Also quietly and without fuss, this ran from Euston to Princes Street without stopping, for the first time in history, while the London & North Eastern was still resting on its marks before the summer services.

It was a stunt of stunts, and in retrospect seems to have been a rather childish one, but it courted popularity at the time, which, one supposes, is the object of Publicity Departments. Various papers made a story of it, though of the specialists *The Locomotive* commented rather tartly that it was doubtful if these long non-stop runs "had done much towards re-establishing the supremacy of 'the rail' over 'the road' as a means of transport for passengers and goods. Vigorous efforts to meet the comfort and convenience of the public interested in general travel, with a drastic reduction in rates, would probably have done more".

Of course, there had been some indication of what was afoot. As far back as 1926 the company had started running the "Royal Scot" non-stop from Euston to Carnforth, using on the initial run two London & North Western engines: No. 5299 (old number 1137) *Vesuvius*, being a Precursor rebuilt with superheater, and No. 5934 (old number 186), a Claughton in Bowen Cooke's original form. On September 26, with the new and magnificent engine *Royal Scot*, the first stop was made at Carlisle, the 299½ miles having been covered at an average speed of 52 mph with 420 tons behind the tender.

Really, this was not very brilliant, even by the British standards of the middle 1920s, and it was not entirely agreeable, either. From 1928 your author recalls such a run made from Euston to a point opposite Kingmoor Sheds, Carlisle. The usually happy music of the train had degenerated into an extremely dull symphony lasting over five hours with no pause between movements. And as the train stood alongside those bleak running sheds, an anxious lady was rushing up the corridors with a dog, looking for a platform with the lamp-posts he much desired. Now one has always travelled, when possible, with one's well-behaved dogs at holiday-time, and for those the ordered sequence of Crewe and Carlisle came just rightly. This was, as remarked, stunting.

Nevertheless it was popularly admired and from 1927 one recalls the enthusiatic astonishment, on a journey from London to Edinburgh, of a Swiss girl who had previously thought that steam trains were an old-fashioned sort of thing that covered short distances, very slowly, as between the Austrian frontier and Winterthur. France had subsequently surprised her, but *this* was *fabelhaft*! Certain French trains at that time were considerably faster than any "Royal Scot". These things are quoted simply as examples of what might be called public-impressionism. Be it added that the Swiss young person was equally, and much more properly, impressed by the British third-class carriages of the period. This shows that both Mr. Loftus Allen and his colleagues on the LMS and the Brothers Bell of *The Locomotive*, were right, though from different approaches their opinions crossed, like those of the London & North Western and the Midland drivers at Derby Junction, Birmingham, in 1892.

So during this time, the LMS company carried on its business outwardly much as it and its constituents had done before; its passenger trains marching along in the low and middle fifties as to speed and gradually improving as to rolling stock on the best trains, while Stamp economies made themselves felt satisfactorily in some ways, to the accompaniment of a creeping shabbiness in respect of others, though this was not to become really disgracefully apparent until the 'thirties were advancing. Sir Josiah was certainly not popular, in the writer's early experience of conversation, in Scotland, which was the least remunerative country served by the system and therefore an early target. The running-down of Lochgorm Works, Inverness, was one of the rings of that target. It was thereabouts that one first heard about the appearance of that modest cream-panelled saloon as being indicative of a "sacking jaunt". Even in 1928 a Wick engineman, apologising for the dirtiness of all the visible locomotives to a young man come to enjoy and admire them, referred to the President of the Executive as *that old sod Sir Josiah*. ("Where did he come from, anyway? He's no railwayman!") In the words of a sometime Great Western director, later Prime Minister of the Realm, the *Winds of Change* were beginning to blow all over the place, but even then we had little inkling of what it would be like when it was really coming on to blow. The callow youth among the engines in Caithness was having starry-eyed dreams of the Highland lines, as well as many others, becoming an electrified marvel.[1]

That exploration of the railways in Caithness (by no means one's first) was at a good time to see engines anyway. The line had been badly washed-out between Golspie and Helmsdale, trapping a lot of strange locomotives in the Far North owing to the grouse season and its traffic. There were three engines on the Thurso branch alone, while south of the washout one could see expresses being hauled by an engine (*Ben Mholach*) which had just been in a minor accident but which, though visibly battered, could still steam all right.

The end of the decade saw several noteworthy LMS appointments. In 1930 Ernest Taylor succeeded J. F. Gee as Chief Accountant. He was a Midland man who had joined the Service in 1923. G. L. Darbyshire, a

---

[1] Expressed, about eighteen months later, in a well-meant but immature slim volume called *Highland Engines and their Work* (Locomotive Publishing Company, 1930). The brickbats were considerable. The book later became a collector's piece.

London & North Western man, succeeded W. Clower as Chief Officer for Labour and Establishment. For this year, G. H. Loftus Allen, by now well established in his LMS office, was Chairman of the British Railways Advertising and Public Relations Committee. Just after this, another big gun came to the LMS from outside.

R. W. Reid, sometime Carriage and Wagon Superintendent, and then a Vice-President as already remarked, joined his ancestors, and his successor was not a railwayman, though he was destined, like Stamp, to become an eminent one over many years. Early in 1930, Sir Harold Hartley, CBE, FRS, became Vice-President (Works and Ancillary Undertakings) and Director of Scientific Research. It was not, of course, the first time an eminent scientist had been recruited. Richard Deeley of the Midland had been one. Hartley had been a Fellow and Tutor of Balliol College, Oxford, since 1901. He was Bedford Lecturer on Physical Chemistry, and had later had much to do with chemical warfare in France, where he became a Brigadier-General, won the MC and was three times Mentioned in Dispatches. From 1922 he had been a Director of the Gas Light and Coke Company.

One ex-London & North Western man, doubtless thinking of Sir Henry Fowler, wearily remarked in less than proper privacy: "Lord! Not *another* gas-man!"

Well, one supposes it was so. But Hartley, already a most distinguished academic personage, was to become a very great railwayman of his time. Stamp, of course, was the nigger in the scientific woodpile. Side-by-side with his evangelical Christianity he had a more than tacit reverence for Science, just as some advanced scientists have been deeply religious men. Stamp, elected President of the Institute of Transport in 1929, took for subject and title of his Presidential Address in October: *Scientific Research in Transport.* So into the railway industry moved Sir Harold Hartley, a Balliol don with a mandate to supervise the technical departments of the LMS. One wonders what Victorian Oxford – or for that matter Sir Richard Moon of the London & North Western – would have thought of such an appointment!

The 1920s continued to be unfortunate for the company in respect of accidents. Only ten months after the Lytham smash, that was, on September 3, 1925, there was a most destructive head-on collision at Hope on the Dore and Chinley line. The signalman at this place, who afterwards most honestly admitted his failure and its circumstances, had put back on the down line a ballast train, headed by Midland 0–6–0 locomotive No. 3773, in order to pass an up mineral train. On the Hope Valley line, "up" meant in the direction of Chinley, beyond which, of course, the direction became "down" over the northern section of the Midland main line into Manchester. At Dore and Totley, trains from

Sheffield were running in the "up" direction as they entered the Hope Valley section.

Now this Hope signalman was occupied with a telegram for the signalman at Bamford box, which he proposed reading over the telephone as this man was still telegraphically illiterate, a circumstance which an Assistant District Controller, who had passed him, had not ascertained. The Hope signalman was covering his colleague's, and incidentally Control's failings, and had so much on his hands that he forgot about the up train standing on his down line. He was handling this telegram when he accepted and offered-on the 3.0 pm express from Manchester Central to Sheffield. Under clear signals, this train, headed by 4–4–0 engine No. 384 and fortunately lightly loaded, but steaming strongly up the valley, ran hard into the engine of the ballast train.

Fortunately the leading carriage of the express was a brake-third, not a full coach. Its interior was gutted by the tender of No. 384. No passengers were killed. But the two engines were practically destroyed; the driver and fireman of No. 384 were killed and a platelayer on the ballast train died in hospital soon after.

Lieut.-Col. (Sir) Alan Mount inquired, and reported that the curious circumstances which had been sufficient to cause forgetfulness in the unhappy signalman at that time would not have led to the collision if the extra safeguards afforded by the *blocking back* bell signal, and the use of the lever collar, had been in operation. He recommended improved siding accommodation for side-tracked trains such as this one which had fatally occupied the other through road; the regularisation of the extent to which, even over a limited period, one man might perform telegraph work for another, under the system of certification of fitness for a signalman's duty, and thirdly the gradual substitution of telephone for telegraph under conditions such as these at Hope.

About five weeks later, on October 12, there was an opposing sidelong collision at Llandudno, between an outgoing pull-and-push train and an incoming ordinary train. The circumstances were uninteresting – the old thing about starting a train on the guard's signal without an eye to the semaphore – but were sad on personal grounds. The outgoing train's driver was at fault, after a long and honourable career, often with the most important expresses. The train he struck, full of girls and boys coming in to school, was driven by his son. One of the children was very severely injured and six other passengers seriously. The older driver earnestly exonerated his guard. Colonel Mount did not.

Social and economic impact of the road motor coach has been mentioned already. Many such were good, new vehicles, but some were botched jobs improvised with old chassis. Control of commercial motor vehicles and those responsible for them was of the laxest sort at that time;

there were spiv proprietors, hideously overworked drivers (as were to be under Belgian auspices in the middle-1960s) and also happy-go-lucky local men who would buy or knock up a coach of sorts for the village outings. One such coach (truly a courtesy title!), rammed the crossing gates at Fenny Stratford on the Cambridge–Bletchley line on December 8, 1925. It broke through the gates and thus encountered the 6.30 pm train from Cambridge, headed by Jumbo 2–4–0 engine, ex-North Western No. 1170, *General*. The wretched flivver, with six of its company, was smashed to pieces and three more died afterwards. It had been a Ford one-tonner, converted. It had been suggested that there was a brakes-failure, also that crossing arrangements were questionable, and on the latter account Government inquired into the collision as a train accident. The Ministry of Transport did not inquire into road-traffic accidents. One carriage of the train, however, had been derailed by passing over wreckage. Major Hall, who inquired and reported, said that human error of judgement was more likely than mechanical failure of the bus, the driver of which was well aware of the position of the crossing and the fact of its gates being closed. The accident attracted attention through being a very early example of collision between train and motor, with a serious death-roll, through level-crossing accidents of one sort and another had occurred ever since such crossings had existed, sometimes through railway fault and sometimes through road user's.

The LMS got safely through the General Strike of 1926 without serious consequences to trains, though the neighbouring LNER had two collisions and, as remarked, one case of major sabotage. On November 19, however, there was a bad accident at Parkgate and Rawmarsh, when a goods train became derailed and the wreckage ripped the sides out of two coaches on a train from York, killing nine passengers. Both the carriages severely damaged were old; one Midland and one Lancashire & Yorkshire, but the consequences would have been the same with any wooden bodies. On May 11, 1927, there was a tunnel collapse at Cofton, killing five men at work.

A bad year was 1928, though its worst trouble was at Darlington on the London & North Eastern, with the heaviest casualties in any British train since 1915. On the LMS one and two persons respectively were killed in a derailment at Swinderby and a collision at Ancoats. On October 13, there was a horrible collision with fire at Charfield on the Bristol and Gloucester line, killing fifteen. In view of its circumstances and consequences, its description belongs to the next chapter, dealing with rolling-stock design and equipment. But in the same month, on the 25th, the north-bound "Royal Highlander" ran into the back of a goods in the same block section at Dinwoodie on the Caledonian main line north of Carlisle, and provided something of an object lesson. The leading engine of the express, an old Dunalastair III, went over to the left and was completely jumped by the train engine, a standard compound, and the leading van. All four enginemen were killed and the old Caledonian engine completed its existence, but the leading van remained coupled to the tender of the compound, in one piece, with its electric lamps still on. The van was a steel one, and behind it the train, though partly derailed, stayed fairly well in line with no serious passenger casualities. The admirable behaviour of modern steel stock, light as it was, and the absence of fire from gas, were both favourably remarked. It had been very different at Charfield.

On January 8, 1929, there was a collision in fog at Ashchurch on the Birmingham and Gloucester line, killing four, and on February 12, a Midland Scotch express, headed by an immigrant Claughton 4–6–0 engine, was in collision at Doe Hill, killing both enginemen. As at Lytham, the locomotive was taken away in pieces.

These lurid events are enough of this sort for the time being. They were indeed enough in all conscience, and there were more to come in the succeeding years.

Still the company maintained and even increased its interest in long non-stop runs, which were ever sure to impress that powerful majority, the Philistines. A remarkable business excursion was made on July 21, 1929. The Bussey Coal Distillation Company had opened new plant at Glenboig in the Scottish Industrial Belt, and gave a good outing to its guests from the South. Of these, 120 were entrained in ten sleeping cars which left London, Euston, at 12.15 am. (From recollections of a later, marine-engineering jaunt to Yoker, one can image a reasonably wet beginning in the Euston Hotel!) The night special train ran to Lanark Racecourse where a day train was laid on to give breakfast to the visitors on their way to Glenboig. After the official festivities this day train, consisting chiefly of dining cars with two cinema cars, covered the 395½ miles non-stop back to Euston in eight hours, with the Royal Scot class engine *Novelty* (more later about this memorable class). There was a banquet on the train, which was wired throughout to relay the speeches through loudspeakers from the High Table (or perhaps the High Car). Travel was very noisy on the descent from Shap, and it was most difficult to hear the speeches above the continual squealing of the brake-blocks just below. Doubtless, however, everybody was happy except the teetotallers, if any.

The year 1930 saw the London Midland & Scottish still looking very much the same sort of undertaking as it had been soon after the grouping. Many of the carriages were becoming ancient, certainly in Scotland, and old types of locomotive had continued to be built, especially from Midland designs. Only crack trains like the "Royal Scot" were consistently up to date. The best thing about them was the use of end vestibules only and of wide "landscape" windows, which were very pleasant indeed.

Curtailment of the system had been as yet negligible. Counting joint lines such as the Somerset and Dorset, it stretched from Poole in the South to Thurso in the North, while its ultimate terminus was at Lybster on the east coast of Caithness, reached by a trailing junction at Wick. Its Northern Counties Committee lines in Ireland, on both broad and narrow gauge, were almost intact, and were yet to be improved by the junction improvements at Greenisland which would enable, for the first time, the running of trains from Belfast to Derry without reversal.

British closures were generally on a small scale, but there was a burst of them during 1930. The few occurring up to and including the little Burton and Ashby Light Railway in 1927 have been noticed. Subsequent closures, to the end of 1930, were as follows:

Congleton–Milton (passenger traffic)	July 7, 1927
Desford–Leicester, West Bridge (passenger traffic)	September 24, 1928
Gilgarran branch (all traffic)	February 14, 1929
Harrington–Lowca (passenger traffic)	April 1, 1929
Sowerby Bridge–Rishworth (passenger traffic)	July 8, 1929
Mansfield–Southwell (passenger traffic)	August 12, 1929
Halifax–Stainland (passenger traffic)	September 23, 1929
Deansgate branch, Bolton (all traffic)	February 25, 1930
Garstang–Knott End (passenger traffic)	March 31, 1930
Brownhills–Aldridge (passenger traffic)	March 31, 1930
Walsall Wood–Brownhills (all traffic)	March 31, 1930
Little Eaton–Butterley (passenger traffic)	June 1, 1930
Preston–Longridge (passenger traffic)	June 2, 1930
Lancaster–Glasson Dock (passenger traffic)	July 7, 1930
Chesterfield–Mansfield via Bolsover (passenger traffic)	July 28, 1930
Staveley–Pleasley (passenger traffic)	July 28, 1930
Pleasley–Glapwell (all traffic)	July 28, 1930
Denny and Bonnybridge branches (passenger traffic)	July 28, 1930
Harecastle–Wheelock and Sandbach (passenger traffic)	July 28, 1930
Deighton–Kirkburton (passenger traffic)	July 28, 1930
Irvine–Kilwinning (passenger traffic)	July 28, 1930
Mansfield–Alfreton via Teversall (passenger traffic)	July 28, 1930
Pleasley–Tibshelf Junction (passenger traffic)	July 28, 1930
Caernarvon–Llanberis (passenger traffic)	September 22, 1930
Melbourne–Castle Donington (passenger traffic)	September 22, 1930
Prestatyn–Dyserth (passenger traffic)	September 22, 1930
Aspatria–Mealsgate (passenger traffic)	September 22, 1930
Holland Arms–Red Wharf Bay (passenger traffic)	September 22, 1930

Skipton–Grassington (passenger traffic)	September 22, 1930
Tarleton Canal Depot branch (all traffic)	November 1930
Dewsbury branch (passenger traffic)	December 1, 1930
Giffen–Kilburnie (all traffic)	December 1, 1930
Ayr–Turnberry (passenger traffic)	December 1, 1930
Holytown–Morningside (passenger traffic)	December 1, 1930
Airdrie–Newhouse (passenger traffic)	December 1, 1930

No item, as suggested, was in itself a very big closure. But the 1930 closures were certainly many, indicative of both the impact of the motor bus and the world industrial slump following the Wall Street smash of the previous year. The former accounted for the passenger suspensions; the latter meant much distress. Closures in Scotland were less than some might have expected. Various unremunerative branches were in country where it was often worth nobody's while to run a bus. It was not until July 23, 1931, that the Railway and Canal Commission reminded people that it was not reasonable to require a railway company to maintain an unprofitable passenger service, a consideration that had escaped some. Certain closures were curiously saddening, such as the end of passenger trains on the little Garstang and Knott End line, ever a frustrated dream. In the old Maryport and Carlisle country, up in the real North of England, people remembered wistfully the famous porter at Aspatria Junction, who had gone along the train exhorting the passengers in accents variously suited to their caste and class of travel, eg "Aspatriah! Change heah for Meals-gate!" and "Spatthry! Get oot!" Why not, indeed? Such announcement was far better understood than that of the Thames–Forth express, whereon the Midland ticket collector told one to change for Melrose at Oyke while the Scots guard said something about changing at Hike, and the place of transit turned out to be Hawick.

But those 1920s made a pleasant time, for those who loved steam railways for their own sake, to know the LMS. One could see the shape of things to come, but the vision was not too brutal. The advent of the third-class sleeping cars in 1928 was a wonderful thing; the sum of seven-and-sixpence could deliver one from nocturnal misery. One could still see the things of the past, with affection, and not too keen a regret as they gently faded away. To catch them with a camera once more before they departed – engines such as *Hardwicke* at Oxford and the shapely *Strathcarron* at Inverness, and luscious old dining cars from before Victoria's Diamond Jubilee – brought excitement to one's journeyings, just as did the puissant presence of a Royal Scot all the way from London to Glasgow. Euston, St. Pancras, St. Enoch, and that splendid Grecian station at Huddersfield were all their, old, magnificent – if rather unkempt – selves.

CHAPTER THREE

Mechanical Development to 1930

It was scarcely unexpected that the first locomotives built for the London
Midland & Scottish Railway followed existing designs of certain constituent companies, and even some already prepared but not yet carried
out. That George Hughes, though advancing in years, would perpetuate
Lancashire & Yorkshire practice, was bound to happen, and before he
retired he produced some quite admirable designs, one of the most
useful of which was to be carried out in Fowler's time.

There was urgent need for new express passenger engines. The Midland
was going its old sweet way with good but relatively small engines,
working in pairs rather more often than some people would consider
economic. On the West Coast main line, where double-heading had been
much less in favour, it was nevertheless being done. A frequent combination was the piloting of a Claughton 4–6–0 by a Precursor 4–4–0.
The Prince of Wales class superheated 4–6–0 locomotives and the four-
coupled George the Fifths were perhaps the best express engines to have
been bequeathed by the London & North Western. North of Carlisle,
double-heading was even more general with the West Coast expresses,
and while the Caledonian company had been an early user of massive
six-coupled engines, some of the most useful work was being done by
the superheated Dunalastair IV 4–4–0 engines. North of Perth on the
Caledonian main line, the expresses were much more frequently hauled
by one engine per train, but on the Highland line double-heading was
very general as far as Inverness, with a third in rear up the Big Hill from
Blair Atholl. A Jones 'Loch' piloting a 4–6–0 Castle was a favourite
combination. Both designs were by now old, but the Castles still worked
on the same duties as Christopher Cumming's much more modern Clan
class. On the ex-Glasgow & South Western lines, trains were noticeably
lighter, with one engine to each.

It was to the ex-London & North Western line that the first new Hughes
passenger engines came, and here again the design was not new. It was
Lancashire & Yorkshire in every respect, and appeared in the middle of
1923. A development of designs executed in 1918 and 1921, it made a
very much better engine than the old pre-war Hughes 4–6–0. The new
engines were four-cylindered with divided drive, that of the outside
cylinders being to the middle coupled axle. The inside cylinders were set
farther forward, as in Great Western practice, but unlike the latter, this

57

design incorporated outside Walschaert gear with operation of the inside valves through rocking levers. Cylinder diameter was 16½in, with 26in stroke, and the cylinders were the largest then in use for a British four-cylinder engine. General dimensions of these, and other engines from the pre-Stanier period, will be found in Table 1. The tender, as usual in Horwich designs except for heavy goods, was relatively small. Distances were short on the L&Y, and the main lines were well equipped with water troughs. The new Hughes engines, however, were very soon to be seen on the West Coast expresses, working through from Euston to Carlisle. The tenders were indeed bigger, with this is view, than the absolute L&Y article – or perhaps "less small" is a better description – for they carried 3,000 gallons of water and six tons of coal. One of these was among the first LMS (apart from existing Midland, Furness and North Stafford) engines to be painted red. Another was the ex-London & North Western Claughton No. 5971 (LNWR No. 2511) *Croxteth* which had been in an accident about Castlethorpe, and consequently hauled-in and repaired about the right time. But I heard that the very first was another Horwich engine which was ex-L&Y Aspinall 4-4-0 No. 10163. This may have been the guinea-pig when it came to painting the LMS engines. I never saw these first examples. But the red, as it became under Standard, was not quite the old Midland red, which entailed an artistic technique of overlaying crimson-lake on chocolate. (The former is a transparent and ultimately fugitive colour, as anyone will know after painting pictures with it and watching how they work out after some twenty years.) My sometime colleague the late Harold Wyatt, an architect who quitted British Railways London Midland Region to join the Council of Industrial Design, once gave me the respective ingredients of true Midland and LMS reds, neatly set out on two sheets of paper. To my shame they went missing in the years, but they were certainly rather different, and the LMS version never had the lustre of the Midland. All the same, it was a fine handsome colour for the best engines of one of the largest railway companies in the world. One recalls with affection an agreeable lady of riper years, met at luncheon in the "Royal Scot's" diner in 1931 and never again, who said at Carlisle: "Aren't the engines lovely, nowadays! Those are 'Royal Scots', aren't they?"

Certainly the Royal Scots, to which we shall shortly come, were most imposing engines, and it was very pleasing to find any woman appreciating a steam locomotive.

As first painted, these first LMS-red locomotives had the initials LMS transferred on the cab splashers, but very soon after, the company produced a handsome badge (still persisting last time your author went up in the lift at Euston House) which presented national emblems *proper* in a field *or*, with the company's title between surrounding concentric bands. It was not a coat-of-arms, such as the London & North Eastern produced with the full authority of the College of Heralds, but it was a nice thing.

Goods locomotives were less ornately treated, for they were painted black with the number in black-blocked yellow on a vermilion panel (quarter-circular cut-outs at corners) on each cab- or tank-side. This last was perpetuated into the late 1920s, but it was altogether too showy a thing to be permitted to the humble Kirtley, Cauliflower or Barney under the Stamp economies. Perhaps this was just as well. If engines were going to be dirty anyhow (and, my hat! – dirty they became!) it was better for them to be unadorned. The larger passenger engines remained red for a long time, though the red became more and more maroon, and one remembers from the late 1940s that tough old puritan, General Dobbie, solemnly naming *Malta GC* at Euston, what time the engine, previously just *Malta*, was still in the cleaned-up remains of the old LMS red. Then as before, the red was styled by black borders with intervening yellow lines. The Northern Counties Committee perpetuated the red for all passenger engines – even Bowman Malcolm's 2–4–0 von Borries compounds – for much longer than the guardian company allowed in the larger island.

To revert, after these kickshaws, to the then new Hughes 4–6–0 express engines. No. 10474 headed a train of LMS main-line passenger rolling stock in the remarkable procession of old, recent and contemporary engines and vehicles at the London & North Eastern's Stockton and Darlington Railway Centenary celebrations in the summer of 1925. The London & North Eastern company invited the other three main-line companies, as well as Irish and Belgian authorities, to exhibit, which was handsome of it, especially when one considers the habitual cageyness then still persisting between railway companies which, even if they were not in an actual state of cold war, were still not in a state of open alliance as the London & North Western, Caledonian, and Lancashire & Yorkshire had been for so long. Of the other three British main-line companies, one regretfully recalls that the Southern Railway made a beggarly show with one 'King Arthur' (*Sir Torre*) heading some adequate but commonplace side-door corridor carriages with a Pullman car over the processional course, which had belonged to the primeval Stockton and Darlington Railway, between Darlington and Eaglescliffe. As for the Great Western, it furnished its *North Star* replica which had to be towed on a crocodile wagon because of the broad gauge to which it was built, a 2–8–0 fast goods engine, a 2–8–0 coal tank engine, and two Castles (*Windsor Castle* and *Viscount Churchill*) respectively hauling the 1897 Diamond Jubilee train minus Queen Victoria's carriage, and some articulated carriages just to show that the London & North Eastern was not the only British railway capable of making these. Altogether a masterpiece of Paddingtonian stodgy conceit!

But the LMS, while producing nothing really startling, was decently represented by both new and old equipment. In the procession, apart from the train just mentioned, there was a Webb four-cylinder compound 0–8–0, No. 1881 (a number which some innocently industrious party put down for the date of construction, which in fact was 1901); one of Bowen Cooke's last 0–8–0 goods engines, No. 9446 of 1922; the London & North Western veteran *Cornwall* whose wheel centres, at any rate, dated from 1847; Johnson's Midland bogie single No. 679, one of the most beautiful of the older exhibits; Bowen Cooke's original *Sir Gilbert Claughton*, and Hughes' 4–6–4 tank engine No. 11112. So, on the whole, the LMS came quite well through this memorable jamboree.

On the West Coast expresses the Hughes 4–6–0 engines remained for quite a long time without trouble, even after the arrival of the more puissant Royal Scots, though their 6ft 3in coupled wheels and 180lb pressure imposed limitations, at least to conventional English eyes upon paper, when it came to fast long-distance running. In retrospect, only the unexciting pressure seems to have been inadequate. One of M. Secretan's older, and best, water-colours showed one on a West Coast Scotch express with the original, though by then red-painted, carriages of 1908. It was published in the Railway Centenary Supplement of *The Locomotive*, 1925.

In 1926 one of Hughes' 4–6–0 express engines, No. 10456, was rebuilt as a four-cylinder compound with 16in high-pressure cylinders outside, and 22in low-pressure cylinders inside, with 9in piston valves having a maximum travel of $6\frac{3}{8}$in. A control valve working off the reversing gear produced compound working when the cutoff was brought below 70 per cent, which was quite different from existing Midland practice, in which control of steam supply was by regulator. The engine seems to have been much improved by this radical alteration – and the Hughes 4–6–0 was a good engine anyway in its later form – but it was not Sir Henry Fowler's way, which was the Midland's, and so it is scarcely surprising that to outside observers no news was leaked, and that this remained a mystery locomotive for some years. Nothing like her was made thereafter. At the time she was the most powerful compound locomotive that ever had appeared on a British railway. The alterations made little difference in the external aspect of the familiar Hughes 4–6–0, apart from the wide steampipe casings at the front end.

If only George Hughes had been ten years younger, yet still in that position which he all-too-briefly held! Such wishes are idle now, anyway. Let it suffice that of the ordinary engines one recalls a very pleasant – if not spectacular – run behind one of these northwards from Euston in

1930, on an immensely heavy night Scotch excursion packed with passengers. (After all, who but a fanatic – with whom one has indeed travelled from London to Edinburgh – wants a spectacular run at night, so long as the train keeps time, does not run too fast, and in the course of its long rumble stops as infrequently as possible?) Enough, just now, that the Hughes 4–6–0 express engines were sufficiently adequate for the relatively leisurely post-grouping express services between London and Scotland by the West Coast route.

Over shorter distances, as between Manchester and Blackpool or Manchester and Southport, which were traversed by critical commuters of the more hard-boiled Northern-English sort, this kind of engine did remarkably well. The little tender scarcely mattered, and now one wonders why George Hughes had not already produced a 4–6–4 tank engine version of his design. In 1924 he did so, and quite incidentally made one of the three most beautiful 4–6–4 tank locomotive designs in Europe (the others being on the London Brighton and South Coast and the Netherlands Railways). It was unusual for Horwich to bring forth a really artistic design.

The first of ten such engines, No. 11110, all of them built at Horwich, was, on her appearance, the only four-cylinder tank locomotive on any British main-line railway, with the exception of Hookham's experimental design on the North Stafford, to which we shall come later. She was also painted red for a while. Even in the middle 'twenties this still applied to passenger engines of all types – even ancient Highland tank engines, but soon black was to be the rule for all except the larger express locomotives, so brief was the company's initial window-dressing.

From the table it will be seen that these very handsome tank engines were closely comparable, in dimensions, to the 4–6–0 class, though higher in evaporative and lower in superheating surfaces. They had plenty of steam for the sort of traffic they handled, which was generally on the residential express services from Manchester to Southport and Blackpool. Some mechanical details may be added to those tabulated: Horwich "top-and-bottom" superheaters were used. The 9 in piston valves had $6\frac{3}{8}$ in travel with $1\frac{3}{16}$ in lap and $\frac{1}{4}$ in lead. A front-end feature was the shortness of the direct steam passages; something that in later years was called "internal streamlining".

Though they came later, and were officially accredited to Sir Henry Fowler who provided them with very Midland-looking tenders, the Hughes 2–6–0 mixed-traffic engines may be opportunely mentioned at this stage. There was an awful need on the LMS at that time for an engine which could work anything from fast goods to an express passenger train over heavy gradients, and Midland standard designs could not furnish this from scratch, nor were small-wheeled 4–6–0 engines of London &

North Western type to be trusted. It seemed as if Fowler had gone rummaging in Mr. Hughes' abandoned luggage and found what he wanted. Main dimensions are given in the table. Two cylinders only were used, of considerable dimensions by the standards of the time. The piston valves were 11in diameter with 6½in maximum travel. Styling apart from the tenders was that of Horwich and these were scarcely beautiful engines to the eye, with their cylinders and valves steeply inclined below irregular platforms.

But they were very useful, which to be sure is the primary object of locomotive design, and for the rest one simply remembers a most won-drous-impudent letter on their appearance which a future general manager sent (delicious irony!) to Sir Henry Fowler. He kept a copy, and showed it to me about 1930. Soon after, he joined the railway service, which shows that one cannot be too rude to people in high office, so long as one aspires to a different department, and so long as one knows one's own particular war-aims. As for the Mogul engines, they came to be seen and appreciated – as engines, if not as works of art – over much of the LMS system. They were peculiarly welcome between Perth and Inverness, a line in tricky territory, for Scottish Highlanders, with some historical reason, are people suspicious of both things and other people. An Inverness man who had grown up on Lochs, Castles and Clans remarked to me (also about 1930) that the 13000 class were grand engines. They were at work for many years after.

Scottish engines – of purely Scottish-constituent design, that is – did not cease to be built with the end of 1922. In 1926, Nasmyth Wilson and Company trotted out ten standard Caledonian 0–4–4 tank engines, whose origin went back to the days of McIntosh. Most of these went to what had been the Glasgow and South Western Railway, which had been very short of smaller tank locomotives, but the class made a fairly brief appearance even on the Midland suburban services out of St. Pancras. One doubts the Plain Average Briton of Radlett and St. Albans often noticed any difference from the familiar Johnson article of those parts.

On a more grandiose scale, there was a new building of William Pickersgill's 60 class two-cylinder 4–6–0 engines, which had first appeared in 1916 and had 6ft 1in coupled wheels with 20in by 26in cylinders. They were good, strong, simple engines, to which Scots enginemen were already accustomed, and altogether better than a late Pickersgill design which the LMS first brought out in 1923, though it was a Caledonian order. The latter were the last of several Caledonian designs specifically intended for the long (and now partly vanished) Callander and Oban Railway, which had maintained its identity through all the years of Caledonian working and whose old servants were still quick to remind one of that fact, even in the 1960s.

Pickersgill's Oban engines were 4–6–0 with 5ft 6in coupled wheels, having piston valves over the 19½in by 26in cylinders and 185lb pressure. Weight in working order was 62tons 15½cwt (tender, 37tons 15½cwt) and the engines were all built at the Queen's Park Works of the North British Locomotive Company. They were not popular. Some said the wheels were too big and others, possibly with more reason, said that the boilers were too small. They were ungainly engines, too; the adequately high platforms each side were crowned by what seemed to be quite needless splashers, as if the engines had been intended to have 6ft wheels at least. For want of a new design, the Oban line might have got along better with a repeat order of old McIntosh engines, and long before it had any more recent designs, its traffic was being worked by old Clans and even older Castles off the Highland Railway.

Much more interesting was a solitary Glasgow & South Western design, and that was nominally a rebuild of a very much older engine. Back in 1897, James Manson had built for the "Sou' West" one of the first two four-cylinder simple express engines to run in Great Britain. (The other, a Crewe product, was a simplified version of the standard Webb 4–4–0 four-cylinder compound, probably built to demonstrate by comparison the economies of the latter.) Manson's engine No. 11, very beautiful to look at, but sadly underboilered, was later given a larger Manson boiler by Peter Drummond, but R. H. Whitelegg in his latter days at Kilmarnock schemed and carried out a complete reconstruction in which very little of the original fabric could have been left, though the shape of the platforms, with a supplementary splasher to cover the throw of the outside cranks, was perpetuated. It was to all intents and purposes a new engine, an enlargement of the old No. 11 with a very capacious Drummond style boiler and a new tender. There was even a new number, 394, and the name *Lord Glenarthur*. Under the LMS general renumbering, this unique locomotive became No. 14509. Main dimensions are given in Table 1. It was a very useful engine with the limits of uniquity, which on a big railway are awkward when it comes to maintenance and replacements, and one feels that had the Glasgow & South Western had a substantial number of such, it would have been a very good thing indeed. The solitary was often to be seen between Glasgow and Ayr.

One wonders whether a son of Crewe, such as George Hughes, knew his *alma-mater* so well that he considered it idle to interfere with its traditions, however supreme were his command. Certainly Captain H. P. M. Beames at Crewe went on with some purely Crewe practice for some time, and with interesting results at that. One of the best investments on the part of the London & North Western's Locomotive Department had been C. J. Bowen Cooke's superheated 4–6–0 locomotives of the Prince of Wales class, whereof the initial engine had appeared as early as October 1911, though a fresh series had been turned out by Beardmores in these early 1920s. Locomotive building by this firm, generally regarded as a marine one though it also built motor cabs at this time, was a fairly blatant *boondoggle* (to borrow a term from America, somewhat later in Franklin D. Roosevelt's first Presidential term); that is to say that such contracts were to keep in work men who otherwise would be tramping the streets on the narrow kerbstone of despair.

In 1923 several Princes were rearranged for outside Walschaerts valve gear while retaining inside cylinders. This arrangement was by no means unknown abroad. Many Italian locomotives had it, though in these the big piston valves were outside too, which practice Crewe eschewed. The London & North Western engines now thus modified were Nos. 56, 867 *Condor*, 964 *Bret Harte*, and 2340 *Tara*. One of the Beardmore lot, LMS No. 5845, was built new in this form and was shown on the firm's stand in the 1924 British Empire Exhibition at Wembley. It was given new 1924 *Prince of Wales* nameplates to excite the Dim Many (one could see HRH *in butter* across the way in that fortunately ephemeral monument of British vulgarity, the Palace of Industry!) The real *Prince of Wales* went delicately nameless at the time. Further to Wembley, the Beardmore exhibit was an elaborate one, with motors mounted to turn the engine's coupled wheels and show the gear in motion, though on the occasion of both the present author's visits something seemed to have broken down, for the Pretender to the Principality was in dignified quescence.

Another curiosity of this exhibit was that it persuaded many of the anxious Faithful among amateurs of Crewe that Premier Line locomotive traditions stood firm, and that they needed not to worry about threatened alien influences from Horwich, of which there was already some evidence, and (horrid thought!) from Derby.

As to the technics of this modification; for many years the London & North Western Railway had been very partial to Joy gear, which had its disadvantages when applied to larger engines, owing to failure of the pierced connecting rods. The alteration of *Bret Harte* (the engine featured in the official photograph) and of the others, was successful up to a point, though not everybody liked the change in the engines' appearance, which was considered un-Crewe-like and therefore very improper. Further, the appearance of the gear in motion and, more seriously certain cases of bent rods in its earlier days, suggested to old London & North Western men the crossing of legs with its ensuing downfall. Consequently they nicknamed the engines "Tishies" after a race-horse of the time who had that particular foible. The authorities seem to have liked the idea of the modified engines being named after a race-horse, and even went to the length of making *Tishy* nameplates. Probably one never will know whether Captain Beames put a quiet tenner for a win on the original Tishy, to have

Loading the "Royal Scot" locomotive for
North American tour.

Stowing the "Coronation Scot"
locomotive for North American tour.

Steel-panelled third-class coach, 1926; outside and inside.

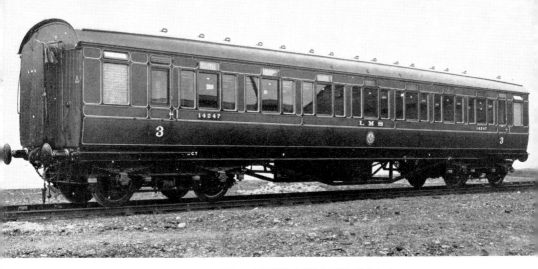

ABOVE AND LEFT: Third-class
sleeping car, 1928.

First-class diner, "Royal Scot", 1928.

Cold winds for commuters.

Becontree, London, Tilbury and
Southend line.

the horse fall down on his plans. But the horse's habits penetrated high official awareness at last, and the new nameplates were hurried away to oblivion in the Crewe brass foundry.

In all humility – for he was neither born nor brought up on the London & North Western Railway – the present author must admit a liking, even a preference for the aspect of the modified engines. But there! He always liked, as a mere spectator, the movement of Walschaert's gear on a big engine, a preference for which Robert Urie's on the London & South Western and first encounters with large foreign engines may have been responsible. Most tastes, whether professional or amateur, were thus governed, though the former sort was generally the more conservative when it came to new construction while the latter was most offended when old favourites departed, however much something new may have been appreciated on its appearance. Now and then the professional, as was proper, called his own new tune. One remembers such grand originals, down a century and more, as Crampton, Stroudley, Churchward, and Bulleid, though these were outside LMS experience, unless one counts the three little Stroudley tank engines on the Highland which came, in their dotage, into the LMS stock.

Of new construction, Captain Beames brought out from Crewe in 1923 his memorable – yet by many forgotten – 0–8–4 heavy tank engines. Save that they had the initials LMS, widely spaced on the tank sides, they were as London & North Western a sort of locomotive as the old company's fondest admirers could have expected, from the formidable Webb chimney cap to the bunker-tank filler. They were even given the full London & North Western livery treatment, richly puritan, which had been part of the Crewe way of doing things since 1873. Basic dimensions are given in Table 2 of this chapter. These may well have been the last locomotives to have been built with Joy's valve gear, and its incidence is quaint, seeing that Beames was already devising his arrangement of Walschaert's gear for the London & North Western Princes. The traditions of Crewe, as remarked, were strong. Someone who for one reason or another liked them less than those of Derby, said it beat him that Crewe had not produced a compound Claughton on Webb's system, possibly when Mr. Bowen Cooke was away on holidays.

The Beames 0–8–4 tank locomotives have been described as banking engines but the term is somewhat ambiguous. They were not for pushing heavy West Coast expresses up to the top of Shap; they were for working all sorts of heavy traffic on what had been the London & North Western lines in Monmouth and South Wales. From Abergavenny to Brynmawr the line rose a thousand feet in about eight miles, with a maximum gradient of 1 in 38, and much of the rise between that inclination and 1 in 50. That called for heavy pulling in all conscience, but an even more severe

c

factor was the restraint of unbraked coal wagons in huge convoys on the descent. Certain Continental engineers would have had a collective fit at the very thought, yet little Webb o–6–2 coal tank engines had been on the job for years, and their axleboxes had a bad time in consequence. The engines became speedily run-down, in most senses of the term.

The Beames o–8–4 tank was certainly a more powerful engine by far than its predecessors, both in tractive and in brake power, but it had its snags. It was long, and rigid for so tortuous a course as this line, especially when new and extra stiff, as in the early 1920s. The permanent way gangs had a bad time straightening distorted track and derailments were fairly frequent. The third pair of coupled wheels had wide treads and no flanges, but that did not prevent them from sliding off the rails altogether and dropping on their springs. Old-sweat enginemen acquired the habit of letting things be until the wheels rerailed themselves with an extra-special bump.[1] Then, although the coupling rods were liberally jointed in front of the driving and in rear of the third cranks each side, the move-ment allowed was in a vertical plane only. The massive rods were laterally rigid from front to rear, although separate short rods, allowing for much easier movement, had been used in the old Webb o–8–0 coal engines many years before. One feels that there have not been adequate correspondence between the Civil and Mechanical Engineering sides, but that was a failing of British railways over many years. Each was ready to blame the other, but in retrospect one is sometimes forced to the conclusion that the locomotive men were insufficiently briefed and the civil engineers were most parsimoniously treated by companies out to spend as little as possible on way and works beyond current maintenance. (In this connec-tion there was a scandalous business on the Highland Railway about 1916, which resulted in six new – and very good – engines built by Hawthorn Leslie being *flogged* to the Caledonian Railway because they were too heavy, and the resignation of their able but embarrassed designer.)

For many years, however, the Beames o–8–4 tank engines continued to work from Tredegar, and though there were anxious moments, especially before they had somewhat loosened their joints, nothing monumentally awful overtook them. In 1924, the Great Western Railway had flatly refused to have them running over any portion of the old Rhymney Railway and, after all, any railway company had some right to be restrictive about foreign workings by suspicious locomotive types.

These were the last locomotives to be built in pure London & North Western style, though there were those – and many at that – who expected an absolute Crewe restoration as soon as George Hughes might be out of the way. He was a veteran, though destined, when that retirement

[1] A masterly – and graphic – account of the engine's vagaries, by J. M. Dunn, appeared in *The Railway Magazine* of April 1953.

came, to live to a great age, and to the deep London & North Western enthusiast, the fading-away of Crewe traditions in design seemed as impossible a prospect as the impending disappearance of steam locomotives seemed to many others forty years after. But though there were no more new designs to be carried out from the Crewe drawing office – not even that small-wheeled, small-axled-loaded 4–6–2 engine which once turned up as a cover design for bound volumes of *The Locomotive* – there was yet some most interesting rebuilding to come.

In the middle 1920s, while the steam reciprocating locomotive was still soaring to its prime, there was much interest in new forms of valve gear. The Caprotti gear, an Italian invention which was to be much applied in its native country, essentially comprised a rotary member with three cams to each cylinder, one working the two exhaust valves and the other two the admission valves. William Beardmore on Clydeside was the sole supplier in Great Britain, and, this firm having already supplied a lot of Princes and thus got a good connection with Crewe, it was not surprising that the latter essayed the gear. The ex-LNWR Claughtons were selected for experiment, and of these, early in 1927, No. 5908 (LMS number) *Alfred Fletcher* was matched against No. 5917 *Charles J. Cropper* with the ordinary arrangement of Walschaert's gear and piston valves. Captain Beames was both executant and umpire.

On these trials, *Alfred Fletcher* burnt 38·5lb of coal per mile with a 389·6ton train from Crewe to Euston. That was equal to ·078lb per-ton-per-mile compared with ·099lb per ton-per-mile consumed by the unaltered engine. Between Crewe and Carlisle the respective figures were ·078lb per-ton-per-mile and ·143lb per-ton-per-mile. As there was an old London & North Western tradition about the superiority of fuel economy over nearly everything else, dating back to the days of Francis Webb, the thing might have gone much farther (as it did in Italy) had it not been for the subsequent triumph of Derby methods over those of Crewe.

Still something had to be done with the Bowen Cooke Claughtons, whose only fault, in the retrospective eye, was that, as so often before, their boilers were not big enough. One suspects that – again as so often before – civil engineering had something to do with the old reluctance to put on as big a boiler as possible. To criticise an engineer of the calibre of C. J. Bowen Cooke, even after all these years, might cross the borders of impertinence, even though the old railway companies are now fair game, for what that is worth. Anyway, to put on a bigger boiler the Powers of Crewe now proceeded to do, and the result appeared in 1928. The essential Claughton remained itself, save that the 16in cylinders were now lined down to 15¾in. The coupled wheels, with their huge bosses reminiscent of the later Webb compounds, remained at 6ft 9in. But the new boiler was visibly bigger with a 5ft 5⅜in barrel. Total evaporative heating surface was 1,733 sq ft (firebox 83 sq ft and tubes and flues 1,560). Superheating surface (24 elements) came to 365 sq ft, giving a combined heating surface of 2,098 sq ft. The grate area was 30 sq ft and the working pressure 200lb per sq in. As rebuilt, the engines weighed two tons more. Outwardly there was little change in aspect, apart from the stout boiler with very squat mountings. The classic Crewe cab and splasher arrangements wrre retained. Only heretics dared say that a raising of the platforms with exposure of the gear, even on the modest scale of the "Tishies", would have been an improvement whether in the matter of keeping the motion cooler or out of aesthetic considerations.

Briefly to summarise the Claughtons under LMS ownership: Numbered 5900 to 6029, only two combined Caprotti gear with the old boiler: Nos. 5908 as mentioned and the last of the series. Both subsequently received the bigger boiler. Altogether there were eight others with Caprotti gear (Nos. 5927/46/48/57/62/75, 6013/23/29, and of these the first, third and fourth, and Nos. 6013/29 had 135 deg crank setting. The Kylälä blast-pipe (a Finnish form) was experimentally applied on Nos. 5908 and 5975, as well as on No. 5912 with the old boiler. The five engines with the 135 deg cranks were balanced 50 per cent against the reciprocating parts, all in the leading coupled wheels except for No. 6013, wherein the balancing was distributed over the three coupled axles. The first of the bigger boilers was put on No. 5999, *Vindictive*, a Walschaert-geared engine, in 1928, and ten more of these, thus rebuilt, were Nos. 5906/10/53/70/72/86/-93/99, 6004/17. Unrebuilt engines of the class were broken up in the early-to-middle 1930s.

While on the subject of four-cylinder locomotives in the 1920s, and particularly in view of that 135 deg crank-setting item, one may regard J. A. Hookham's interesting experimental locomotive for the North Staffordshire Railway, though its first appearance was, strictly, pre-amalgamation. It was originally a tank engine, 0–6–0, with four cylinders in line driving to the middle axle. Dimensions were modest, but one would have thought that four cylinders 14in by 24in were exacting for a boiler carrying but 856·7 sq ft of evaporative heating surface with 195 sq ft in the superheating elements. The pressure was 160lb. The interesting part of Hookham's engine – and one must repeat that she was an experiment concerned with that part – was the arrangement of the cranks inside and out to give eight impulses to each revolution of the wheels. The outside cranks were at 90 deg with each other and the inside likewise, but the inside and outside cranks at each side were at 135 deg instead of being opposite. There were four sets of Walschaert's gear, which, though necessary to such an arrangement, made for a complex engine. On the credit side were easy starting and running with an early cut-off, with consequent economical steam distribution. This modest-looking engine had an estimated tractive effort of 23,694lb at 85 per cent of boiler pressure, or 16,725 at 60 per cent. The cylinders were steeply inclined.

Hookham's engine appeared in 1922, and very soon after construction, in the early days of the LMS company, the side tanks were removed together with the bunker and the backs of the frames, and a standard Adams tender of the North Staffordshire variety took the place of these. No other eight-impulse four-cylinder engines were built in LMS days, though Richard Maunsell on the Southern Railway took up the arrangement, first with an old Drummond four-cylinder engine and then in the Lord Nelson class of 1926. The North Stafford engine – a rare bird to those who observed locomotives for their own sake – deserves its niche in the recorded history of steam locomotives. The LMS number was 2367.

Before we consider what might be called the Derbyan Conquest, two more Horwich essays should be noticed. In 1923 appeared a set of heavy o–8–o coal engines of pure Hughes design, carried out in L&Y days and really belonging, like some others mentioned, to pre-grouping history. They had 4ft 6in coupled wheels, with drive to the second axle, two 21½in by 26in cylinders inside, and piston valves with Hughes' automatic release valve for reducing back pressure. Boiler diameter was 5ft 8in with a working pressure of 180lb. The tube heating surface was 1,656 sq ft with 192 sq ft in firebox and 430 sq ft in the superheater, giving a combined heating surface of 2,278 sq ft. Grate area was 25·6 sq ft. Tenders were eight-wheeled with double opposed laminated springs above the axleboxes and rigid frames. Tender capacity was for 3,600 gallons of water and five tons of coal. Rigid eight-wheel tenders were quite old in L&Y practice, dating back to the early 1900s, but were used only for heavy mineral engines whose work entailed a good deal of waiting about. The usual small L&Y tender would not have done at all on such duties. For the same reason, such tenders had been used with the ordinary small L&Y o–6–o engines sent to France and Flanders for, *inter alia*, gun-spur construction behind the British lines. The heavy o–8–o were most useful engines and lasted for many years.

In 1925, George Hughes retired, and was succeeded by Sir Henry Fowler, KBE, who until 1923 had been already Chief Mechanical Engineer of the Midland Railway. Fowler was an all-round mechanical engineer rather than a locomotive engineer in particular. Persistent legend has it that on one convivial occasion he slapped a fellow guest on the back and remarked, laughing, that he never designed a locomotive in his life, a remark which, if it were indeed made, people may take according to the way they take the word "designed". He had been Gas Engineer to both the Lancashire & Yorkshire and the Midland companies in succession,

but long before that he had been a pioneer in heavy commercial motor
engineering, at a time when the motor car had been regarded as a new
and rather doubtful sort of pleasure carriage. In this connection he had
worked on the *Engineer* trials of 1897 and the Liverpool trials of 1898,
1899 and 1901. As to his later career, seconded to service under Government in the 1914–1918 war, he was appointed Superintendent of Royal
Aircraft Factories and that office brought him his knighthood. He was an
extremely clever organiser, and if ever a man deserved high office by the
exercise of energy, he did so.

Although, during Hughes' office, Fowler was without that supreme
command which he had already attained on the Midland, he was able
nevertheless, like Beames over at Crewe, to work well enough on his own
in the traditions of the works he had already headed. He had been
Works Manager at Derby since 1907, and had succeeded R. M. Deeley in
1909. He was thus senior to Beames in the hierarchy. The second-named
had succeeded to Crewe only at the end of 1920, having been Bowen
Cooke's Deputy Chief Mechanical Engineer since June 1919, and his
Personal Assistant since 1910. So the old, old feud between Crewe and
Derby was at last resolved, by a simple matter of promotion by seniority.
That Fowler was also Sir W. Guy Granet's man was a factor which
fortunately did not need to enter the picture.

Already, while Hughes was still in office, Fowler was seeing to it that
Midland design prevailed, at any rate on the Midland Division, and once
Hughes had retired, that practice was to extend to the Western and the
Scottish lines also, though it was never to make any heavy penetration of
the Highland system. The former Glasgow and South Western lines, on
the other hand, were to see a tremendous influx, realising, on the
mechanical side, that fusion of Midland and Sou'-West which had been
proposed but squashed many years before. That for general service
Midland, or quasi-Midland, locomotive design was entirely commendable,
none could deny save on the grounds of sentiment or regional loyalty.
Whether the backwash of the Midland small-engine policy was such a
good thing was a more open question when it came to the working of
heavy trains, of the West Coast sort, over the succession of Grayrigg,
Shap and Beattock.

The most interesting development under Fowler was the burgeoning
of the 4–4–0 three-cylinder compound engine, of the Smith-Deeley
arrangement, with alterations carried out under Fowler. These last were
matters of dimensions, and entailed no radical alterations or improvements. The Midland had been getting along very nicely with them since the
days of good King Edward, and from their viewpoint, now was the time
to show that they could work the principal express passenger trains
over much of this enormous London Midland & Scottish Railway.

To begin with, the Midland Division was quite urgently in need of such engines itself. As the Midland Railway, in its last years, it had probably had in heavy main-line traffic the largest proportion of very old engines of any major railway in Europe. One did not count Spain, and at that time nobody seemed to know quite what was going on in Russia. Austria had some veterans, indeed, but also many very advanced designs. So in 1924, forty new Deeley compound engines were built, following the classic Midland model in all main features of design and very closely in dimensions. The original 7ft coupled wheels were indeed *out*. There was something positively *Victorian* about the sound of such a dimension, and people nowadays, looking back to an era in many ways fearsome but in certain other ones rather successful, often can scarcely realise what a pejorative adjective that was in the 1920s. Fowler's first Deeley compounds had 6ft 9in coupled wheels (blessed three-inches-off!). The high-pressure cylinder was 19¾in in diameter and the two low-pressure were 21¾in with 26in stroke. The pressure was 200lb. In a hundred subsequent engines, half an inch was put on the coupled wheels and the cylinder diameters were down to 19in (high-pressure) and 21in (low-pressure) with the pressure remaining the same. The second variety in particular was subsequently to be found anywhere between London and Perth by all LMS routes. Mountings were cut down to suit Scottish loading-gauge restrictions, rather marring this initially very handsome design.

London & North Western, and Scottish men of Caledonian nurture, were at first extremely suspicious. The former, of the current generation, had been told shocking stories about compound engines in the days of their fathers' dreadful chief, F. W. Webb. The Caledonian enginemen knew nothing of compounds. It takes a well-taught artist to handle a relatively complex locomotive, whereas all sorts of men had successfully flogged Georges and Princes along the many miles between Euston and Carlisle Citadel, while the others had been perfectly happy with a Caledonian 140 class (Dunalastair Four) north of that place. The latter class, indeed, was to last for many years yet, particularly north of Perth on the Aberdeen road.

By degrees it was found what a very good engine the Deeley compound really was, within the limitations of its modest dimensions and often outside those. All the same, a mechanical historian cannot help wishing that Sir Henry Fowler had been permitted, or had had the gumption, to build at last the much bigger Deeley compound 4–6–0 which the Midland itself had funked. (Whether the Paget family, or Granet as one of Richard Deeley's relatives has rather testily suggested to me, were responsible for the memorable Deeley row, is now irrelevant. The design was undoubtedly made, and I have a tracing which I am not, by mutual agreement, to publish.)

In general – and one should not lay the blame on any one department – the company was for the present content to allow construction of *the engine, as before* and some time was to elapse before (it seems) the Executive turned on some of those who had been serving it, with something like an ultimatum. Six years after formation of the LMS, fifty Class 2 4-4-0 engines, bearing much the same relation to the Midland Railway version as did the compounds to theirs, were being churned out to replace still older engines which by then were becoming worn out. In the 1928 series, the cylinders were reduced in diameter from the original Midland 20½in to 19in, with 26in stroke, and the coupled wheels from 7ft 0½in to 6ft 9in. The pressure was 160lb, which was scarcely enterprising for that time. This series was initially numbered 563–612, but Nos. 575, 576 and 580 were immediately drafted to the Somerset and Dorset Joint Railway, in whose stock they became Nos. 44–46. Many of the others were soon to be found on the Glasgow and South Western lines, whereon the pre-group locomotive stock suffered a much more abrupt eclipse than did those of the Caledonian and the Highland lines. As already suggested, the Midland had always had its eye on the Glasgow and South Western as a slice of *Lebensraum* which only the obtuseness of Parliament had denied it. All the same, before we start being too beastly to the Midland, or over its traditions, be it remembered that the Glasgow and South Western had been a railway whose locomotive stock was more various than extensive. Though this were even more so on the Highland, much of that railway's stock was closely akin to that of the Caledonian, and under David Urie at St. Rollox, Caledonian boilers were easily put on to many Highland locomotives as these came in for rebuilding.

Urie had been, albeit very briefly, the last Locomotive Superintendent of the Highland Railway Company. In that time he had arranged for the rebuilding of Peter Drummond's bigger variety of Ben class 4-4-0 engines, which were largely used between Inverness and Wick, and Inverness and Aberdeen, with Robinson's superheaters and extended smokeboxes. The result, which appeared after the LMS had taken over, was very much like that of his father's (R. W. Urie's) operation on Dugald Drummond's very similar S11 class on the London & South Western Railway. In both cases the engines were much improved. Locomotives of the Glasgow and South Western Railway, however, in spite of the fact that Peter Drummond had held his last office thereon, could not be brought into the Caledonian/Highland scheme under first William Pickersgill and then David Urie.

Company Minutes being, quite properly, a closed book until half a century has elapsed, it is inexpedient to record here just what happened between the Executive and the Chief Mechanical Engineer's Department on the LMS during the years 1926–27, but fairly obviously, something did happen. That Executive had been formed, and Sir Josiah Stamp took office as its President, in January 1926. This is part of company, not mechanical history; but with Stamp in, things began to happen in the way of pulling together this ramshackle edifice of amalgamated companies. Abolition of the old office of General Manager was announced in October 1927, and its last holder, H. G. Burgess, was to retire in March 1927. Sir W. Guy Granet had given Stamp a mandate to manage the railway in his own way. He did.

If Midland methods were not exactly thrown overboard, they were called to severe account, and one persistent Midland method, as we know was that "small engine policy". As noted already, the Midland had built only one engine which could possibly be called a big one; the solitary ten-coupled "Big Emma" on the Lickey Incline. Still, up and down the Midland main line in particular, the heaviest coal trains were still trundling along behind small and often ancient 0–6–0 engines in pairs. The situation was comparable to that of the London & North Western about 1850, when Edward Bury had apparently considered that the same little locomotives could effectively work the traffic for ever.

To cut out this sort of thing on the Toton–Brent goods and mineral trains, in 1927 three Beyer-Garratt articulated locomotives, 2–6–0 + 0–6–2, were supplied by Beyer, Peacock and Company, the patentees and at that time the sole builders apart from Maffei in Munich. They were far and away the largest locomotives yet built for the LMS or its constituents. Main dimensions are given in Table 2, but here it should be remarked that the total wheelbase of each articulated unit was 25ft 9in of which 16ft 6in was rigid, and the combined wheelbase came to 79ft. At 85 per cent of boiler pressure (190lb per sq in) the tractive effort was 45,620lb.

One wonders whether Beyer, Peacock and Company, to which firm R. H. Whitelegg of the Glasgow and South Western had gone to be General Manager and Engineer-in-Chief, quite liked the wheel arrangement. They were building steadily increasing numbers of such engines for overseas railways, often on narrower gauges and relatively lightly laid track, and liked to have carrying wheels, latterly in a four-wheel bogie, at each end of each unit. There seems, however, to have been no trouble in the way the LMS variety felt its way up and down the solid Midland permanent way. It was a less exacting course than some other lines, such as the Hex River Pass and the Mau Escarpment.

Thirty more Beyer-Garratts were built during 1930, so whatever trepidations Mr. Whitelegg may have had about them needing inner carrying wheels and running off the road through lack of them, the type clearly was suited to Midland heavy goods traffic. These thirty-three engines worked up and down between Toton and Brent until they wore out, and obviously impending changes in traction, under British Railways,

C*

discouraged thoughts of renewal. No other widespread use of the great engine thought-up by Herbert Garratt took place on any railway in Great Britain,[1] though the type was to be found thereafter over much of Africa, Asia and Australia. On the LMS the 1930 series had the fuel space increased to nine tons (in the original three it was seven tons) and a sliding cover provided on the bunker to protect the enginemen from blown coal-dust when running with the boiler in their rear. They were not fitted with mechanical stokers, but in 1931 a start was made with the provision of Beyer Peacock's patent self-trimming bunker which gently rocked the fuel down into the hopper.

For all the excellence of the Midland compound 4–4–0 engines, the company's crying need was for a reasonably heavy and powerful engine for working the fastest West Coast expresses. It was in this connection that a sort of ultimatum was alleged to have been delivered from the Executive to Sir Henry Fowler and his Department. It was not the time to trot out Deeley's compound 4–6–0 from the old oak chest; nor to try flogging to the Executive that experimental rebuilding, as compound, of a Hughes 4–6–0. At that time first the Southern Railway, and then quickly after it the Great Western, had produced heavy 4–6–0 express engines with four cylinders and simple expansion, a type of which both Eastleigh and Swindon had already quite considerable experience, the latter more successfully than the former. Here or there was some sort of a prototype. Further, Gresley's three-cylinder Pacific engines, especially since their pressures had been bumped up, initially with one called *Enterprise*, were doing very well on the London & North Eastern.

One may impertinently imagine some sort of conversation taking place in the Derby Drawing Office, rather on the lines of one in Kipling's *Just-So Stories*:

"Well, don't let's have a Pacific! There is some sort of Pacific in those drawers, isn't there? Didn't old Hughes draw one? But I wouldn't have us look like the East Coast lot for ever-so!"

"No! Of course there's Swindon's King class! But I wouldn't have us look like the Great Western for ever-so!"

Just what sort of a huddle then took place, with Sir Henry Fowler in the Chair, one dare not imagine, but the upshot was that a big 4–6–0 must be built; something like Maunsell's *Lord Nelson* on the Southern Railway, but with three cylinders instead of four. The North British Locomotive Company undertook to build fifty such engines, provided there was something of a guide to work upon. Mr. Maunsell of the Southern Railway kindly lent from Eastleigh a complete set of Nelson drawings, which

[1] The London & North Eastern had a solitary 2–8–0 + 0–8–2 which it used on the Worsborough Dale loop, in the South Yorkshire coalfield, from 1925 onwards, and a few were on industrial service, beginning with Vivian and Sons' 0–4–0 + 0–4–0 at Swansea in 1923.

were hurried to Glasgow for the magicians to deal with. The result was the famous Royal Scot class.

It was unlike anything that had appeared hitherto under Midland, London & North Western or Lancashire & Yorkshire auspices. To be sure, William Pickersgill had built three-cylinder 4–6–0 engines for the Caledonian, but the new design was otherwise different. There was certainly a resemblance to the Southern four-cylinder Nelsons, just as, some time later, E. C. Bredin's three Irish giants on the Great Southern Railways were destined to bear a distinct resemblance to these LMS engines, which Mr. Bredin greatly admired. Nevertheless, there was nothing quite like a Royal Scot. They were not conventionally beautiful engines; the great drum of a smokebox with an almost frivolously small chimney on its camber suggested a most mountainous lady with a plate hat on. They were not big engines by current French or German standards – let alone American or Spanish. They had the usual sort of Midland six-wheel tender. But – remembering one's first sight of one, on a winter night at Euston in 1927 – they were extraordinarily impressive loco-motives. A woman's reaction, valuable because of its rarity, has been already noted. The engines were painted red, and unlike many LMS examples, now that the Stamp Presidency was really getting into its swing, they were kept clean.

Apart from art and its appeal, they were very successful engines, which was just as well for many people. The Emperor Napoleon – by which one means the great general, not his much junior relative who was broken by Prussia – used to query confidential reports on his officers with the note: "*Is he lucky?*" Certainly Sir Henry Fowler would seem to have been a lucky man, all down his career, for although a brilliant all-rounder and an undoubted organiser, he left us with no great evidence of originality. The ordering of fifty untried express locomotives from an outside works was a gamble of gambles. It paid off. NB Loco in those happy days was a great whale of a firm, and it was well briefed, for which fact we must give Fowler his due. Main dimensions of these excellent engines are in Table 1. They were not yet expected to run at any really tremendous speeds, but they were to work heavy West Coast expresses, keeping time, at speeds which were higher than anything elsewhere in Europe other than in France or on the Great Western, and surely as good as anything in America. They did so. The West Coast line, between London Euston and Glasgow Central, formed their first habitat, with its Manchester and Liverpool spurs for good measure. The name of the first engine, and of the class, was taken from that bestowed on the time-honoured ten o'clock morning express in each direction. It was not an old name (except regimentally) but the company had marched well into the Public Relations and Publicity business on its own account, following the course of the Southern when that company had engaged the future Sir John Elliot to such ends. At Euston, G. H. Loftus-Allen moved-in on the new engines, for what they were worth in public estimation, which was liable to be much more than many third-generation railwaymen ever would have admitted to believe. This man had on his books, though not on his staff, such able writers as Edmund Vale and S. P. B. Mais, and before long the second-named had produced for him an engaging little book called *The Royal Scot and her Forty-nine Sisters*. Naming the first of the engines after the old but newly-named train started a train of another kind, one of thought that other engines of the class should bear regimental names. In the name *Royal Scot*, there was something of a punning nature, or at least an ambiguity, for the Royal Scots formed one of the oldest regiments in the British Army, while as for the train, the ten o'clock West Coast day expresses used the Royal Mail Route. At first, however, many of the new locomotives were named after pioneer engines on the Liverpool and Manchester and other early railways embraced within the LMS system. The thing was hand-somely done, too, with the likenesses of the original namesakes engraved on oval brass plates. By degrees, more and more regiments came to be represented, often with elaborate naming ceremonies. The first fifty engines were these:

NO.	NAME		
6100	*Royal Scot*	21	*HLI*
1	*Royal Scots Grey*	22	*Royal Ulster Rifleman*
2	*Black Watch*	23	*Royal Irish Fusilier*
3	*Royal Scots Fusilier*	24	*London Scottish*
4	*Scottish Borderer*	25	*Lancashire Witch/3rd. Carabineer*
5	*Cameron Highlander*	26	*Sanspareil/Royal Army Service Corps*
6	*Gordon Highlander*		
7	*Argyll & Sutherland Highlander*	27	*Novelty/The Old Contemptible*
8	*Seaforth Highlander*	28	*Meteor/ The Lovat Scout*
9	*Royal Engineer*	29	*Comet/The Scottish Horse*
6110	*Grenadier Guardsman*	6130	*Liverpool/The West Yorkshire Regiment*
11	*Royal Fusilier*		
12	*Sherwood Forester*	31	*Planet/The Royal Warwickshire Regiment*
13	*Cameronian*		
14	*Coldstream Guardsman*	32	*Phoenix/The King's Regiment Liverpool*
15	*Scots Guardsman*		
16	*Irish Guardsman*	33	*Vulcan/The Green Howards*
17	*Welsh Guardsman*	34	*Atlas/The Cheshire Regiment*
18	*Royal Welch Fusilier*	35	*Samson/The East Lancashire Regiment*
19	*Lancashire Fusilier*		
6120	*Royal Inniskilling Fusilier*	36	*Goliath/The Border Regiment*

37   Vesta/The Prince of Wales'
        Volunteers (South Lancashire)
38   The London Irish Rifleman
39   Ajax/The Welch Regiment
6140 Hector/The King's Royal Rifle
        Corps
41   Caledonian/The North
        Staffordshire Regiment
42   Lion/The York and Lancaster
        Regiment
43   Mail/The South Staffordshire
        Regiment

44   Ostrich/Honourable Artillery
        Company
45   Condor/The Duke of Wellington's
        Regiment (West Riding)
46   Jenny Lind/The Rifle Brigade
47   Courier/The Northamptonshire
        Regiment
48   Velocipede/The Manchester
        Regiment
49   Lady of the Lake/The Middlesex
        Regiment

These comprised the original series. There were more to come. With the greatest respect to the regiments commemorated, never had the practice of naming locomotives achieved a more dismal Nadir of systematic sycophancy, than in these ponderous titles. Regimental nicknames would have been better, even though it would have involved No. 6106 being *The Kaiser's Bodyguard*.

Now to a much more seriously unfortunate essay, which was that of the high-pressure compound locomotive *Fury*. Basically, this was a specialised Royal Scot, but the boiler and machinery were very different. Late in the 1920s, there was the liveliest interest in very high pressures plus compound expansion, and the Schmidt Superheated Steam Company of Kassel in Germany produced an extraordinary boiler which was made for locomotives in several lands, notably Germany, Grance and Canada. This was the boiler which Fowler put on to LMS No. 6399 *Fury*, built in Glasgow by the North British Locomotive Company in collaboration with the Superheater Company, agents in Great Britain for the Schmidt firm. The boiler was in three parts; the sides, crown and back of firebox comprised a range of Perkins closed-circuit tubes connected at bottom to a foundation ring and expanded at the top into equalising drums. Evaporating elements fed by pipes from the equalising drums were placed in a high-pressure drum supplying steam to the inside, high-pressure cylinder of the locomotive, which was $11\frac{1}{2}$in in diameter by 26in stroke. Pressure in the closed-circuit system, which was filled to a predetermined level with distilled water, varied from 1,400lb to 1,800lb per sq in. That in the high-pressure drum, heated by these closed-circuit tubes and supplying the h.p. cylinder, was 900lb per sq in. This drum was of nickel steel, and was fed by hot water from the low-pressure boiler, the third component of the boiler unit, which was fired by tubes from the firebox in the normal way, and carried a working pressure of 250lb per sq in. The high-pressure drum naturally raised steam more rapidly than the low-pressure boiler supplying the two 18in by 26in outside cylinders, so an intercepting valve was provided to bypass surplus steam from the first-mentioned to the second, to avoid needless (and one would imagine deafening) blowing-off from safety-valves with its consequent waste. The low-pressure boiler was of fairly ordinary type, occupying a nickel steel boiler barrel with mild steel tube-plates.

Working was in this wise. The regulator handle in the cab simul-taneously worked both high- and low-pressure regulators. Steam from the 900lb drum passed through superheating elements in the lower flues of the main boiler barrel to the single inside cylinder, and exhausted from this into a mixing chamber where it was met by steam at 250lb from elements in the upper part of the low-pressure barrel, and whence the combined force of steam passed to the two outside cylinders. There were the usual piston valves, with three sets of Walschaert's gear; as suggested, the chassis of the locomotive was that of a standard Royal Scot, and so was the general outline, apart from the semi-elliptical casing above the high-pressure drums towards the rear, which followed the same contours as the upper part of the cab roof, producing a very straight-backed aspect.

The *Fury* was delivered for trials early in 1930, having been completed at the end of December 1929, but apparently no road trials were made in January. On February 10, while travelling quite slowly at Carstairs on the main Caledonian line, a tube of the closed-circuit system burst in the firebox, blowing the fire out on to the footplate. There were three men in the cab. One came off with miraculously light injuries. Fireman Donald Blair was severely scalded and burnt, but managed to jump before he could receive the full force of the blow-out. Louis Schofield, who was responsible for the engine at the time and was driving her, was over-whelmed by the appalling eruption, yet not instantly killed. He was rushed to the Glasgow Royal Infirmary by special train, and died there soon after from his terrible injuries. The *Fury* was not, as some might have expected, blown to pieces like some other locomotives down the years. Eyewitnesses noted simply a great cloud of steam and ash blown out through the cab.

Few people have seen the *Fury* in her original, fatal form. An F. Moore painting was made, showing her in standard red, but she was in works grey from delivery to the time of the accident. Five years later, when (Sir) William Stanier was in command of the LMS Locomotive Department, he used her wheels, frames, tender and gear for an additional engine of Royal Scot type, but with his own taper boiler. This was No. 6170, named *British Legion*, and formed a prototype for future rebuilding of this famous class. Later Royal Scots were:

NO.	NAME	NO.	NAME
6150	*The Life Guardsman*	61	*The King's Own*
51	*The Royal Horse Guardsman*	62	*Queen's Westminster Rifleman*
52	*The King's Dragoon Guardsman*	63	*Civil Service Rifleman*
53	*The Royal Dragoon*	64	*The Artists' Rifleman*
54	*The Hussar*	65	*The Ranger (Twelfth London*
55	*The Lancer*		*Regiment)*
56	*The South Wales Borderer*	66	*London Rifle Brigade*
57	*The Royal Artilleryman*	67	*The Hertfordshire Regiment*
58	*The Loyal Regiment*	68	*The Boy Scout*
59	*The Royal Air Force*	69	*The Girl Guide*
6160	*Queen Victoria's Rifleman*	70	*British Legion*

As for the names of the last two, Sir Henry Fowler was very keen on the Scout Movement, and had himself photographed in front of No. 6168, complete with Scout's hat and short pants. Some of the engines' titles could be described only as monuments of brass-foundry verbosity. To be fair to the LMS, other authorities achieved things as absurd as these. The Russians named a locomotive after *Isvestia*, but giving the newspaper's full title, which was as long as an American freight train. Of our own, one which named a lot of engines after supposed country seats, found that it had thus honoured a lunatic asylum. The name was quickly and quietly changed. On the LMS, regimental badges were applied to many engines, a nice redeeming feature to an absurd programme.

Still the company had not enough express engines of the larger, more puissant sort. There were many portions of the system which needed something nearly, but not quite as heavy, as a Royal Scot. The London & North Western Claughtons, even with bigger boilers, were by now somewhat old-fashioned in some other people's eyes, and surely much too Crewey for Derbyan tastes. So a start was made with their "reconstruction" (more actuarial ingenuity?) beginning with No. 5902 *Sir Frank Ree* and No. 5971, which had no name, though previously she had been *Croxteth*. Not even the old tenders were retained, but the enormous bosses on the coupled wheels suggested that the old wheel centres had faithfully reappeared. The result was really a light Royal Scot with three cylinders and three sets of Walschaert gear as in the big version. Drive was divided, with the inside cylinder well in advance of the two outside ones placed symmetrically over the bogie. The boiler was that which had been designed for rebuilding the old Claughtons. Main dimensions are given in Table 1. The engines were almost immediately dubbed Baby Scots, a name not much fancied in official quarters, though with many other people it was to last for as long as the engines did. Forty more of this new class were rebuilt (or "reconstructed") though this later operation involved even less of any recognisable Claughton components. Crewe turned out fifteen in 1932 and fifteen more in 1933, when Derby also, produced ten. At first they took old Claughton numbers as replacement engines, but later the series of forty-two were renumbered 5500–5541. In 1934, Crewe built ten more, Nos. 5542–5551, and in these there was no more fiction about rebuilding. They were entirely and officially new engines.

Now for the suppression of that repugnantly borne nickname "Baby Scots"! As is well enough known, the London & North Western had specially named one of the Claughtons *Patriot* and numbered her 1914, as a war-memorial engine. She became LMS No. 5964, keeping the name and the commemorative plates, but at some time acquiring a Great Central type tender from one of the ex-Railway Operating Division 2–8–0 locomotives. At that time people were not keen on knocking down war-memorials, and one remembers speculating on what would happen when the war-memorial locomotive became obsolete one-day-some-day. The thing was done as nearly tactfully as possible. When the old *Patriot* went the way of most engines, the name and dedication passed quietly to that "Baby Scot" No. 5971 which contained the old *Croxteth's* wheel centres. With the renumbering, the new *Patriot* became No. 5500. Now the entire series could safely be called the Patriot class, and so they remained until they, too, fell to the scrappers' torches as ageing engines must.

Ere that came to pass, the class became one of the best locomotive investments a railway company could have wished to make. They were much liked, even by old London & North Western men. They could go where Royal Scots were not allowed at that time, notably on the Midland main line which had been small-engined for so long, and with Manchester–London expresses via Stoke. They were fast engines too, with a very well-designed front-end and long valve-travel. Working with a wide-open regulator and very early cut-off they could go soaring up to the lower nineties. Highest recorded speed, one believes, was 93 mph clocked on the Midland.

Most of the class received names, some of them inherited from London & North Western predecessors. There was a bit of an overflow from regiments and other bodies left out of the Royal Scot list. That had contained *The Royal Air Force* but not, somehow, *The Royal Navy*. Probably too much of the company's crockery was kicked about the resounding platforms of Carlisle Citadel a-nights by jolly Jack Tars for these to be in favour. These, with their final LMS numbers and names, were the Baby Scots/Patriots:

NO.	NAME	NO.	NAME
5500	*Patriot*	2	*Royal Naval Division*
1	*St. Dunstan's*	3	*The Leicestershire Regiment*

4	*Royal Signals*		(presumably named after a
5	*The Royal Army Ordnance*		Borough Council)
	Corps	27	*Southport*
6	—	28–9	—
7	*Royal Tank Corps*	5530	*Sir Frank Ree*
8--10	—	31	*Sir Frederick Harrison*
5511	*Isle of Man*	32	*Illustrious*
12	*Bunsen*	33	*Lord Rathmore*
13	—	34	*E. Tootal Broadhurst*
14	*Holyhead*	35	*Sir Herbert Walker, KCB*
15	*Caernarvon*	36	*Pte. W. Wood, VC*
16	*The Bedfordshire and*	37	*Pte. E. Sykes, VC*
	Hertfordshire Regiment	5538	*Giggleswick*
17	—	39	*E. C. Trench*
18	*Bradshaw*	40	*Sir Robert Turnbull*
19	*Lady Godiva*	5541	*Duke of Sutherland*
5520	*Llandudno*	42	—
21	*Rhyl*	43	*The Home Guard*
22	*Prestatyn*	44–5	—
23	*Bangor*	46	*Fleetwood*
24	*Blackpool*	47	—
25	*Colwyn Bay*	48	*Lytham St Annes*
26	*Morecambe and Heysham*	49–51	—

That made fifty-two engines. Whether some went nameless through wartime economy in non-ferrous metals, one dare not argue, for as we have seen a later engine was renamed in order to acknowledge the collective award of the George Cross to Malta. Certainly the Home Guard got in. Quite a few old North Western names could have filled up the gaps, and noting with honour the perpetuation of two VCs, one wonders sadly about L/Cpl Christie, for whom also the London & North Western company had named one of the Claughton class. Following this long list of titles, one had best get back to a modest commentary on design. It is convenient – if technically premature – to remark here that from 1946 onwards, ten of the Patriot class were rebuilt with taper boilers carrying 250lb per sq in and raised in classification from 5 XP to 6P. Rated tractive effort went up from 26,520lb to 29,570lb. The rebuilt engines, immediately after State ownership succeeded the company (1948) were Nos. 5512/14/-21/26/28–32/40. British Railways renumbering added 40000 to the LMS numbers of these and of other LMS engines.

December 1927, saw the appearance of Fowler's 2–6–4 passenger tank engines, which were mechanically somewhat similar to the mixed-traffic 2–6–0, though the styling was undoubtedly Midland. In the author's opinion, they were not handsome engines, having a gawky appearance, like that Miss Sichliffe who reminded Rudyard Kipling of a camel when she knelt down to make a fuss of a puppy. One felt that if anything broke about the leading truck, the engine would do just that, though to be sure, when one of them was in a bad collision at Holmes Chapel, years after (in 1941), she lay down on her right side, as decorously as the circumstances would allow. Still, they were useful engines, destined to do good work for many years, and the forerunners of many engines built by Sir William Stanier for the same railway, as of the ultimate British Railways standard 2–6–4 tank engine.

As to the camel-lady's vital statistics; there were two cylinders 19in by 26in, and 5ft 9in coupled wheels. The evaporative heating surface was 1,220·25 sq ft with 266·25 sq ft in the superheater elements, giving a combined heating surface of 1,486·5 sq ft. The grate area was 25 sq ft and the working pressure 200 per sq in. Tanks held 2,000 gallons and scoops were fitted for water pickup. The bunkers held 3½ tons of coal. Weight in working order was 86tons 5cwt. Seventy-five were built, Nos. 2300–2364, and in consequence of a royal visit, No. 2313 was named *The Prince*, after His Incipient (and Beloved) Majesty, King Edward VIII. These engines did useful, if not startlingly brilliant work on many sorts of train, from heavy-passenger to parcels, over moderate distances.

Akin but on a smaller scale were Sir Henry Fowler's 2–6–2 tank engines. The type had been used, and built, by the Great Western Railway over many years, and in 1930 both the London Midland & Scottish and the London & North Eastern essayed it. On the LMS much of the local passenger traffic was entrusted to 0–4–4 (Midland and Caledonian) and 2–4–2 (London & North Western) tank engines, some of which were of very considerable antiquity, though the Caledonian variety was of fairly robust sort. These 2–6–2 engines were intended to replace some of the pre-grouping four-coupled types.

From the early part of 1930, fifty of these engines were built at Derby. They had each two cylinders 17½in by 26 in, 5ft 3in coupled wheels and 200lb working pressure. The boiler was not very big, even by Victorian standards, having a combined heating surface of 969 sq ft, divided into 692·75 sq ft (tubes and flues), 103·5 sq ft (firebox) and 172·75 (super-heater). The grate area was 17·5 sq ft. Weight in working order was about 70·5 tons. Apart from the initial twenty, the engines were given surface condensers and trip-cocks to the braking system for working Midland trains down to Moorgate via the Metropolitan Widened Line. On these duties they superseded Johnson 0–4–4 tank engines which had worked this service for many years. The non-condensing engines one remembers as having superseded Webb 2–4–2 tank engines on what had been the London & North Western system, even on pull-and-push trains such as those between Harrow and Stanmore (the last perfectly idyllic branch line in the London Area).[1]

There were ever the handmaidens of freight and shunting, and as on so many railways, these had on the LMS a high average age. That meant that many of them were worn out, and it was most expedient to replace them with something more or less the same, which could be built in large quantities *and would do*. The Midland recipe seemed the obvious one. In 1927, Andrew Barclay at Kilmarnock built 25 engines, the first of many additions to a standard Midland 0–6–0 design. It was a good solid engine, and lasted for a long time. The author remembers seeing one, at Crianlarich (Upper) in 1954, which had gone down the mountain on Loch Treig side because the snowslide she was bucking happened to have some sizeable boulders inside it. She was only chipped a bit. Such stocky, substantially-made engines were very useful.

Cylinders of these were 20in by 26in, driving 5ft 3in coupled wheels. The boiler with 175lb pressure, had a total evaporative heating surface of 1,133 sq ft (136 sq ft in the firebox) plus 338 sq ft in the firebox. The grate area was 21·7 sq ft. Weight of engine in working order was 48 tons 15 cwt and of tender 41 tons 4 cwt. The latter held 3,500 gallons of water and four tons of coal. The engines had inside admission valves worked by Stephenson link motion through rocking shafts. There were automatic air relief valves. The class was to be seen over most of the LMS system, sooner or later. Unlike the compounds and the Class 2 4–4–0 engines it even gave good service on the Highland Railway as far as Inverness, what time the Jones and Drummond goods engines moved farther north and west, and in the early days of British Railways it moved into what had been certain London & North Eastern territory, witness the specimen that hit a boulder somewhere south of Tulloch.

These were sufficient for most ordinary purposes in the way of dragging about the timeless unbraked British goods train, but even under Sr Henry Fowler there was recognition of a need for a somewhat bigger engine, to be still as ever-so-ordinary as could be managed. So from March, 1929, onwards came a delivery of a hundred 0–8–0 engines. The main object, as seen by a disinterested observer, seemed to be production of a Midland version of the London & North Western standard 0–8–0 coal engine. Cylinders were 19in by 26in, coupled wheels 4ft 8½in and working pressure 200lb. Inside Walschaert gear was used (see Table 2).

Of much older sort were the standard 0–6–0 shunting engines, sometimes called "Jinties". (These nicknames were often purely local; your author has heard this one sometimes in Scotland, often among amateurs, but not on the Midland.) They were as typically Midland as the 0–6–0

---

[1] It even had an accident of the *Titfield Thunderbolt* sort; a buffer-stop collision which destroyed the Stanmore "Ladies", fortunately with nobody *in situ*.

goods, and the first lot came from orders placed in 1923 for fifty; 20 from Vulcan Foundry, 15 from Hunslet Engine and 15 more from the North British Locomotive Company. There was an extended smokebox, and the first of them had Ramsbottom safety-valves, Derby style. Coupled wheels were 4ft 7in; cylinders, 18in by 26in and pressure 160lb. Total heating surface was 1,074 sq ft, and grate area 16 sq ft. Many of these serviceable but stodgy-looking engines were yet to be built. In 1928 Beardmore turned out ninety, 25 of them with vacuum brakes making them eligible for branch-line passenger service.[1]

During 1928–29 the company invested in a set of dock-shunting engines. As in such cases the requirement was for something which could shift good loads (by dock standards) on very sharp curves, which in this case were of 2½ chains radius. They had 3ft 11in wheels on a wheelbase of only 9ft 6in, the trailing axle having sliding Cartazzi boxes. Walschaert gear and cylinders (17in by 22in) were outside. The boiler, carrying 160lb pressure, had 1,008 sq ft of heating surface including 85 sq ft in the firebox. Grate area was 14·5 sq ft. Styling was inevitably Midland, though for this sort of work the old Midland Railway had used 0–4–0 tank engines, themselves large of their sort.

In 1928 the LMS produced its first diesel-electric train, which was converted from a four-car Bury electric set, at Horwich. In one car was mounted a 500hp Beardmore engine, with eight 8¼in by 12in cylinders, having four speeds: 350, 600, 750 and 900 rpm. It was coupled to a 340kW 600 Volt dc English Electric generator with an 8kW exciter. There were two motors on one bogie, rated at 280hp. The gear ratio was 18/60. As to design, officially, of course, Fowler was the Old Man, but much of the work was done at Beardmore's and by Lieut.-Col. F. A. Cortez-Leigh, Chief Electrical Engineer, and Ernest Lemon.

This train was a modest vision of the shape of things to come many years later. But for the time, steam was still triumphantly universal. Electric traction was limited to the Lancashire and the London suburban areas, and the Lancashire seaside traffic. New London suburban trains followed London & North Western design, plus a really sumptuous improvement of the first-class which seemed, while one was riding in it, to attain better main-line standards than some other people's, apart from the lack of lavatories such as much rougher suburban trains possessed in Munich, Stockholm and several other cities one knew.

A very interesting experiment was carried out during the winter of 1930–31, and that was the introduction of a rail-motor which could run on ordinary roads, or perhaps more properly a motor-bus which could

[1] One remembers some disappointment on finding a "Jinty" on the ex-Highland Burghead branch about 1931, having expected some wondrous Highland antique as at Fochabers, Dornoch or Lybster!

also run on rails. Certainly the idea was not new. One remembers an American agency photograph, c 1919 showing a motor-lorry of such a sort, appearing in that most educative, yet by-many forgotten magazine called *Everyday Science*. But to make such a thing go satisfactorily needed more than an initial idea, as Leonardo de Vinci no doubt was aware when he invented the helicopter at the end of the fifteenth century, not having produced a suitable engine to make it rise.

The LMS vehicle, quickly dubbed in vulgar language the Ro-Railer (for nobody produced a more academic substitute) was built by Karrier Motors of Huddersfield, with body by Craven's of Sheffield, to the requirements of John Shearman, Road Motor Engineer to the LMS.

To make either a motor bus or a rail-motor was simple enough, but the thing had to have two sets of limbs, both for ground locomotion. So the pneumatic-tyred road wheels were mounted on eccentrics fitted to outward extensions of ordinary flanged railway wheels, which nevertheless had to be mounted on axles of road motor type for steering in front and differential at the rear. When the Ro-Railer ran as an ordinary bus on the road, the wheels were concentrically locked, and as the pneumatic tyres gave a larger diameter to the outside pair, fore-and-aft, all was well.

While running on rails, the outer wheels, raised by a half-turn on the eccentric mountings, were locked out of gear and secured by locking pins to the chassis. At the same time the road steering gear was locked so that the bus ran as a rigid-wheel-base four-wheeled rail-motor. The transformation could be carried out in as little as $2\frac{1}{2}$ minutes, and under normal working conditions it was done in less than five. The change-over was made on a sort of ramp like the timbers of a road level crossing. A light buffer frame could be mounted fore and aft, making possible the towing of the vehicle, out of gear, by an orthodox train. Unlike ordinary road buses, the middle entrance was made double, so that railway running was unaffected by the left- or right-hand position of platforms. Normal top speed was 50 mph on the railway, though maxima of 60 mph on road and 75 mph on railway were possible. The engine developed a maximum output of 120hp, and the transmission included a supplementary gearbox to give increased rail speed at low engine speed. Top gear ratio (road) was 7 to 1 and (rail) 4·2 to 1. Corresponding fuel consumption, using petrol, was 8 mpg on the road and 16 mpg on the railway.

Rail-to-road conversionists of the period, of whom the most prominent enthusiast was the pioneer motorist S. F. Edge, did not quite like such a demonstration of the superiority of rail over road efficiency with the same motor vehicle, though one remembers with some amusement an exuberant motor-coaching exponent[1] who saw a glorious possibility of bus com-

---

[1] Charles Rudy of the *Coaching Journal*.

panies seeking and getting compulsorily-granted running powers over longer-distance railway routes and beggaring their wicked landlords.

A few other leading dimensions of the Ro-Railer: gauge of road wheels was 6ft 3½in, with 36in by 6in Goodyear tyres in front and 42in by 9in in rear. The chassis wheelbase was 17ft 1in. Overall dimensions were: Length, 26ft; width, 7ft 5½in; height (on road) 9ft 9¾in, (on rail) 9ft 6½in, (inside saloon) 6ft 4¼in; weight (tare) 7 tons 2¼cwt; passenger capacity, 26 persons; freight equivalent, 3 tons.

Following demonstration, this most interesting sort of car saw some public service on the Stratford-on-Avon and Midland Junction line, at the western end of which it would make its change-over and drive off with its passengers to the Welcombe Hotel in which the company was interested, but its only lasting application was as a departmental ballast vehicle for the Engineer's Department on the West Highland Railway, a component of the neighbouring London & North Eastern system. One feels that more might have been done with it in wide and remote places, as in Sutherland and Caithness, and in parts of Wales. All the same, though small as a railway vehicle, it was rather a large bus for such roads as radiated from places like Larig, Thurso and Lybster. Of the coast road westwards from Thurso at that time one recalls in particular its crossing places at intervals and its extraordinary mail bus whose body resembled a stage-coach "inside" with boot at the rear, mounted on a light commercial motor chassis and comparable with nothing else earthly. Certainly the Ro-Railer was what a Victorian youth would have called, with enthusiasm, *a crumby dodge*, and deserved better success than it was allowed. One must take into consideration the resistance of both railway and commercial motor people to any sort of collusion between what both at the time regarded as natural enemies.

Before turning to standard LMS rolling stock, we may notice several Pullman cars, which were a result of a contract between Dalziel's Pullman Car Company and the Caledonian and Highland Railways, over which they ran as far north as Aberdeen and Aviemore. Pullman cars had been built for Caledonian Railway service just before the 1914 war outbreak, and the "Caley" remained faithful to them for as long as it lasted. Apart from the sumptuous observation car *Maid of Morven* on the Glasgow–Oban run, the Pullman in Scotland primarily provided dining or drinking service. People could ride all the way in it by paying a supplement, but others could come in and simply eat if there were room for them. The cars were of classic Pullman style, quite unlike ordinary British coaching stock, with more than a whiff of American constructional conventions and a high Edward VII style of decoration and furnishing within. They were of their kind very handsome vehicles, much more so than some objects which were to be presented with ill-merited pride later on.

When the LMS moved in, there were built for Caledonian/Highland service by Clayton Wagons four more Pullman cars, all eight-wheelers with 10ft bogies at 43ft 4in centres. Bodies were 63ft 10in long by 8ft 7in over mouldings. Three of them were first-class diners, named according to the custom in Scotland after various interesting girls of the past: *Meg Dods*, *Lass o' Ballochmyle* and *Mauchline Belle*. The fourth was a third-class "buffet" car (Pullman No. 80) but in fact there was no bar, but small kitchen-pantry arrangements. The cars seated thirty-three first-class and thirty-nine third-class passengers respectively.

The London Midland & Scottish Railway was fortunate as to the sequence of its coaching design. That of its constituents had been very variable indeed. Midland, London & North Western, and Caledonian had all three made very handsome carriages indeed: Glasgow and South Western stock included some really excellent vehicles and had a good general standard. Highland, and Lancashire & Yorkshire coaches were on the severe side; the one company had ever lived on a shoestring of sorts, while the other had to carry men grimy from the factories and women both woolly and cottony from the mills, leaving between them an extraordinary mixture of residues to which woven horsehair alone could stand-up. Furness carriages were fairly elaborately uncomfortable, with heaps of upholstery in what seemed to be the wrong places, at any rate to a person of normal stature. The carriages' sanitary appliances were generally good except on the Caledonian. For lighting, there was far too great a predominance of oil gas on the big lines, especially on the L&Y and the Midland, though it was very general on most lines. The North Stafford shone exclusively electrically.

But there were also the differences between best and usual practice. The London & North Western had many very old-fashioned coaches, with less excuse than a line like the Highland. For all the excellence of the best Caledonian vehicles, the worst, in the Glasgow area, were very awful indeed, while the ordinary ruck was somewhat scruffy. We named the gas lamps "fly-cemeteries", borrowing the nickname from a form of currant-biscuit to which boy and girl were both very partial in spite of appearances. Beyond all doubt, the general standard of the former Midland Railway, from the Scotch expresses to the local trains about Leeds, was far above everything else, and it was at Derby works that very noticeable advances were made in the mass-production of railway carriages, during R. W. Reid's time and soon after the amalgamation.

Standardisation of coachbuilding components was, of course, nothing new. For many years, the major railway companies had turned out scores and even centuries of identical coaches whenever a generally useful design had been achieved. At Derby in the early 1920s the sawmill was over-hauled with a view to the production of more rapid accurate work, with

new woodworking machinery. Much more use was being made of stop
bars and jigs, one component being marked out to make a template for its
successors. A very careful study was made of the cramping and assembling
of carriage doors, processes in which Ernest Lemon is believed to have
done much valuable work. Roofs and bodies were made separately, and
the former dropped neatly over the latter at a relatively advanced stage
in erection. The carriage bodies were still all of wood, but one might add
a rider to that, in remarking that the wood in those days was properly
seasoned, which cannot be said for much stuff about nowadays, except,
perhaps, for the best Swedish household furniture. Considering these
things, it was therefore fortunate that R. W. Reid succeeded in command
of the LMS Carriage and Wagon Department, to be followed by E. J. H.
Lemon. Midland carriages were comfortable, and that they were in some
respects old-fashioned was an entirely secondary consideration.

That last particularly applied on some business block trains for the
service between St. Pancras and Bradford in 1924. The carriages had end
vestibules and medial gangways, like dining cars; further, the brake thirds
at the ends had not only the standard form of Midland clerestory roof,
used on all Derby main-line stock up to 1917, but oil-gas lamps in the
lower decks on each side. It was a clear case of make-do-and-mend, with
either old bodies or at any rate old components. Nobody at the time
publicly remarked any anachronism. The "new" train was proudly posed
for official photograph, with one of the first of the post-grouping Midland
compound engines at its head.

But the open saloon carriage with end entrance, used for so long in some
other European countries such as Sweden, came to stay for certain inter-
city traffic, and was built in large quantity for long-distance excursion
trains. Each section at that time had two windows, a fixed light and a
drop-light with a strap, thus perpetuating what had been Midland
"dining carriage" practice over many years previously. The seating was
remarkably comfortable, comparable with German second-class carriages
which then were about the best of their kind in Europe, and far in advance
of anybody else's third-class stock, allowing that term to embrace North
American "day coaches". After that solitary lapse with the Bradford
brake-thirds, all new passenger coaches had electric lighting.

All the same, there was no particular hurry over converting existing
stock from gaslighting until after a horrible accident in Charfield on the
old Midland–West of England main line, between Gloucester and Bristol,
early in the morning of October 13, 1928. The westbound mail and
passenger train from the Midlands, running through signals, struck the
engine of a shunting Great Western goods train under a brick road bridge
and further fouled an LMS goods passing through on the other road.
The Mail was a typical old Midland gaslit train which jammed up into a

great mass of wreckage under the bridge and between its own engine, which turned over, and the still upright Great Western one. Fire broke out at once, and burned for many hours. At least seventeen persons were killed, but identification was in many cases quite impossible: a mass grave had to receive the human debris when it had been more or less sorted out from the mass of scorched frames and axles, as at Abergele on the London & North Western, sixty years before.

The thing was too bad for much academic discussion, but thereafter one noticed the incidence of electric lighting on many vehicles which certainly had not been built with it, even old-stagers on Highland locals to Keith and the Kyle of Lochalsh. The conversion was never quite completed. By 1939, only the Southern Railway, in Great Britain, could claim that all its passenger coaches had electric lighting and that there was no gas whatever in vehicles publicly used. For this one must partly blame the Midland. Its fatal attachment to oil gas had luridly paid-off several times before, in carriages having all-wooden bodies.

In 1925 the company had placed massive orders with carriage builders about the country for all-steel passenger coaches. Steel under-frames were old, and there were many carriages with steel-panelled skins mounted on wooden pillars, rails and carlines. These at last were the real thing, yet extraordinarily light compared with the frigate-like steel Pullmans and other cars in the United States. To begin with, 235 third-class carriages, including thirty-five brake-thirds, were ordered from Birmingham Railway Carriage and Wagon, Cammell Laird, Leeds Forge, and Metropolitan Carriage, Wagon and Finance. These handsome vehicles began to go into service during the spring of 1926. At an inaugural luncheon in Birmingham, W. L. Hichens, Chairman of Cammell Laird, who was also a director of the LMS, regretted the absence of the latter's chairman, Sir Guy Granet, and remarked that the latter had always advocated steel coaches. Nobody queried this interesting statement, but some may have thought privately of their peculiar absence from the late Midland Railway, and recalled a certain proneness on the part of that company to burn night Scotch expresses to ashes somewhere or other on the bleak Pennines. It was not the time for sick jokes, however; everybody was very glad to see the LMS offering these handsome steel carriages to the *Publick*.

A standard third-class of this series was 57ft long by 9ft wide: there was no inclination to copy the more nearly American dimensions of the Great Western company's largest stock. Nine-foot bogies were used at 40ft 6in centres. As for internal features, the lavatories had hot and cold water service (though in summer time only the cold taps did what their labels proclaimed). Seats were two-by-two in facing sections, each side of the gangway, and the tops of these sections, with their headrests, were recessed from the gangway to allow more space for the elbows of passengers moving up and down the train. Seating capacity was for fifty-six passengers in an ordinary third-class and for forty in a brake-third, and the tare ranged, according to type, from 29 to 31 tons. The gangway connections were an old-fashioned feature; they were of the ordinary narrow bellows sort, used in conjunction with screw couplings; Mr. Reid was clearly in no mind to ape others with buckeyes and Pullman vestibules. The general aspect of the carriages was extremely "Midland", and though the moulded wooden outsides were gone, the lining-out followed the old pattern, as if the mouldings were still there. This traditional decoration persisted for a long time on British trains, though the Great Western dropped it a few years later.

In 1928 came the long-promised, long-deferred advent of the third-class sleeping carriage, and in this case there was clearly some agreement between the British main-line companies, for all except the Southern, which scarcely needed sleeping cars, produced the British version of the *couchette* simultaneously, in the autumn of that year. It was not thought that the passengers would expect bedclothes beyond pillow and rug. By the standards of the time, at seven-and-sixpence a night (or five shillings on internal English services) they had good value for their money, with four berths to each compartment and Marshall's Vi-spring mattresses, an early and very comfortable variety of the cellular-spring sort. The upper berths were made to fold down from the partitions and to receive mattresses which had formed the upper seat cushions by day, a very much more comfortable arrangement than that of hinging up the cushioned seat-backs, as in some foreign countries. Windows were in coach-style threes, though there were no side doors except those serving narrow vestibules between the sleeping compartments and the lavatories, which were paired on each side of the end gangways. Side corridors were used, though some of us not-in-the-know had speculated on the probability of the Pullman sleeper making a British come-back, especially in view of LMS favour for the middle-gangway coach. There was no absolute segregation of the sexes, but it was generally understood that couple be paired with couple, or that parent-and-child parties were to be similarly assorted. Clearly Mr. Reid and his staff had no idea of people bringing supplementary bedding with them and putting themselves to bed in the usual way. But so they did! After all, there was safety in couples. One recalls, all the same, a curious journey to Perth in 1934, when, owing to a booking-clerical slip, a married couple was put in with two maiden ladies, one of whom was much amused. The other was not.

First-class sleeping cars continued for some time to follow the London & North Western model, long standardised for West Coast Joint stock, and a very good sleeper at that. Single-berth compartments were usual, but with connecting doors which could be unlocked as desired.

Some composite sleepers were improvised from that old London & North Western sort which devoted half the body to first-class sleeper arrangements and the other to third-class ordinary. In these, the original two-and-a-half "thirds" were turned into two four-berth sleepers with longitudinal bunks. They were to be found on the London–Preston run and also between Glasgow and Inverness, but they were very inferior, in the third-class, to the genuine article. In 1930, however, when Ernest Lemon was in command at Derby, some twelve-wheel composite sleeping cars were built, each having six first-class and sixteen third-class berths. They were 68ft long by 9ft wide. As it has been stated and published that the upper third-class berths were formed out of the seat backs, it had better be denied here. They opened down from the bulkheads, as usual, with access from a combined carriage table and step-ladder. One could be very comfortable in them so long as one maintained the camping-out spirit, was untroubled by other people's snores, sick children overhead, or other men's wives who uncorseted themselves in bed with extraordinary contortions. Passengers were generally well behaved. One had no re-collections of that abominable character, sometimes liable to haunt the day coaches of night Scotch or Irish expresses, the travelling drunk. This last, be it added, was more to be seen on the regular trains than on the old 26/6d. excursions between London and Glasgow, which may surprise some who never knew such trains. The staff used to lock the bellows doors once the diner was detached at Crewe, in the case of the London–Inverness and Aberdeen trains, and right at the beginning with later ones, which suffered most. That at least ensured that the official sleepers slept.

During 1930, new side corridor coaches, with end vestibules only and a single long window to each compartment, Central-European fashion, appeared on the best expresses, including the "Royal Scot". In these initial specimens, balanced, frameless droplights were provided, with louvre ventilators above. The lavatories set a new, and very high standard, much appreciated in a feature of the railway carriage about which people had long complained. In the past, a few had been good, many indifferent, and some truly awful. At the same time, there appeared what might be called a sort of *prestige-carriage*, a first-class *lounge car* (horrible title!) with enormously long, brown leather arm-chairs of that hideous sort which, in all domestic history, only the late 1920s could produce. They took up most of the space down the middle of the carriage unless they were turned strictly fore-and-aft, in which case they mixed up people's extended feet. Only a man over 6ft 8in could be really comfortable in one. Still, they served that fraudulent old meretrix, Auntie Fashion, and were much admired and proudly offered. These were not, of course, real club carriages, which had long been used by the richer business men travelling daily to and from northern cities, particularly Manchester.

For ordinary passenger services, standard carriages, although of the traditional British compartment type with side doors and no corridors, were rather good. There was the old English puritan ideal about them, so that one had to go snooping up and down the train to find out, in advance, where the lavatory might be, but they were comfortable to ride in, and by 1930, they had got far as the local trains between Perth and Blair Atholl, whereon previously one had been able to study at first hand the railway coaching history of half a century. Perhaps it was already too late. For by then, even Blair Atholl had got a bus. Over twenty-five years later, however, they were still there. Main-line trains on the Highland line, even as late as 1930, were of most picturesque variety owing to the enforced influx of corridor coaches in the middle 1920s. One recalls dining cars, both North Western and Midland, of the old and famous Vintage '93.

One cannot record much novelty about freight rolling stock. In the 1920s British wagons were generally about as antiquated as ordinary French coaches at the same time, which is saying something. Some four-bogie trolleys for carrying electrical transformers and comparable heavy pieces of power and works equipment, built in 1930, tared 31½ tons and were rated to carry 60 ton loads, though their capacity was somewhat higher. Under such a load, the maximum weight per axle was 11·44 tons. Main bolster centres were 40ft apart, the diamond frame bogies were of 5ft 6in wheelbase, the carrying girder was 2ft 4½in deep in the middle and the overall length was 62ft 6in. In their design, Ernest Lemon was in collaboration with the manufacturers of the transformer units which they were intended to carry. At that time there was a great increase in the country's industrial electrification; we were going on what was already called the Grid, and vehicles such as these were in demand, as the new, big power stations went up here and there about the land. British railways, however, apart from the Southern under Sir Herbert Walker, funked major electrification schemes on account of their high capital cost, though pressure from Big Business, with the welfare of oil and motor companies in mind, was as yet fairly weak. For better or worse, the steam locomotive had yet a long way to go, and as a lover of that most noble of engines, your present author cannot altogether regret that. Besides, when the London & North Western lines were at last electrified, on credit, in the 1960s, the result was a better one than might have been achieved thirty years before with 1,500 volt dc, though it came too late to stop much of the Oil Revolution which probably will lead to the ultimate undoing of Western Civilisation.

Of Sir Henry Fowler, as a Chief Mechanical Engineer serving the largest railway company in the world, working one of the most concentrated of the world's railway systems – even allowing for those far-flung lines in remote Scotland and that rather unremunerative investment in northern Ulster – one may write in a facile way, calling him an overgrown Boy Scout (as Winston Churchill once called Rudolf Hess) and a great many other things. Certainly he had a good Scout's ability to be a remarkable all-rounder, acquiring badges for doing with efficiency all sorts of very different duties. Whether he were a man of much imagination is a question less easy to answer favourably. He was, as we have noticed, a very great organiser, but great organisers are about as often men of imagination as imaginative men are great organisers, which is singularly seldom. The combination produced a genius; men like Caesar, or Napoleon, for of such stuff have been made the few really great military emperors.

Fowler's energy abounded. When that somewhat formidable Technical Editor the late Charles S. Lake visited him, Fowler immediately took his guest inside a firebox where the two of them tapped all the staybolts and made chalk rings round every one which made an unpromising sound when hammered. Of an LMS locomotive submitted as an example of repair methods, Fowler made the withering remark that it "was not a Derby product at all". For he was a Derby men, as clannish as ever the Midland made such, whatever might have been his previous history on the Lancashire & Yorkshire, and that explained a great deal of the LMS company's locomotive policy during those critical 1920s. It is doubtful whether a commander from another place – Crewe, Horwich or St. Rollox – would have shown much less bias. Locomotive chiefs were like that. They had their old loyalties like many other sorts of men, and such loyalties were bound to meet with disapproval from other quarters in an amalgamated undertaking like this one. Was it through the wisdom of Josiah Stamp that the later CME, who during the 1930s really made LMS locomotive practice and organisation into something whole, was chosen from the foreign ranks of the Great Western? For only thus could old loyalties be sublimated and old jealousies put down.

Fowler's influence on LMS locomotive practice cannot be decried as wholly bad. Though the only really original locomotive designs were cooked-up outside, as in the Royal Scot class and the Beyer-Garratt goods engines; though too many of the others were built new to obsolete or obsolescent designs; at least there was produced an economy through standardisation which the scores of types contributed by four major constituents[1] and several other smaller main-line railways could not possibly furnish. For that we must give Sir Henry Fowler his due, and we should also remember his enterprise in trying the Schmidt high-pressure boiler, unfortunate though the result should be. In retrospect, he would seem to have been a brave man who put that boiler on any locomotive!

[1] The London & North Western and the Lancashire & Yorkshire are here taken as two constituents, although, as noted, these had amalgamated just before formation of the LMS.

TABLE 1

London Midland & Scottish Passenger and Mixed Traffic Locomotives, 1923-1930

	Chief Mechanical Engineer	Year	Type	Cylinders (inches)	Coupled wheels ft in	Heating surface in sq ft				Grate area (sq ft)	Pressure lb/sq ft)	Engine weight in W.O. (tons)
						Tubes and flues	Firebox	Total Evaporative	Superheater			
1.	G. Hughes	1923	4-6-0	16 ×26 (4)	6 3	1,511	175	1,686	552	27	180	79.05
2.	Sir H. Fowler	1924	4-4-0	19¾(1)×26 21¾(2)	6 9	1,169	147.25	1,316.25	290.75	28.4	200	61.7
3.	G. Hughes	1924	4-6-4T	16½×26 (4)	6 3	1,817	180	1,997	430	29.6	180	99.85
4.	R. H. White-legg	1923	4-4-0	14×24 (2) 14×26 (2)	6 9½	1,443.4	148	1,591.4	211	27.6	180	61.35
5.	Sir H. Fowler vice G. Hughes	1926	2-6-0	21×26	5 3	1,361	160	1,521	307	27.5	180	66
6.	Sir H. Fowler	1927	4-6-0	18×26 (3)	6 9	1,892	189	2,081	445	31.2	250	84.9
7.	Sir H. Fowler	1930	4-6-0	18×26 (3)	6 9	1,550	183	1,733	365	30	200	89

NOTES: 2; Later compounds were built with 19in and 21in cylinder diameters; first 40 as shown. 4; *Lord Glenarthur*, a solitary. 6; Royal Scot class. 7; Patriot class ("Baby Scots").

TENDERS

George Hughes' tender on the 4-6-0 engines: 3,000 gall, 6 tons coal, weight in working order 40 tons. Sir Henry Fowler's tender: 3,500 gall, 5¾ tons coal, weight in working order 42 tons 14 cwt. Whitelegg's tender weighed 37·25 tons in working order.

TABLE 2

London Midland & Scottish Goods Locomotives, 1923-1930

Designer	Year	Type	Cylinders (in)	Coupled wheels ft in	Heating surface in sq ft				Grate area (sq ft)	Pressure (lb/sq ft)	Engine weight in W.O. (tons)
					Tubes and flues	Firebox	Total Evaporative	Superheater			
1. H. P. M. Beames	1923	0-8-4T	20½×24	4 5			1,687.4	358.6	23.6	185	88
2. (Beyer, Peacock & Co.)	1930	{2-6-0 + 2-6-4}	18×26 (4)	5 3	1,854	183	2,037	500	44.5	190	152.5
3. Sir H. Fowler	1929	0-8-0	19×26	4 8½	1,434	149.875	1,583.875	352.5	23.6	200	60.78

NOTES: 1; Beames heavy tank engines had 2,030 gall tanks capacity. 3; The 0-8-0 goods had the standard Fowler 3,500 gall tender.

CHAPTER FOUR

The Viziership of Ernest Lemon

IT IS EASY for one who loves steam to have a mechanical engineering bias in assessing the renaissance of a railway company, and there is indeed some justification in identifying that of the London Midland and Scottish company with the locomotive improvements carried out while William Stanier was in command. While Sir Henry Fowler had produced – one cannot use the word *designed* in its fullest personal sense – a really good modern express locomotive in the Royal Scot class, and had built hundreds of traditional types in which the old Midland small-engine policy was faithfully perpetuated, the system was still full of engaging old veterans representing scores of different classes and in many cases dating back to the days of Queen Victoria. The same could be said for the carriage and wagon stock, though Ernest Lemon had been most praiseworthy in extending the practice of mass-production.

In his brief office as Chief Mechanical Engineer, January to November 1931, Lemon had left no visible marks of impact on the Department which Fowler had vacated: people scarcely expected him to have done so. Rather to people's surprise, it was in operation, not traction, that this man was to do work of great and lasting value. His career up to this point deserves a brief *resumé*.

Ernest J. H. Lemon was Cornish by blood, Dorset-born, and Scots by adoption and training: a promising mixture of Celt and Saxon. He certainly looked like a Scotsman, narrow-headed with a straight mouth and prominent dark eyebrows. He served his time in Glasgow at the old Neilson Reid, Hyde Park, Works, and had his academic training at Heriot Watt in Edinburgh. Later he served with Brown Brothers, the hydraulic engineers, in Edinburgh; then under Peter Drummond on the Highland Railway at Inverness, from which he went to Hurst Nelson and Company, the famous carriage and wagon builders in Motherwell. To the railway service he returned in 1911, with the Midland at Derby, he being then twenty-seven. He rose rapidly with the Midland and with the LMS – a first-rate carriage man who believed in exacting standards – and when his Chief, R. W. Reid, became Vice-President for Works and Ancillary Undertakings in 1927, under the new Stamp dispensation, Lemon was promoted Carriage and Wagon Superintendent of the company before he stepped into the chair which had been occupied by Hughes and Fowler, in command of all mechanical engineering on the LMS.

At this time the Vice-Presidents of the Executive, under Stamp, consisted of S. H. Hunt, J. H. Follows (both for the Railway Traffic Operating and Commercial Sections), R. W. Reid, as stated, and J. Quirey for the Accounting and Service Departments. Late in 1931, on Follows' retirement, Lemon succeeded him. Now the latter's mechanical training began, in conjunction with his organising ability, to set the undertaking on its legs as a machine for transport, whereas previously it had been simply a company owning machines for transport, which was not quite the same thing.

The Railway Rose which had budded was now full blown. No longer could it blossom untroubled in the vase of local monopoly, big as were both the rose and the vase. The motor had broken that monopoly already, and a railway company could scarcely expect increased revenue simply through a constant growth of traffic, as such had done in the Victorian Era. Indeed, even had the railway monopoly persisted, this was a time of world-wide trade depression. America was floundering in that slump from which F. D. Roosevelt was to save it by methods which conservative American opinion regarded, in the words of some commentator or other, as *un-American, unethical, anarchistic and lousy.* And world economics, for better or worse, were coupled to that huge American locomotive which had suddenly collapsed its firebox. British unemployment ran into millions. Many of us remember those glum-faced Welshmen who slow-marched along the London gutters, singing Methodist hymns until their once grand voices grew broken in the fog. The Germans, perhaps the hardest workers in Europe but dominated by a Big Business that was frightened out of its wits, believed they faced a choice between Marxist Communism and what was speciously called National Socialism. They made their unholy selection soon after, with the consequences we know.

Under such circumstances, a great railway company could keep itself going only by some continual and radical sort of retrenchment, and outwardly that showed itself in the peculiar and increasing shabbiness of the LMS during those early thirties. Within its territory it had some of the most depressed areas in the realm: Clydeside, Merseyside and the Scottish and South Welsh coalfields, which it shared to some extent with the London & North Eastern and the Great Western. (The Southern Railway was least vulnerable, with no great industrial interests apart from docks and a predominantly aristocratic, agricultural and bourgeois user.)

If more traffic could not be expected – and there were few signs that it was to be expected for a very long time – there must be improved methods in handling what traffic there was in order to save expense. Overheads must come down somehow, and any attempt at reform would be up against tradition, against the case-hardened convictions of veteran railwaymen and their sons that there was only one way of running a

D

railway, and that this had been invented in Queen Victoria's Golden Days.

From his succession at the end of 1931, to 1938, Ernest Lemon held steadfastly to the preparation and implementations of schemes to improve both operating and commercial procedure. To have induced the ascetic puritan J. H. Follows (an admittedly admirable man of his type and time) to change anything much would have taken some doing. But Follows had retired, as we know. Sir Josiah Stamp was likewise a puritan, and one with a Civil Service training at that, but he was a man of fresh ideas and very formidable intellect. He could be convinced where a traditionalist was not always to be persuaded. If Lemon drank whisky while Stamp's most abandoned tipple was fizzy water, let Lemon have his way if that kept him supercharged as he needed to be.[1]

Improvement of freight handling was a priority. In March 1933, with the President's approval, Lemon engaged an outside observer, Lewis C. Ord, a man with great experience in works reorganisation and industrial investigations, to carry out such a private inquiry into goods handling at stations, which involved the company in an annual wages bill of about one-and-a-half-million pounds. (Mr. Ord, by the way, was engaged on a £500 monthly contract.) Crewe Tranship Shed was the first object of investigation. Lemon described it as "one of the largest and most difficult cases of its kind".

Mechanisation, Lemon thought, was the master-key to the problem. He aimed as far as possible at the entire elimination of trucking, quicker clearing of traffic, speeding-up and more cheaply handling container traffic and extensions of the use of containers, reductions in the use of shunting locomotives by the use of cheaper mechanical means, to keep in mind that reductions in shed handling costs were not to be lost by increased cartage costs, to get quicker release of wagons under load, to concentrate work as much as possible to reduce walking time and aid supervision, and "to bring the work to the men in every case that was possible, and not having the men moving all over the place to their work".

Lemon emphasised that he wished for no criticism of past results so long as each man did all that was possible henceforward, and that there should be no attempt to split economies due to physical change or mechanisation from those which might have been made without these.

There was as always, but particularly in those lean early thirties, a fear of redundancy among the men. They had come to fear the dole-queue[2] as their grandparents had feared the workhouse. It seemed a hopeless point of no return.

[1] One is reminded of President Lincoln during the American Civil War, sending to know what brand it was that General Grant habitually consumed, and requiring that a case be sent to each of the other generals, though one cannot quite imagine Stamp doing such a thing.

[2] One has good reason to recall that for a young married man who had lost his job, the weekly amount was £1.3.3.

Reporting the following March, Lewis Ord believed that all Lemon's points could be met except that he was doubtful about speeding morning deliveries. His report was lengthy, and must have summary. He suggested the remodelling of five stations: Lancaster, Chesterfield, Kettering, Preston (Butler Street) and Blackburn, with similar facilities. To cut handling costs, road vehicles should go to the railway wagons without the use of conveyors, and the remodelling of the last three goods stations mentioned, approved by the Board, incorporated this arrangement.

Many stations were not being efficiently worked. It had been suggested that economies shown by analysis to be possible should be made before mechanisation, that to be carried out subsequently if shown to be worth while. At Blackburn, mechanisation of forwarded traffic resulted in a drop from about two hours per ton to just over one hour, and it was hoped to bring it down to ·85 hr Ord believed in, and described as "a reasonable figure", a rate of about ·65 hr per ton on forwarded traffic. On the basis of experience at Blackburn, he recommended further experiment with the mechanisation of Forwarded Goods handling, and that as this would involve removal of shed decks and some alteration to the Received shed decks, where traffic was being worked at a high figure, consideration should be given to the mechanisation of the Received traffic also. He was much in favour of removable tops for lorries and drays,[1] and the use of tractor-trailer motor units. From this last dates the beginning of the railway's widespread subsequent use of the "Scammell Mechanical Horse", a three-wheel motor tractor with a dray articulated to it. (Scammells were naturally ready to do business even with a railway company, though there was a scandal when this firm circularised advertisers in *Modern Transport*, suggesting that the paper had a railway bias, and that formidable Editor, F. C. Coleman, got hold of the correspondence and published it, with the righteously-wroth observation that his paper was not to be coerced.) How salutary! How holy! Some of us who had nothing to do with any of the parties fairly hugged ourselves!

To return from the occasional jollities of journalism to hard company history: Lewis Ord reported at this stage that investigation into mechanisation was not yet complete and added rather pungently: "If accurate analysis of a proper sort had been possible in the Department, layouts such as Ancoats and Heysham and the complete Huddersfield layout would never have been attempted. It would have been apparent even on paper that they could not succeed." There had been a sheeplike following of Victorian leaders, as in so many other places. But there was also the question of human, as well as of commercial and technical antiquity. The men engaged were much older than the average on such work. Their

[1] A pioneer was the London & South Western Railway with its "demountable flats" about 1920.

physique was correspondingly inferior, "and they and their foremen are set in their ways and it will be a very difficult thing indeed to speed them up, in a class of work with conditions and methods under which they have been working for the past thirty years, to a figure representing nearly double the pace at which they have worked in the past.".

This was a consideration as old as the Cuillin Hills, and one which ever recurs in a deeply established industry. That average age was bound to increase in the next few years. Lemon's suggestion on the reduction of physical effort and walking became an important one to what later was known as *work study*. At the same time, with the increasing habit of the motor, the very act of walking, to any extent, was destined to be regarded by many as a hardship.[1] Lewis Ord's report concluded with the words: "In training all concerned to the new methods and new points of view which are necessary if the best possible results are to be obtained for the company, with or without mechanisation, no more useful suggestion has been put forward than Mr. Lemon has made – the use of the movie camera – both to analyse the work in more detail and to enable the very great amount of instructional work to be carried out cheaply, quickly and effectively."

To put over a system of work-study at this stage in social and industrial history must have needed some nerve. It was liable to be resented, and feared, as a means for finding out how one man could be made to do the work two had previously done, with a view to making one of them redundant and tossing him on to the nearest labour exchange counter. The time was 1934, and things were not as bad as they had been, but Unemployment was still the Ogre, the Giant Despair from whose dungeons escape was so difficult. The idea that work-study could lead, by greater efficiency, to increased prosperity, and therefore to more and not less employment, was not easy to absorb. The Luddite mentality was still with us after more than a century, and will doubtless remain for as long as there is any threat of unemployment.

Much pioneering work had been done on work-study in France. During the inter-war period, Raoul Dautry's memorable reorganisation of the once nearly-moribund French State Railways was much in the mind of railway officers and commentators elsewhere, but with the greatest respect for that memorable Frenchman, one would record a forerunner, who was Carlo Crova in Italy, the man who made Italian trains run to time like German ones;[2] (among non-Italian people, the credit was larded on

[1] In Steinbeck's novel *The Grapes of Wrath*, those *Deputies* whose job was to hound transients in the United States during the depression-migrations, were supposed to be identifiable by their posterior development through spending more time at the wheel of a motor car than on their feet. A similar remark was later to be made by some soldiers about their latest allies.

[2] To be quite fair, German trains at that time were distinctly sluggish. There was not much to choose between a *Schnellzug* (express) and an *Eilzug* (fast train without supplement) except in the quality of the rolling-stock. Both were slow.

B. Mussolini, who happened to pull-off his *coup-d'etat* at the same time.) It must be remarked that for all the efforts of Stamp, Lemon and others, London Midland & Scottish punctuality in running was seldom very admirable when it came to express trains over longer distances. Ere this, the London & North Western had publicly boasted about such a virtue which one remembers as being very partial. In pre-grouping days, late arrivals at Euston were always blamed on the Caledonian and the Highland. In the North – the real North – working over long stretches of single line could be made chaotic by any serious delays south of Perth, and recriminations often were made with more justification. The Midland Railway – once a byword for unpunctuality – deserves the highest credit for its universal adoption of Control long before the amalgamation, and wisdom of those who had been its officers was to make great improvement in LMS services – in time!

A senior officers' tour was made late in 1934, and criticism was made of parcels' office arrangements at stations, describing these as not having kept pace with the development of traffic, and being "seriously inadequate" at some places. The Chief Commercial Manager was requested to make a system-wide review of the position and to prepare a priority list. Some small schemes were authorised, but in April 1937, Lemon arranged for the setting up of a special section in the Chief Operating Manager's Department to carry out time-and-motion studies on handling of parcels traffic. This, the Parcels Development Section, reported in November 1937, on its studies at Northampton, Holyhead, Leeds, Sheffield, Liverpool, Birmingham and Hanley, as well as at some smaller centres. Euston also entered the picture, and whatever its architectural merits it was a fearsome old station from the operating point of view. A section of conveyor was installed with success on No. 1 Platform, and was not only useful in itself, but furnished data for the ultimate solution of parcels problems at other places.

Old Euston's days, even then, were numbered, though owing to the intervention of war that particular sentence never was carried out. It was the LMS that was going to demolish Euston and build a new terminus. There was even a more or less ceremonial firing of charges at Caldon Low, which were to bring down the rock, out of which would be hewn the foundation stone of the new station. One seems to remember also that there was much less rumpus about the destruction of architectural treasures than there was to be when the thing was ultimately done under the auspices of a State railway undertaking. True, the Georgian Group was anxious. The Victorian Society was not yet in existence. However, the LMS failed to demolish Euston, as things turned out, and so did the German Air Force, though the latter made an awful mess of its neighbour termini a few years later.

Keeping to those dicey 1930s: LMS *Memoranda* of this time contains this item: "In connection with the proposed rebuilding of Euston, a comprehensive scheme was prepared for handling parcels traffic with an entirely new and modernised layout and the data assembled for this is available for adoption, with any necessary post-war revision, when it is possible to proceed with the new station scheme.[1] In April 1938, an outlay of £3,756 was involved in the provision of conveyor equipment at Holyhead, for the transfer of mails and other material between trains and ships. Staff economy had been estimated at £829, and subsequently it was noted that this had been "more than realised". Once the war had started, redundancy no longer mattered. Like possibilities of defeat (as noted years before by Queen Victoria) *it did not exist*. At intervals, Lemon met this Development Committee for progress reports. He being a mechanical engineer, machinery of one sort or another frequently provided a solution to some problem, though being a wise engineer, unlike some who had gone before, he did not regard it as the invariable panacea. But some of his best suggestions took the form of parcels vehicles with moving floors, barrows with roller conveyors, wheeled containers, and many other appliances of these sorts. These things were to prove themselves inestimably valuable when war came and business had to be conducted under adverse conditions of which the blackout against hostile aircraft was one of the most severe. One, of the abstract as opposed to the mechanical sort, was the schedule of alternative accommodation for use in the event of normal facilities being put out of action.

Mechanisation of marshalling yards was a thing which attracted overdue attention on British railways about this time. Much had been done abroad, most notably at Hamm on the German State Railway and at Markham on the Illinois Central. Then the London & North Eastern equipped its down marshalling yards at March with Frohlich "eddy-current" rail brakes below the hump, and a good deal was made of it in the technical papers. Humping, in its simplest form, was already a well-established practice in Great Britain; pioneers had been the London & North Western at Edge Hill (on a small scale) and the Great Central at Wath-upon-Dearne; somewhat later the London & South Western had laid out its great yards on the western side of London at Feltham, and the North British did the same sort of thing at Cadder, but as yet it could be scarcely described as mechanised marshalling; it was simply a way of making one big tank engine – and gravity – do the work of several smaller locomotives batting wagons about on the flat. To the LNER be conceded credit for the first mechanised marshalling yard in Great Britain.

[1] The author can put a date to this *Memorandum*; it was in 1941. But he would emphasise that it was not obtained from Minutes in official keeping, in respect of which he punctiliously observes the fifty-years ban. The same applies to later passages.

On the LMS, Ernest Lemon officially brought the notice of the Chief Operating Manager to what was going on at March. Clearly the London & North Eastern was impressed with what it was achieving, on German and American lines, under the influence of Colonel H. H. Mauldin.[1] Lemon suggested that the LMS "might come round to the view of there being something worth while in the arrangement for LMS purposes".

So the LMS, in the persons of its COM and his assistants, became guests of the London & North Eastern out in the Fens at March, and reported. Lemon then went to Toton, and examined its possibilities on the lines of the Whitemoor installation at March, in collaboration with the General Railway Signal Company. The latter in turn reported and made proposals to the LMS which drew up a scheme embracing the provision of centrally controlled rail-brakes and points, which would save brakemen and pointsmen respectively, raising the height of the hump, adjusting the layout at the hump and the entrance to the sorting sidings, and the provision of necessary track circuits, signalling of a suitably advanced standard, lighting, communications and buildings. A report was made and submitted to the Executive.

Outlay for the proposal was estimated at £59,587, and while this estimate carried a rider showing an annual increased cost of £725, it made no mention of the value of locomotive economies, which could not be reliably assessed in terms of money. Annually increased cost, it was however reckoned, would be fully covered by these, by reduced damage to wagons, and in ways less easily specified. Further, mechanisation at Toton would have what might been termed guinea-pig value. Lemon's conclusive Memorandum contained the following passage:

"Whilst the Toton scheme will not produce additional net revenue, the time has arrived when we are justified in adopting such a scheme from the point of view of bringing our equipment up to date. Ever since railways were constructed, shunting has been carried out on the present lines, and no-one shall say that this is the last word. Other railways, both at home and abroad, have adopted other mechanised arrangements, and I consider that in the case of Toton, which is our largest marshalling yard, and also the key yard in connection with the Midland Division coal traffic, the adoption of the scheme will provide *additional capacity* for future utilisation, seeing that the physical considerations restrict any extension or the provision of additional roads, and will also reduce manual labour on the part of the staff. It will be an experiment with permanent benefit

---

[1] A most able man of the Other Line, then its Eastern Section Superintendent, Southern Area; an old Great Eastern man, and understudy to the memorable and modest Fred V. Russell, GER Superintendent of Operation under Sir Henry Thornton. His military promotion had come with the ROD, he having enlisted as a sapper of the RE in 1915. Like all really good soldiers, he respected his enemies, who at that time, of course, included Dr. Fröhlich.

and it is also possible that the lessons we shall learn from it will be capable of adoption elsewhere."

In October 1937, the Board and the Traffic Committee gave their approval to the scheme. In all humility, a student of transport wonders why on earth it had not all been done earlier than this, and whether it would have been if the Lloyd Georgian dream of State railways had been realised. And yet – and yet – the principal German railways had long been in the hands of a company whose initial object had been the payment of German war reparations; in the USA, home of ruthless private enterprise, the only State railway was one in Alaska, which none in his sense would have backed with his savings with a view to getting a fat annual return. All the same, one can imagine the rows which would have torn the LMS – and other companies' – annual general meetings had there been any proposed expenditure on something alien and expensive in first cost, of which the stockholders had no previous knowledge. Somewhere behind it was the British distrust, and the American love, of anything new. Both are good things, and both bad things, according to circumstances.

That real steps were at last being taken towards the application of new techniques to an industry in more peril of becoming moribund than most of its older servants could imagine was surely due to the sagacity of Sir Josiah Stamp. Though no railwayman by training, he had the mind that could grasp quickly all the things that made a railway go. He had, as we have seen, the gift of choosing his deputies well for the tasks that were to be performed. As already noted, he had a great admiration for American methods, both in business organisation and in technical improvement. A mission was sent to the United States, under Lemon, to study these, with the floodlighting of marshalling and other yards particularly in view. A report made in November 1930, stated that while floodlighting had been adopted in new or re-arranged yards, the Committee could make no general recommendation. Each case should be dealt with on its merits. Substitution of floodlighting for ordinary installations could well be left to the discretion of the Chief General Superintendent, who at the end of 1935 reported on general lighting standards for marshalling yards and the provision of improved arrangements to enable work to be carried on in fog to a greater extent than formerly. Commenting on the Report, Lemon urged that the matter be pressed forward so that they could go to the Board with a general proposition on lighting improvements. "I think", he wrote, "the Research Department might be pressed more strongly to see what can be done to obtain some relief by using coloured lights or selenium cell rays".

At the Traffic Committee meeting in April 1963, approval was given to a scheme for the lighting of the down yard at Toton, and investigations were pressed forward on lighting conditions at other big yards. In July, further schemes were approved and at the time of the outbreak of war in 1939, 17 schemes had been sanctioned at a total outlay of £12,158. In the middle 1930s, total annual shunting costs had exceeded £5 million.

There had been some politely tart Memoranda, as in one on the analysis of shunting costs from Lemon to C. R. Byrom, dated February 19, 1935:–

"You have from time to time sent me particulars of the reviews which are being made of the cost of shunting, from which I gathered that it was really a continuous process. I notice from Minute 98 of your Conference of January 15 that in the statement no engines are shewn to have been saved by the Shunting Analysis Committee.

"Whilst appreciating what they have done in the past, I shall be pleased if you will send me some detail as to the Committee's activities, indicating what they accomplished during 1934, both from saving in wages and elimination of engines; who are on the Committee; whether it is a full-time job, and whether the employment of the Diesel shunting units is brought under notice when they are reviewing any particular depot."

As to these diesel shunters, apart from conversion of an old Midland steam locomotive, using again the original frames and coupled wheels, the Board had authorised in January 1933, the purchase of ten 150/200 hp diesel shunting locomotives so that a thorough investigation could be made in the utility of such engines of different capacity and with different forms of transmission, and to accelerate the production of the types found most efficient. These things belong more conventionally to mechanical history, but, with the diesel still emerging from infancy to puberty, are best considered in connection with operation at this stage.

In April 1934, arrangements were made for an English Electric 300 hp diesel-electric shunter to be tried over an extended time under conditions described as *severe*. The same was done when an Armstrong Whitworth 250 hp diesel-electric locomotive was put into service, and comparative tests were carried out at Beeston in June. Considering the replacement of steam tank engines, the more powerful diesel was found a more likely candidate. In July 1935, the Traffic Committee authorised the purchase outside of twenty 350 hp diesel shunting locomotives at a cost of £132,000. Economies by the use of diesels in shunting depended on availability, in which they were expected to score over steam. A diesel working only one daily turn was not expected to save more than £20 annually, and it was a dear thing to buy. Two turns should save £539 and three turns, £1,078 a year. Assuming an effective life of thirty years, there seemed to be "sufficient margin to cover the uncertain repair position but there did not seem to be justification for the introduction of diesels if only one turn per day is required". A recommendation by the Chief Operating Manager to purchase, as part of the 1940 locomotive renewal programme,

D*

twenty more diesel shunters was approved by the Board in June 1939.

War was imminent, and most people had realised that, since the Munich crisis of the previous year, following which the subsequent occupation and dismemberment of Czecho-Slovakia had put the seal on their belief. It is not surprising, therefore, that, in addition to the virtues of one-man operation, and of continuous availability on a week's shunting without need for runs to the locomotive depot for servicing, there was the point that "there is no firebox glow which makes the units ideal for shunting under blackout regulations". (Construction of 100 more 350 hp diesel shunters, at an estimated cost of £910,000, was to be authorised at the end of 1940.)

Going back from the motive power to the rest of marshalling yard operation, anyone who has watched humping under old conditions will never forget, firstly, its primitive nature and hazardous method, and secondly one's own admiration for those agile shunters who leaped on to moving wagons as they came down from the hump, riding on their own poles with dangling legs as they braked on the descent. American brakemen running on the ice-glazed catwalks of car roofs to screw down the old brake-wheels above, certainly had no more perilous occupation than those in the old British humping yards. Either occupation seemed to the observer to be a mixture of Disneyland and the early film exploits of that most gifted actor, Harold Lloyd; the former because it was so absurd, and the latter because one expected every moment to see the principal character meet with a frightful end.

Factors to be considered in the design and construction of future yards, and the modernisation of existing ones, were the choice of most suitable gradients; the speed of wagons on descent from the hump; the introduction of power-worked points from a central installation, whether rail-brakes were necessary or not; the curvature of lines for the most efficient movement; layouts and general design; the use of capstans, traversers or overhead cranes; conversion of flat yards to the principle of hump and gridiron; construction of an entirely new yard, of modern design in a particular area[1], and the closure of neighbouring obsolete yards, and the introduction of mechanical humps.

Proposals for new yards, and the remodelling of existing big yards, were ever dependent on the making out of a financial case for the heavy expenditure. Be it remembered that the London Midland & Scottish was an undertaking whose officers were answerable to proprietors, not a Public Service such as the Army and the Navy which had given up living by plunder and piracy in the seventeenth century, and, thanks to Mr.

---

[1] Recent examples of the 1960s, are those in the Sheffield and Carlisle areas.

Cromwell and Mr. Pepys, were financed under Government for the good of the community.[1]

As with marshalling yards, so with motive power on the running side; the British running shed, or steam shed as one remembers it in Scotland, might or might not be adequate for the storage under cover, and servicing, of locomotives. But either way, very little change had been made about it since Victorian years; indeed, it was incredibly old-fashioned; a stable for iron horses. Servicing, office accommodation and provision for the most basic comforts of the enginemen were alike and all-too-often primitive.

A special committee set up by the LMS organisation in 1931 laid special emphasis on the following possibilities in the mechanisation of running sheds: Mechanical coaling, and ash-lifting plants, and the mechanical removal of smokebox char; arrangements for washing-out boilers, the extended use of portable appliances and cranes; sand supply and drying facilities; improved layout for sheds and locomotive yards; improved facilities for running repairs, and improved steam-raising methods. It was felt that considerable economies could be made by mechanisation and by an overhaul of general arrangements.

To Stamp, Lemon reported on March 28, 1933, that; "The real problem to be attacked is not so much the saving in money by mechanisation schemes but the greater use which can be made of engines. We have, as you know, locomotive stock to the value of roughly £31,000,000 and as I was concerned to know what was really happening to engines at typical sheds on what might be called the 'motion study', I arranged for an analysis to be made of the actual operations over a period of 24 hours."

Examples of engine waste through standing time at three such running sheds tabulated as follows:

| | Time occupied cleaning fires, coalng, water and sand | | |
	Under present arrangements	Under proposed scheme	Number of engine booked turns
	HOURS	HOURS	
Aston	$1\frac{1}{2}$	$\frac{1}{2}$	43
Patricroft	3	$\frac{3}{4}$	53
Farnley	6	1	38

One of the things was that the sheds were very old. They had been designed for smaller engines, and the layouts provided were "not prepared for future developments in locomotive progress". It was indeed a case

[1] Irony lies in the fact that when the LMS and the others had indeed become such a State Public Service, British democracy inclined to the view that the old commercial standards still should be applied. There was much rumpus over a modernisation programme of the late 'fifties which was subsequently nibbled away like a pie amongst mice.

everywhere of new wine in old wineskins, and when, years later, other forms of traction came to displace steam all over the country, new depots altogether were needed.

In that same month, Byrom had reported, emphasising the advantages of quicker engine turn-round, which would mean fewer engines being required to deal with a specified mileage for all. There would be increased productive mileage per engine per day in steam. Shed costs would be lower from engine preparation and steam raising. He felt that to carry out a co-ordinated scheme of improvement, reflecting the benefits as a whole in connection with the more efficient diagramming of engines, consideration should be given to a certain number of sheds which were interrelated and where co-ordination of working was desirable. He gave a list of such sheds in the Western Division, the approximate cost of necessary expenditure, and the expected return of that expenditure, estimates given being at that stage approximate. The list follows:

Shed	Total cost	Total net savings	Percentage return on expenditure
	£	£	
Aston	8,770	566	7·5
Buxton	27,200	916	3·4
Bescot	12,900	95	0·7
Devons Road	8,000	1,198	15·1
Edge Hill	7,875	1,042	13·2
Farnley Jc.	17,770	2,260	12·7
Lancaster	2,024	930	45·9
Longsight	16,430	1,774	10·8
Monument Lane	16,870	463 *debit*	2·7 *debit*
Patricroft	30,230	2,093	6·9
Rugby	13,270	1,063	8·0
Springs Branch	15,430	2,019	13·0
Stoke	13,123	2,211	16·8
Walsall	11,196	108	0·9
	£201,088	£15,812	7·86 per cent

C. R. Byrom remarked that if his estimates were approved, mechanisation of most important Western Division running sheds would be accomplished. He recommended a block allocation for the realisation of this important allocation's instalment *without delay*. He added that his estimates at this stage were only approximate, ("but it is not anticipated that they are likely to be exceeded as in the absence of definite figures liberal allowances have been made"). Should the block allocation be agreed to, firm estimates and plans would be obtained; and each case submitted to, and authorised by, the Vice-President before being carried out and subsequently reported to the Committee.

The watering of locomotives was in many places poorly accomplished. Ernest Lemon, with his Highland Railway experience, knew something of this sort of inability.[1] Two schemes were approved in Traffic Committee late in 1937, and further schemes set in motion. Outlay on these at the end of April 1940, came to £14,602. Pressure at water column was a variable and often unsatisfactory matter.

Up to the early 'thirties, the London Midland & Scottish was describable as a railway running, in addition to its tremendous goods and mineral traffic, a very adequate service of fairly fast trains. Frequency was much higher than in such advanced foreign countries as France, the United States and Germany[2]. Speed, however, was lagging. British railways as a whole were behind Germany in the provision of cross-country through trains and coaches. Our "Sunny South" and similar services bypassing London were exceptions. One never heard of any real express between Oxford and Cambridge via Bletchley; it was unthinkable. In all fairness, one must remember that the British railway system as a whole was at once more metropolitan in conception and more radial in planning than that of Germany. Most of its provincial centres were still on direct lines from London. The negative aspect of inter-company competition was still only too evident. Such services as those between Tyneside and Merseyside owed their being to past alliance between the Lancashire & Yorkshire and the North Eastern, whose interests had not clashed.

On the main lines, however, there was obvious scope for acceleration of passenger trains, and certainly competition was the spur when it came to the Anglo-Scottish services. But side by side with this came the need for the greater utility of fewer locomotives, and the elimination of unproductive time of enginemen. As to the former, in July 1934, monthly meetings were arranged between representatives of the Headquarters and Divisional Chief Operating Managers, to consider "a further and sustained effort to achieve a more intensive and economical use of engines". Results for the period August 1934 to June 1935, reviewed in October of the latter year, showed that there had been a saving equivalent to 362 engines, and that 230 old ones had been withdrawn from service during that time. (One recalls that the knife moved most freely amongst the former stocks of the London & North Western and the Glasgow South Western; in

[1] One recalls a placard at Blair Atholl: NO WATER AT DALWHINNIE; and others like it. There were troughs on the Caledonian, and plenty south of the Border. Those at Garsdale on the Midland line sometimes bred pack-ice.

[2] In proportion to population, however, Sweden was pre-eminent.

the latter case towards the point of virtual annihilation.) The scheme was ruthlessly pursued. Total stock of locomotives, including those stored, declined as follows: Year 1933, 8,226; 1934, 8,004; 1935, 7,894; 1936, 7,691; 1937, 7,688; 1938, 7,644. Average miles run per locomotive per day increased from 106·77 in 1933 to 117·87 in 1938. As to the first two war years, at the end of 1939 there were 7,589 locomotives in service or stored, and 7,546 at the end of 1940. War brought an embarrassment. Old engines had to be borrowed, notably from the Southern Railway which had many made redundant by electrification, and, fortunately, had not broken them up.

In 1935, the neighbouring London & North Eastern Railway put on a very fast service – the "Silver Jubilee" – between London and the Tyneside, using streamlined steam locomotives, and the train achieved on a preliminary press run sustained speeds well over 100 mph, with a maximum of 113 mph. While Newcastle-upon-Tyne was outside LMS territory, it was clear that the same sort of thing would be done in a Scotch service from London before very long. In the Locomotive Department, as will be detailed later, William Stanier was doing things very different from those in the days of Sir Henry Fowler. Veteran engines were being rapidly retired; new and much more reliably puissant ones were being turned out on the same scale as Fowler's previous production of moribund-Midland pratice.

At a meeting of the LMS Executive Committee on November 2, 1936, the question of running certain long-distance passenger trains at very high speeds was discussed. Stanier and Lemon had clearly been in some sort of a huddle, and at the meeting, the latter advised that the company should run such a train. Line capacity had been studied, and a train could be scheduled to leave Euston at 4.0 pm and to arrive at Glasgow Central in 6½ hours or even six. Such a train ought to be streamlined; it would cause little interference with the evening fast freight services to the North. A Pacific locomotive of the Princess class should be used. The Executive agreed in principle. (Goodness knew what the London & North Eastern would be up to next!)

On the question of fast trains generally, the Vice-President said that while the company's aim was for a uniform speed-up of all on a scale consistent with passenger comfort, it was necessary to make one or two special high-speed trips "in order to judge what alterations and improvements to the stock could be made to give comfort at the speed reached".

On November 16 and 17, with engine No. 6201 *Princess Elizabeth*, the experimental runs were made from Euston to Glasgow Central and back, with about 200 tons behind the tender. Northbound, the 401½ miles were covered in 5hr 53min, making an average speed of 68·11 mph. On the return, the run was made in 5hr 44min; average speed 70 mph. Maximum speeds were expected on the levels in the Lancaster district. The highest figure was 95·75 mph on the northbound journey. This performance was used in preparing schedules for daily services between the two cities, and these were announced at the Annual General Meeting on February 27, 1937, with departure times at 1.30 pm in both directions, and a journey time of 6½ hours, making an average speed of 61·8 mph. The new service, as is well known, was inaugurated with the Coronation Scot train on July 5, 1937. With its special locomotives and rolling stock, it will be more fully described in a later chapter.

At the same time one may mention here an interesting consequence of the company's high-speed policy, which came soon after, with the war. Government caution resulted in the maximum speed of all passenger trains being reduced to 45 mph (a limit which, one remembers, was rarely observed). About October 1939, it was increased to 60 mph. When the real air attacks came, even this resulted in very severe congestion. From February 11, 1941, the limit was placed at 75 mph which was reasonable enough, even under normal conditions, for ordinary passenger traffic of the period.

With the West Coast main line thus stealing much thunder, in much the same way as it was to do with 25 kV electric traction some thirty years later, something had to be done about the Midland. Indeed, in 1936 the Chief Operating and Chief Commercial Managers, *pressed* by the Executive (Lemon's term) arranged for a joint investigation into the problem of remodelling the services of the Midland Division. Dynamometer car tests were conducted in April of the following year to decide the maximum permissible speeds at various points and over various sections of the Midland Division. The company had a good dynamometer car of Hughes design, yet destined for use on such tests over many more years. The Engineering and Operating Departments set about working out revised train schedules from the results of these. (Presumably the Locomotive Department, then well under Stanier's sway, felt quite competent to execute whatever performance these nabobries might require.)

Proposed accelerations were given effect in the winter timetable of 1937–38, and as a result of speeding up, there were on the Midland Division 34 daily start-to-stop runs at speeds of 60 mph or over, covering a total of 2,663 miles.

One factor had been what in former days the London & North Western would have claimed as a crushing victory over its old enemy, the Midland. Lemon, as an old Midland man, was to be forgiven for writing to Byrom that it was a *lamentable* feature of the Western Division acceleration that the faster trains had become so popular that they were pulling-in user which would be more conveniently accommodated by the Midland trains. A. E. Towle, Controller of Hotels, Refreshment Rooms and Restaurant

Car Services since January 1, 1923, and before that on the Midland since 1919, told Lemon about this time that his staff could not manage to serve sufficient dinners on the 6.0 pm from Euston to Manchester, and on the corresponding 5.45 pm up from London Road, while the lack of custom on the Midland route between the cities was demoralising his staff there. He, Towle, also wanted more business on the Midland–Scottish services, but they could not compare in journey time with those of the West Coast Route. In *The Times* of November 19, 1936, reference had been made to the 9.40 am Midland train from Bradford to London making up fifteen minutes of lost time from Leicester to St. Pancras. Lemon was surprised. Of the driver concerned, he wrote "Presumably he had clear signals, which makes me wonder whether many of the delays which arise to-day are due, not so much to the engine performance, but to having distant signals against express trains en route." He concluded his message: "All this leads me to the view that a complete remodelling of the Midland Division timetable can justifiably be undertaken. It will be a long job before completion and I doubt if it can be carried out within the day-to-day work of the staff concerned. Some relief from such daily duties will therefore be required and additional staff may be necessary." Then followed a *coda* which, for polite compulsiveness, was worthy of Brunel in the early days of the Great Western Railway; "Unless you have very good reasons against the wisdom of my suggestion I shall be very pleased to hear how you propose to tackle the problem."[1]

As we know, Byrom tackled it, after what he called a chat with Ashton Davies, deep in the science of the God Mercury.

Better inter-city timings were the main goal. It was already being realised that in such journeys was the future role of railway passenger traffic apart from the movement of commuting passengers in and out of such great centres as London, Glasgow and the Lancashire cities, and that rural passenger traffic was fated to suffer a lingering decline. The most important improvement was in the London–Manchester service which since the end of the last century had been in heavy competition with both the North Western and the Great Central routes.[2] All the principal day expresses between London and Manchester via Derby were accelerated up to a maximum of 42 minutes per train. The fastest through journey times were reduced to 3hr 35min down, and 3hr 38min up. In the Western Division, the crack service between London and Manchester was the "Comet" (a punning name jointly significant of Cottonopolis and Metropolis, bestowed in 1932 and possibly thought up by Loftus Allen), and at this time it ran from Manchester London Road (5.45 pm) to Euston in

---

[1] Memorandum to Byrom; November 19, 1936.
[2] Sheffield, however, was the apple of Marylebone's eye, and this again was a most important Midland goal.

Horwich mogul.

Class 2 4-4-0 with
feed-water-heater.

Beyer-Garratt double-
mogul with self-trimming
tender.

Vintage Royal Scot;
Sanspareil.

Rebuilt Royal Scot;
Seaforth Highlander.
Eric Treacy

"Dieselled Jintie";
hydraulic transmission, 1933.

Diesel-electric shunter
(Armstrong-Whitworth),
1934.

Diesel-electric shunter
(English Electric), 1939.

No. 10000 (English Electric/
Derby), 1947.

3hr 15min via Styal, with one stop at Stafford, whence 133·6 miles to London were covered in 128min. In the down direction, the "Comet" left Euston at 11.50 am and reached Manchester at 3.20 pm, with stops at Crewe and Stockport. From London to Crewe, 158·1 miles, 165 minutes were allowed. To relieve the "Comet", which had been suffering, as noted, from dining-car congestion, a new Midland express was put on, leaving Manchester Central at 6.20 pm and reaching St. Pancras at 9.58 pm. Much was done for the Midland towns, notably those which depended chiefly on the Midland main line, with some extra reliance on the Great Central. Standard start-to-stop timings for the fastest trains in the new (1937) programme included 99 minutes (60·05 mph) for four down and six up trains over the 99·08 miles between London and Leicester, and 123 minutes (60·2 mph) for four down and two up trains between Nottingham and London. Kettering, Melton Mowbray, Wellingborough and Manton all had mile-a-minute non-stop runs to and from St. Pancras, and there was also mile-a-minute running between Luton and Kettering. The fastest run in the new programme, on the Midland Division, was one of 61·7 mph from Kettering to St. Pancras, last lap of the 7.0 am express from Leeds.

On the hilly section between Derby and Manchester, 61½ miles, the fastest non-stop timings were now at 77 minutes. Old Cinderella, the Thames–Forth Express, was accelerated by 38 minutes in the up direction, with the last stop made at Melton Mowbray instead of Kettering and the 105·3 miles thence to St. Pancras covered in 103 minutes – 61·3 mph.[1] There were improvements too in the timing of Midland – West of England trains. Savings in journey time included 83 minutes from Leeds to Bristol and 53 minutes from Nottingham to Bristol. Northbound, Lickey Incline and its banking ever provided an obstacle, but 38 minutes were cut from the timing of the best train from Bristol to Leeds.

British methods of freight handling in the 1920s were all too archaic, and the LMS was certainly no exception. Up and down the country there trundled and banged the old, often immensely long, loose-coupled goods trains with no continuous brakes whatever. Sensitive British subjects, travelling in company with visitors from abroad, were sometimes irked when some businesslike German, peering out-of-window at something running on parallel goods lines, said it was *merkwürdig* and the American's "cute" was somehow even worse.

Following the formation of the Chief Operating Manager's organisation in 1932, much attention was given to the acceleration of freight traffic – which, for all the passenger heroics, was the main source of company's-

---

[1] A most agreeable train for the more reactionary type of traveller. It traversed country of great loveliness in the North, and even in the late 1920s its composition could be described as Vintage Midland.

bread-and-butter on all except the Southern Railway – and three forms of "fast goods" were decided upon, all to be fitted, more or less, with continuous automatic vacuum brakes. *Fitted* was the magical adjective. In Fitted Freight No. 1, the maximum load was one of 50 wagons all piped for automatic vacuum brake, which should be effective on not less than half the load. In 1932 there were 28; in 1938, 47, an increase of 19. Fitted Freight No. 2 had a maximum load of 55 wagons, with AVB operating on not less than one third, and a maximum speed of 50 mph. There were 55 in 1932, 123 in 1938, showing an increase of 68. Express Freight involved a train with a maximum load of 60 wagons, four of them fully-fitted and next the engine. There were 111 in 1932 and 169 in 1938; increase, 58. It really was not very brilliant by some foreign standards, though one hates to say so even after all these years. Nevertheless, raising of freight trains to the fitted-freight and express-freight classes resulted in a total acceleration of 9,015 minutes in the period 1932–38. Other accelerations of booked freight trains represented 5,808 minutes more.

That term *freight*, by the way (German *Fracht*), was at the time officially used on the LMS, though England still generally regarded the word as American, the usual terms being *goods* for a train and *cargo* for a ship. Doubtless Sir Josiah Stamp encouraged it.

There was another examination at this time, on the possibilities of increasing distances which freight trains were allowed to run without stopping for examination. For Fitted Freight No. 1, or equivalent train, the maximum distance allowed was 160 miles; for Fitted Freight No. 2, and for Express Freight with oil axleboxes, it was 125 miles; for Express Freight and other freight trains with grease axleboxes, it was 85 miles. To meet demands for later departures and/or earlier arrivals, just before the outbreak of war in 1939 a scheme was worked out for providing what were called high-speed freight services in each direction between London and Glasgow, using specially converted vehicles and running the trains at express-passenger speeds. Such would entail various alterations to passenger train services. The war interfered, of course, but the scheme was shelved rather than pigeon-holed, for post-war revival, subject to review at that stage of the commercial value of such services. At the outbreak of war there were about 350 fitted freight trains of each and every description. Most had to be withdrawn, but by June 1941, nearly half were back again.

The still extensive use of grease axleboxes will have been noted, and the archaic sort of British goods wagons at that time has been deplored. To the average British official mind, the use of roller-bearing axleboxes on British freight trains was an exotic supposition, such as might have been expected of those fussy people, the Swedes, who were trying to sell the things anyway. One trouble with British railway operation was that it had not yet recovered from the surprise of the original Liverpool and Manchester Directors, during the year 1830–31, when they discovered that there was a great demand for goods transport when they had been expecting chiefly passengers. Through a century, many of their heirs and assigns had often got along with the idea that the goods must be fitted in somehow, but made to know its place.

Centralised Traffic Control was a thing pioneered by the Midland Railway. But to those whom one might call the old stick-out-a-mile railwaymen – certainly those of companies which had no Control – the whole thing was some modern fad, which was to be kept out of sight, like an eighteenth-century water-closet tucked into the cupboard under the stairs. ("Early in 1937 Mr. Lemon, during an Officers' Tour, visited the Control Offices at Westhouses and Rowsley and found that the accommodation was very unsatisfactory and that the staff had to work under considerable difficulties."[1]) A review of the layout and equipment of Control offices was speedily ordered, and it was further decided that an ideal "theoretical" Control should be built with a miniature geographical board, incorporating all of what were then the latest ideas in respect of cabinets and telephones. In designing the equipment of this "model", every endeavour was made to eliminate operating and electrical difficulties experienced with existing Control office layout.

The new layout had many advantages. Firstly there were hand micro-telephones, none fitted below table level. Next, all telephone cables were concealed and out of the way of operating staff. All lamp signals were directly associated with the circuit telephone. Fourthly, an *engaged* lamp signal was given throughout the office on any circuit when that was in use, thus preventing a member of the office from ringing on a circuit while it was being used by a colleague. Apparatus was to be standard for any Control office. Duplicate independent telephones were to be provided, one on each side of the table on all omnibus control circuits. All telephone circuits were to be wired in parallel, to avoid complete failure of a circuit through a fault in any one unit. Lastly, indirect lighting should be installed. Difficulty had been experienced through highlights and shadows under ordinary direct lighting, then very general in business places and almost universal in private establishments.

The model Control room was installed in No. 19, Euston Square,[2] London, and Lemon went to have a look at it on December 22, 1937. The equipment was approved subject to some minor alterations, as being suitable for the improvement of the company's Control offices. The first of these to undergo the *treatment* was at Wellingborough, which received

[1] Memorandum dated August 1941.
[2] One of a terrace of stucco-fronted houses on the north side of the Square, divided by the old main entrance to the station and facing Friends' House. They were picturesque, but most inconvenient.

part of the equipment from the old house in Euston Square. Improvement was also carried out at Kirkby and Westhouses before war interfered with further progress of a constructive sort.

In October 1933, Lord Knutsford suggested the use of a public announcement system, of a very simple form; simply the appointment of more staff to direct passengers at big stations. Lemon seems to have said: "What about loud-speakers?" Just over a year later, these had been installed at six of the company's larger stations, anyway. By October 1937, they were in use at 22 stations and 18 yards on the LMS, and the system was of tremendous value during the war years, under conditions of blackout. A portable-pack type of amplifier serving one loud-speaker and carried by one man was found invaluable under such conditions. Thirty sets were on order by June 1941. Out of those years, which were *very* dark when there was neither moon nor the light of a burning, comes the echo of some unknown girl at her microphone: "The train at Platform Five will call at Watford Junction, King's Langley, Hemel Hempsted, Berkhamsted, Tring, Cheddington, Leighton Buzzard, Bletchley, Wolverton, Castlethorpe, Roade, Blisworth, Weedon, Welton, Rugby and – " (Deep sigh, clearly audible through the loud-speaker) " – all stations to Stafford by the Trent Valley Line. This train is *very* crowded. *Was* your journey really necessary?"

One hopes that the announcer did not later find her feet on too hot a carpet. While the strain of war sometimes made people's tempers shorter, in civil as in combatant life, ties of common funk (Kipling) seemed to make us much nicer to each other. The slow train to Stafford was probably overcrowded because of misfortunes which were publicly unmentionable, but this sort of thing really belongs to a later chapter.

Strictures on goods vehicle design have been made already, and your author still believes that archaism in this respect, coinciding with the advance of the commercial motor, lost all British railways traffic they should have retained. Much fragile goods, consigned to the bangs and bumps of our wretched wagons, arrived at destination in pieces. The railway paid claims. The customer was further irritated by delay. In June 1932, Lemon wrote to J. Ballantyne at Euston: "In conversation with a Mr. Turner recently he referred to the use of road transport for his traffic (sanitary piping) from Swadlincote, explaining that while he would like to use the railways, his customers frequently stipulated for road transport, on the grounds of delivery to site, less breakage, and frequently cheaper rate. He also made a point of the heavy use of straw for packing purposes when loading railway wagons, whereas by road I gathered that little or none was necessary."

As usual Lemon gathered that the traffic had been *under Mr. Ballantyne's notice*, and he would be glad to know the facts. He was sending a copy of the letter, he said, to the Chief Mechanical Engineer (William Stanier) and suggested that Ballantyne and he should consult. Doubtless they did so. Slowly ground the mills of whatever gods govern railway administration. Late in November 1936, the Board authorised the construction of a hundred shock-absorbing wagons. Delivery was completed by July 2, 1938. Half of them had been allocated to the transport of pottery-products in the Derby area and the rest to fragile goods in other districts.

On November 7, 1938, T. E. Argile, Acting Chief Commercial Manager, and T. W. Royle, Chief Operating Manager, reported to Ashton Davies at Euston, that in the 14 weeks from July 2 to October 8, 1938, 652 loads were conveyed in these wagons, made up as follows: sanitary tubes and conduits, 543 loads; other sanitary-ware such as water-closets, six; chimney-pots, 10; concrete tubes, two; stone and concrete paving slabs, one; firebricks and grate-backs, 23; sheet glass in cases and crates, 35; beer in cask, two; unpacked machines and machinery, 15; acids in carboys, 15. Receipts from these loads were approximately £2,150. Except in isolated cases, loads had been carried without damage.

One feels that but for the use of unbraked vehicles, damage might have been *nil*, but that was not remarked in the report. Argile and Royle continued their joint report in this wise.

Traffic in sanitary ware, they stated, had been definitely retained to rail. Previously serious breakages had been common, but with shock-absorbing stock most loads had travelled without damage, or with breakage of one of a few articles only. One firm had forwarded 14,976 pipes in 148 wagons, with only 103 breakages, which was 0·69 per cent. As to unpacked machinery, several lathes and other machines from Scotland, and washing machines from Kendal, had been safely carried from firms which had been either using road transport previously or were threatening to do so on account of damage. There had been marked improvement in the carriage of acids in carboys, and return of the empty carboys. For these, road transport was common, and the railway had had much trouble through breakage in the past. As for concrete tubes, the Stanton Iron Company had stated that with the improved results in railway transport, *they would be prepared* to forward 25 wagon-loads per week of traffic at present motor-borne.

The report was a fairly long one. Clearly the wagons were paying for their construction, but it was emphasised that breakage was not the only factor. Service, delivery to site, and rate must all be considered and in these the hauliers still could offer important advantages. Still, the field should be widened. Argile and Royle were consulting with Stanier on the provision of further rolling stock of this kind; they had suggested to him that the situation might be met by building a number of shock-absorbing wagons instead of standard wagons already on the 1938 building programme, Stanier said this could be done, and delivery given at the rate of 20 wagons a week from February 13, 1939, *if* a decision was given quickly. It was suggested that the 1938 programme be altered to the extent of building 100 non-fitted shock-absorbing wagons out of the programme originally intended for 1,000 ordinary twelve-ton wagons not yet built, leaving 900 of the latter. The price of a shock-absorbing wagon was £190 against £130 for one of the ordinary standard type.

We should turn for a while from the constructive to the destructive, for under the Lemon Viziership, the London Midland & Scottish Railway unfortunately continued to smash up its trains now and then. It was poor consolation to argue that the LMS was a much more extensive railway than the Great Western (whereon few people at that time could remember a major accident). That sort of argument had been advanced over many years for what to all Europeans had seemed to be the smash-happy railways of the United States, taken collectively.

On Sunday, March 22, 1931, a West Coast express was in a spectacular derailment at Leighton Buzzard, and for one reason and another, this accident attracted particular attention. For one thing, the gutter news-papers – and even certain of the more respectable ones – insisted on calling the wrecked train the "Royal Scot". It was in fact the 11.30 am Sunday express from Euston to Glasgow, but its composition was not unlike that of the weekday train. Headed by Royal Scot class engine No. 6114, *Coldstream Guardsman*, it comprised 14 vehicles, mostly of recent con-struction. The ninth and twelfth, however, were ex-London and North Western twelve-wheel diners, which, it should be at once remarked, were not much damaged in what was to occur. The famous Glasgow Orpheus Choir, under their eminent conductor Sir Hugh Roberton, were on the train but fortunately for contemporary choral music, as well as their loved ones, they were in the rear. There was a first-class coach with an attendant kitchen car, in the front of the train.

Owing to permanant way repairs north of Leighton Buzzard, north-bound trains were being crossed on the quadruple main line from down-fast to down-slow. This Scotch express, which was carrying 183 passengers and about 20 staff, ran through the crossover south of Leighton Buzzard at the normal high speed which it would have maintained had it been continuing on the down-fast. The circumstances of crossing over to down-slow had been posted. *Coldstream Guardsman* managed to get round the first turnout, but overturned on her right side at the second. The tender partly jacknifed on to the engine cab, as in some previous accidents of this sort, killing the enginemen. The first three carriages were destroyed, their bodies mostly smashed to bits, but owing to the use of steel underframes they tended first to shoot out in a stellar formation, instead of utterly disintegrating like all-wooden coaches in earlier troubles. In these were killed three passengers and one of the train's cooks who was working in the forward kitchen car. With the enginemen, six people completed the fatal casualty list. There were some odd stories about escapes in those leading coaches. A Dutchman fell through a suddenly-opening carriage floor and survived. Another man was flung out of the wreckage unbreeched but unhurt, and therefore had less reason to resent his indecorous situation than he might have done. Accidents are like that. So, of course, is war.

These first three vehicles were, as remarked, in pieces with some handsomely varied decorations still incongruously recognisable amongst the muck; the fourth was more or less kippered. The rest of the train, though much derailed, kept in line. Fatalities might indeed have been much worse than they were. The train was of course automatic-vacuum-braked, and the engine had steam brakes on all wheels, including the bogie wheels.

There was no doubt about the fact that the enginemen had driven at full speed through a crossover wheron speed should have been greatly reduced. The guard of the express might have been watching signals, but firstly, attention to displayed notices, and secondly, better visibility of signals which were probably quite obscured by exhaust clouds beating down, would have prevented the accident. In respect of this last, the Royal Scot class engines were notorious. One remembers watching them at speed about this time, and there would be, unless they were working really hard, a continual white cloud from the ridiculous little chimney, backwards over the cab. An observer noted, at Leighton Buzzard, a brief show of grey smoke in the last moments, suggesting that steam had been cut off when it was too late. Apart from the express, there was considerable destruction of four horseboxes on a siding between the fast and slow lines. Apart from the humanities the whole thing made an awful mess, blocking the West Coast main lines completely until next day. The author was among the first passengers through, going south. By that time the battered engine was away in the yard to the north of the station, and more gruesome evidence had been removed; all the same, a young woman suddenly confronted with the smashed carriages was somewhat sick.

Sir Alan Mount reported, and certainly noticed the matter of exhaust clouds beating down. The CME told him that wind-tunnel experiments were being undertaken already; indeed, this disability of express engines with very large boilers and short chimneys had been under examination for a time, certainly since the Southern Railway had had its early morning express and mail train, the 5.40 am out of Waterloo, in collision near Fleet in 1926. The Southern company soon after, and the LMS subsequently, paid much attention to smoke-lifting. Side shields, in German fashion, were found to mitigate this dangerous nuisance.

In the end of that year (December 18, 1931) there was a rear collision at Dagenham Dock late at night in dense fog. Visibility was 12 yards at most, probably much less, and a goods train had a breakaway owing to drawbar fracture on a privately owned tank-car. The signalman involved failed, in the darkness and mirk, to observe the lack of a tail-light on the passing goods and accepted a passenger train headed by Tilbury-type 4–4–2 tank engine No. 2139. This struck the stranded goods-brake and wagons, and the impact also caused damage to the coaches in rear. The goods guard and one passenger were killed.

On June 17, 1932, there was a bad derailment at Great Bridgeford, somewhat repeating the circumstances of Leighton Buzzard, though with a much older train. This was the 7.23 pm express from Crewe to Birmingham, an offshoot of the 12.20 pm from Perth to London. Crossing from up slow to up fast at this place, the engine, 4–4–0 No. 5278 *Precursor* (LNWR No. 513, and rather famous in her time) turned over on her left side and thus slid along outside the up-fast road. The train comprised four coaches, two of which were much damaged, and four passengers were killed. The engine was not severely battered; those with inside cylinders and gear were notably less vulnerable than the newer types under such circumstances.

September 1934, was a black month, with two serious accidents. At Port Eglinton Junction, the 5.35 pm business train from Glasgow St. Enoch to Kilmarnock, being crossed from the up-main to the up-fast Canal road struck on the diamond crossing the 5.12 pm train from Paisley to St. Enoch, almost head-on. The engine of the Paisley train was running tender-first, a circumstance which was subsequently noticed, though it was a common practice in the Glasgow area south of the river. Trains were thus run on the Cathcart Circle line, for instance, because it was a very convenient way of turning an express engine productively. The driver of this train, poor man, had run through signals. None likes observing them around a swaying tender with heaped coal while having the regulator, reversing lever and vacuum brake handle behind him. This man survived. The other three enginemen, and six passengers, were killed. It was a messy accident, at the height of the evening suburban rush hour.[1]

Just over three weeks later, there was an even worse accident on what had been the London & North Western system, at Winwick Junction on the night of September 28. In one respect it repeated circumstances which had had really appalling results at Quintinshill in 1915; that of forgetfulness regarding a standing train of secondary importance. Fortunately the results were not so terrible, though bad enough in all conscience.

[1] The author, on holiday at the time in Western Inverness-shire, met a fellow-writer who expressed anxiety about this accident as he had been engaged on signal engineering over this section. His anxiety was quite unfounded; there was just that thought that *perhaps – if –* ! Oneself has had a holiday similarly spoilt, while quite innocent. It was a rotten thing.

A local train from Warrington to Wigan via Earlestown was moving slowly forward from the home signal for the down fast line, up to the Winwick Junction signalbox, so that the driver could ascertain why the home signal for the main line to Preston, and not that for Earlestown, which he had been expecting, had been lowered. His train comprised three coaches headed by a 2–4–2 tank engine. He had stopped a short distance in rear of the home signal, at about 9.06 pm, sending his fireman to the box to carry out Rule 55.

His train was violently struck in the rear by the 5.20 pm express from Euston to Blackpool (nine coaches headed by Prince of Wales class 4–6–0 engine *Queen of the Belgians*). The last coach of the local was broken up and the two leading ones on the express telescoped into one another. The express engine was relatively little damaged, was still able to steam, and was used by the breakdown gang afterwards to pull away some of the damaged vehicles. Ten passengers, and the guard of the local train, were killed.

The signalman at Winwick Junction had accepted the local passenger train, offered by Winwick Quay at 8.57 pm. He had received *train entering section* at 9.03. He did not, as he ought, offer it forward at once to Vulcan Bank, and therefore did not pull off for it his home and starting signals, hence the driver's anxious curiosity.

Now the unhappy signalman had been occupied with the handling, in rapid succession, of eight trains, all during the few minutes before the accident, and several of which involved conflicting movements at the junction as well as telephonic arrangements with adjacent boxes. It was then and thus that he forgot the waiting local train from Warrington to Wigan. He was perhaps most concerned with an express from North Wales to Manchester via Earlestown, and with the Blackpool express from London.

The block-book boy in the box, with 18 months' experience there, said at Colonel A. C. Trench's inquiry that he had completed his entries for the express from North Wales, which had passed about 8.56, and had entered acceptance from Winwick Quay of the down local when he was called to the telephone to take particulars of alterations in the running of excursion trains. Having done so he went to the other end of the box to look at the special weekly notice, and to enter alterations thereon. As he turned back he heard his signalman say "Goodness! I've not given 2–1 here yet." The signalman gave train-out-of-section on his down-fast instrument to Winwick Quay and immediately after was offered, and accepted, the Blackpool express. He had in mind the North Wales train, having forgotten, as remarked, the local.

The boy assumed that the latter train must have passed while he was telephoning. He therefore entered on the book what he thought would be normal intermediate times for the passing of the train and its acceptance ahead without asking his signalman. Colonel Trench ascribed the latter's failure to "mental lapse"; but his action in sending *train out of section* without verification was a most serious breach of the basic principles of block working.

While the fireman of the local train was on his way to carry out Rule 55 at Winwick Junction box, the signalman at Winwick Quay had intimation that the Blackpool express was approaching, and as his block instrument to Winwick Junction still showed *train on line* he gave Winwick Junction the *call attention* with a view to signalling *shunt train for following train to pass*. The Winwick Junction signalman, hearing the *call attention*, looked at his block instrument and saw that it was still at *train on line*. It was then that, forgetting the local and thinking about the North Wales train, he made his fatal mistake, immediately giving *train out of section* to Winwick Quay; being offered, and accepting, the Blackpool express; and having offered it forward and had acceptance from the next box, setting the road for this train. He pulled off the signals for it, thus perplexing the driver of the local train who was expecting to be cleared via Earlestown. The collision followed.

Late at night on March 13, 1935, between King's Langley and Nash Mills signalboxes, the LMS had one of the smashes of the century. But as none of the four trains involved in the cumulative collision was carrying passengers, it was soon forgotten except by railwaymen and some earnest students of transport. It did not even excite the Beaverbrook newspapers into fresh diatribes against one of their favourite targets, the wooden railway carriage.

About ten minutes past eleven the 4.55 pm express freight from Alexandra Dock to London (Broad Street), which was called both for convenience and accuracy the *meat train*, was pulled up about King's Langley owing to a vacuum brake defect. As it stood on the up-fast line, on embankment just above the Railway Arms public house; it was struck in rear by the 5.50 pm milk train from Stafford to Euston, headed by standard Midland compound 4–4–0 locomotive No. 1165. By the impact, this engine was much damaged as to the outside (low-pressure) cylinders and the bogie, and the meat wagons were flung all over the place.

Moments later, into the wreckage pitched the 10.30 pm freight from Camden to Holyhead, running on the down-slow line and headed by standard class 5X 4–6–0 engine No. 5511. This big engine came off very badly, with the outside cylinders broken and the outside motion stripped, and by now the rubbish of dismembered wagons with prodigious spilling of milk and butcher's meat in bulk, lay all over the four-track main line. Into this ploughed the 12.25 pm coal train from Toton to Camden, headed by 0–8–0 engine No. 9598, completing a spread so monumental that it could be fully surveyed only from an inquisitive aeroplane, which came over next day to take photographs for the evening papers.

After the first shock, Driver William Buckley of the Stafford train went back to warn, if he could, the driver of the up coal train which he had previously overtaken, while his fireman, Edward Newns, went with similar purpose along the down-fast road. In these things, as we have seen, they were frustrated, and in the driver's case, tragically so. He was killed by an avalanche of debris when the Holyhead train struck the existing wreckage. Thus he died well, though in vain. It took a long time to find what was left of him.

Fortunately the 10.50 express passenger train from London to Aberdeen, running on the down-fast, had only just cleared Watford Junction and could be held by signals before it might add a fifth and very gory contribution to the chaos.

Whilst, under such circumstances, devoted men should be named, there is no need to name those who fall down on the job in times relatively recent, thus giving hurt to those still with us.[1] The King's Langley signalman had most improperly accepted the second of the trains when the first was still standing, through breakdown, in the block section north of his box. The signalman at Nash Mills, the next box north, might have suspected somewhat ambiguous inquiries made by this man, instead of thinking, as he did, that his colleague had simply omitted to give *train out of section*. Colonel Mount, inquiring, exonerated the Nash Mill's man, with an acid remark that a good deal of his King's Langley colleague's evidence and explanation "was spent in a regrettable endeavour to implicate him". The King's Langley man admitted that "perhaps twice a week" he telephoned to ask whether he had cleared a train. It was altogether a sorry business. Had passenger trains been involved, it would have gone down to remembered history as a blood-bath like that of Quintinshill on the Caledonian, nearly twenty years before. Both had been caused by some quite absurd bungling, without preliminary high drama.

Quite apart from the massive destruction of the King's Langley collision, there was fearsome dislocation of traffic to and from the North, over one of the busiest main lines in the world. The 10.50 pm express train from Euston, and that which followed it at 11.0 pm, were drawn back to Willesden, thence sent down to Acton Wells on the North & South Western Junction Railway, where they reversed and proceeded to the Midland main line by way of Dudding Hill. This route was used next day for many trains in and out of Euston, though the most important West Coast and Irish ones worked in and out of St. Pancras. Reconnection from the Midland main line to the North Western was made from Wigston

---

[1] The author has named those responsible for accidents in books dealing with events more remote in time. The scruple is like the fifty-years' ban on Minutes.

Magna to Nuneaton via Hinckley. While this route meant an addition of only fourteen miles, congestion on the Midland was very severe; few of the through trains were less than two hours late.

Some of the Lancashire trains were cancelled, and so were all those, once the pride and joy of the London & North Western company, between Euston and Birmingham (New Street). Passengers for the great Midland city were directed to Paddington, and the Great Western Railway thus had, briefly, a realisation of its more extravagant dreams about a monopoly of passenger traffic between London, Birmingham and Wolverhampton.

Of course, things would have been much simpler had there been a link between the old London & North Western branch to St. Albans and the Midland main line near Napsbury. Such a connection had been planned very many years before, but it never was built. As things were, everything into and out of Euston, apart from local trains terminating at Watford, had to make that clumsy reversal at Acton Wells, thence passing over a line already under heavy goods-transfer traffic between Brent on the Midland line and Feltham on the Southern Railway. For suburban traffic north of Watford as far as Tring, special buses were put on by the London Passenger Transport Board.

Another adverse circumstance was that of locomotive restrictions. The biggest engines, such as the Pacifics and the Royal Scots, were barred from the Midland main line. South of Crewe, therefore, the heaviest engines had to be the Stanier 5 X three-cylinder 4–6–0 Jubilees, which indeed were found very useful and often took loads much in excess of their rated maximum. For a day, in spite of great skill in coping with these fearsome rearrangements, the West Coast services were a shambles. Control, to be sure, was invaluable. In its lack, there must have been complete stoppage.

Just over twenty-four hours after the initial collision, the down-fast road was cleared. At 6.15 on the following evening, the last of the wreckage was cleared or tumbled from the up-slow, and all four roads were restored and able to carry traffic after nearly two days and nights.

Right at the end of 1935, on December 30, there was another of those accidents which might have been very awful indeed, but in fact were just alarming and abominably inconvenient. About five o'clock in the morning, the down Irish express from London to Stranraer, on the last lap of its journey, was almost completely derailed on Ken Viaduct between Castle Douglas and New Galloway. This train was headed by two standard Midland type Class 2 4–4–0 locomotives – a light steady-running design – and at that time of year it was a short train for all its two engines. In order from the second tender came a van, a Post Office sorting carriage, two sleeping cars (third- and first-class respectively) a brake-composite coach and another van. Everything was derailed from the tender of the leading engine to the rear van. The engines and tenders ran on ahead, round the left-hand curve, while detached from their carriages. These went away on a right-hand tangent, keeping remarkably well in line although partially overturned. The sorting carriage fared worst, with body detached from underframe, and one of the P.O. sorters was the only person on the train to be kept in hospital afterwards; he, poor man, having had a considerable tumbling. As for the passengers, the worst that happened to them was the simple misfortune of being tipped out of bed at a ghastly winter morning hour. Doubtless they were much annoyed; one hopes also that they were grateful, after the initial curses and cries of fright, that nothing worse had befallen them.

Marks of derailment were found on one of the trough girders on Ken Viaduct. A distinguished colleague, asked for his opinion after the accident, said simply: "The usual Scotch bloody permanent way!" Inquiring and reporting to Government, Colonel A. C. Trench regretted that he was unable to reach any precise conclusions. He could only recommend a stricter speed limit than that of 45 mph at this place. As to the viaduct, additional sway bracing to its girder spans, which had been decided upon already, was "certainly desirable".

Before the thirties were out, there were several more accidents on the LMS. Two deserve mention for, respectively, magnitude of destruction and technical curiosity. At Oakley on the Midland line, on January 21, 1938, there was a spectacular head-on collision. An empty-stock train of old wooden carriages, headed by Mogul engine No. 2893 (facing towards London), had been set back on the Northampton branch. The disposal of this train, which earlier had formed an excursion from Bradford, was certainly bungled. Northbound on the main line was the 2.10 pm express from St. Pancras to Bradford, headed by Stanier Class 5 4-6-0 engine No. 5568, *Western Australia*. This train ran through signals, on to the branch, and struck the empty train at considerable speed. Engine frames were broken up so that the locomotives lost their leading trucks and finished in an awful embrace, smokebox-to-smokebox.[1] Three of the old empty coaches were smashed to pieces and two carriages on the express very severely damaged, with the death of two passengers and the subsequent death of a man on the dining-car staff. Lieut.-Colonel E. Woodhouse inquired for the Ministry of Transport, reporting the circumstances mentioned already, but adding that signal visibility was certainly not of the best.

On April 8, 1938, a train from Lanark to Glasgow, approaching Rutherglen at about 50 mph, was derailed by breakage of a coach axle. One passenger was killed in the train and another died of injuries after-

---

[1] To quote an RCTS commentator, showing photographs with an epidiascope: "That was No. 5568, 5 X, 4-6-0. It's 0-6-0 now!"

wards. The accident was ascribed, on inquiry, to a fatigue flaw in the offending axle, extending through 81 per cent. of its cross-section. A photograph of the fracture made it look rather like an almost complete eclipse of the moon. It must be admitted that at that time, and for some years after, equipment on many of the ordinary Scottish train services of the LMS had a marked aspect of decrepitude. About what once had been the proud Caledonian Railway there seemed almost to be a sort of creeping senile decay, and certainly there were more shocks to come on the Glasgow lines in later years.

To what extent, one wonders, was this due to economies of the Stamp regime? How much could be laid at the doors of a mixture of hopelessness and sullen resentment among men who, for too long, had been serving a railway company to which they felt no natural loyalty, in a country which had suffered more than many from depressed trade and frustrated technical improvement? Years after in the early 1960s, the same sort of demoralisation was to be seen in several Regions of British Railways. How, one remembers wondering, was one to sell railway transport to people who were being told in the same breath that their particular line was on the schedule for closure?

Turning to more cheerful things: twice in the 1930s the company made a considerable publicity-gesture by sending a train on tour and exhibition in North America. Visiting Americans were then still very train-minded. Among them, too, was a general impression that going by train in foreign countries was a very rough business indeed. Those without experience expected, on the European Continent, something like early post-Revolution Russian travel, bed-bugs included; and in the British Isles, something like the old narrow-gauge lines of New England. The first of these LMS railway-picnics was the visit to the United States and Canada of the "Royal Scot" in 1933. It was an expensive jaunt, indeed, but was evidently regarded afterwards as having paid, so that towards the end of the decade the "Coronation Scot" train was sent to follow on a somewhat similar tour, which will be mentioned later. The 1933 train was not, strictly, the real "Royal Scot"; rather a train with the Royal Scot class engine bearing the prototype name, with carriages representative of the best West Coast express passenger practice of the time. It comprised a side-corridor brake-third, an open-gangway third class, a kitchen car, an open-gangway first class, a first-class lounge-brake of that sort which had such enormous slab-sided leather arm-chairs, a third-class sleeping car, a first-class sleeping car (twelve-wheeled), and a brake-first carriage.

Unusual coaching features included (for the first time on the LMS) electric cooking appliances in the kitchen car, supplied by two diesel generators, and the first-class sleeper had the Thermo-Reg arrangement of heating and ventilation, which would pass as a sort of air conditioning, and of which a traveller of long experience has never felt inclined to disapprove until, many years later, he detected a distinct and insidious whiff of diesel exhaust, that abomination having by then made its noisome impact on railway travel in the British Isles.

Locomotive (partly taken-down) and carriages were loaded on the steamship *Beaverdale* at Tilbury, sailing on April 11 for Montreal, where reassembly was carried out by the Canadian Pacific company's works with the advice of Fitter W. C. Woods of Crewe. With it went Driver William Gilbertson and Fireman John Johnson, both of Carlisle. The train began its North American tour from Montreal on May 1, after being visited by many people. Perhaps Ontario-Scots predominated, but nostalgia among expatriates led to many others making quite considerable efforts to see the train somehow. In an agency photograph, the author was delighted to spot his elder brother.[1] One believes that then, and on the subsequent tour, the train's advent resulted in many unexpected encounters.

From Montreal, the "Royal Scot" went west to Ottawa, Toronto and Hamilton, then into the United States at Buffalo and eastwards along the New York Central main line to Albany. Then and throughout the tour, the railway companies over whose lines it passed provided pilot crews, each consisting of engineer, fireman, conductor and two brakesmen. From Albany the train struck due east over the Berkshires to Boston, thence south to New York by the New Haven Railroad, and west by the Pennsylvania to Pittsburgh, visiting Philadelphia, Atlantic City, Baltimore, and Washington by the way. Thence it went to Chicago by a designedly round-about route, calling at Cincinnati, Louisville, Indianapolis, St. Louis and Chicago, reaching the latter on May 25, ready for the opening on June 1 of the Century of Progress Exposition there. It was intended the train remain on exhibition until the time came for it to be shipped home via Montreal, but the enthusiastic reception it had received in American, as well as Canadian cities, had evidently taken its sponsors by surprise. Americans, as one often remarks, love anything new, and anything strange too, so long as it does not interfere with their various particular conceptions of the American Way of Life. The "Royal Scot" certainly did not intrude; it was new and it was strange. It was as if something of the Tower of London, Edinburgh Castle, Anne Hathaway's Cottage, York Minster and the Banks of Loch Lomond had all been packed aboard a locomotive and eight of the dinkiest little railroad cars you ever saw. Sometimes they purloined lamps and antimacassars, often they wrote their names on anything from the tender to the first-aid boxes, but they loved it.

Encouraged by this, the LMS company persuaded the exhibition

[1] Christopher Ellis, 1900–1950, sometime Chief Newscaster, Canadian Broadcasting Corporation.

authorities at Chicago to release the train earlier than schedule, so that it could do some more district-visiting. (In Atlantic City, an enormous band of pipes and drums, in terrific Highland dress, had received the train with musical honours.) Of instant impressions among American citizens were these: Royal Scot screamed when American trains hooted; she was small but stylish, and she was red all over, and rounded, while most American trains were mud-green with black locomotives, and square; her cars were unexpectedly comfortable to back and bottom, when thus sampled; she was of course *English* – or was she *Scotch*? What happened to those little cars in a wreck? Where was the pilot?

The train's planned homeward route was to have been from Chicago to Montreal through Detroit, Cleveland, London (Ontario) and Toronto. Instead she headed for the Pacific Coast after over two million visitors had sampled her, making their occasional marks. In the Middle-West she visited Bloomington, Springfield and Indianapolis before turning up for the second time in St. Louis. At the first-named, schoolboys and girls laid cents, and bits, and even dimes over half a mile of rail, as children have done in front of trains ever since they began, but on a grander, more American scale.

From St. Louis, the real Western business began. The train struck out to Kansas City, and thence ran to Denver. Much piffle was written at the time, of course, about the way this little British train managed to do with ease what the enormous American ones were supposed (at home in England) to do with much fuss. Of course this three-cylinder tenwheeler could not have managed her assignment with sixteen standard American Pullmans behind the tender. But with little more than half her normal British load, the engine managed very well. Between Colorado Springs and Palmer Lake she had to climb from 5,992ft to 7,242ft. W. B. Thompson remarked at the time that the bank resembled very closely that between Blair Atholl and Druimuachdar Summit. *Royal Scot* did not need assistance in rear from *Uncle Dick* or, less improbably, some more modern American "pusher".

Salt Lake City was the next big port of call, and thence the train ran over the old, classic, historic, original Pacific railroad down to San Francisco. Thence it ran northwards up the coast, through Oregon to Vancouver, where real British Columbian rain did not deter a crowd which had to be controlled by extra police, and six thousand had to be turned away from their organized inspection. So far, the locomotive had been equipped, to satisfy North American requirements, with a big electric headlamp (rather motor-looking with a clumsy cable) a-top the smokebox door, and a regulation locomotive bell in the middle of the front platform. Purely for publicity reasons, she had an additional *THE ROYAL SCOT* nameplate across her front diameter, which could be

The Hand of War. ABOVE: London
St Pancras, May 10, 1941. BELOW:
Queen's Park, October 15, 1940; engine
Royal Ulster Rifleman.

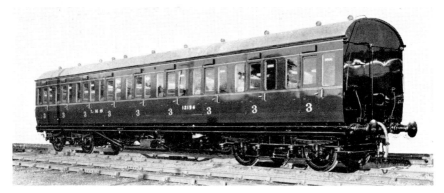

Third-class suburban coach, 1939
(ABOVE), and first-class corridor
coach of 1935(BELOW), converted to
dining trailer in 1945.

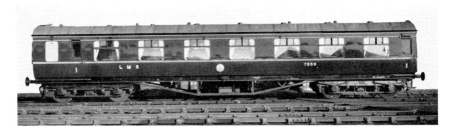

Travelling club coach, Manchester-
Blackpool, 1935

Assorted interiors. ABOVE: *"Coronation Scot"* club saloon, 1939. LEFT: Third-class compartment, 1947. BELOW: Prime Minister's office in Government train, improvised from London & North Western "semi-royal" carriage, 1939–1945.

Motor penetration. ABOVE: Diesel passenger train converted from Lancashire & Yorkshire electric set (Bury line), 1928. LEFT: The Karrier Ro-Railer on the Stratford-on-Avon and Midland Junction line. BELOW: Diesel-electric No. 10000 by the Roundhouse at Camden.

floodlit. But now the Canadian Rockies were ahead of her. In those mountains were grizzly bears and other imposing fauna, and perhaps the occasional fallen pine tree. So her bufferbeam was additionally adorned by a very large pilot, suited to the higher British platform level, and thus very reminiscent of the days when North American trains were indeed headed by long-legged tenwheelers with *cowcatchers* worthy of the name.

Thus armed, the Royal Scot set out, eastbound, by the Canadian Pacific Railway, with a summit of 5,326ft ahead of her. By this time the ancient 1 in 21·8 incline at Kicking Horse was long abandoned and the climb, though long, was by no means so forbidding. The engine cleared it unassisted with a minimum speed of 10 mph. Unfortunately the train's supposed feats were described not only in the Philistine newspapers but even by some official stuff from Euston, which, as W. B. Thompson remarked, "merely tended to bring England into ridicule". So it ever was, and more was the pity, for in Europe it was always America that was accused of telling the big prestige-lie, with some, but not exclusive, reason. If only the train had been left free of Press ballyhoo, the prestige would have looked after itself, and even as things were, it earned a tremendous amount of goodwill among potentially critical people.

So over the Selkirks went the "Royal Scot", and over the Great Divide where a single mountain river split and poured its infant waters to both the Atlantic and the Pacific. Down by Calgary she went and across the great northern wheatlands. So she came back to Montreal, and there the steamship *Beaverdale* once more received her, to bring her home to Tilbury, where she arrived on December 5, minus about 500 electric lamp-bulbs and plus the autographs of men in Moose Jaw and some other places, north and south of the Forty-ninth Parallel. On December 15 there was an official reception at Euston, with old John Bromley, M.P., of ASLEF, and a pipe band, followed by the last exhibition of the trip in Euston Station itself.

It had been a happy jaunt, and a much more ambitious one than the London & North Western's outing to Chicago and back in 1893, with the Webb compound engine *Queen Empress* modestly hauling a train of one composite coach, one West Coast sleeper and some Wagner sleeping cars to make up the *consist* for a run back to New York over the New York Central's Water Level Route. Between the two visits, the Great Western engine *King George V* had been to visit the Baltimore and Ohio company's Festival of the Iron Horse in 1927. In the United States and Canada, the "Royal Scot" had covered 11,194 miles of route and had called at about eighty cities and large towns. Including the exhibition, rather more than three million people had looked at, and in many cases walked through the train. During the sojourn in Chicago, incidentally, Driver Gilbertson had parted with his appendix, which is an excellent thing to do with a few of

E

the physiological gadgets evolution has left on us.

Quite apart from necessities of impending war, of which the nation had at last beome aware, the last pre-war year had all sorts of other changes apparent in the offing, though many of them would have to be shelved, as things turned out. As remarked, the rebuilding of Euston Station was one of them, and part of the scheme, under Government Loan Guarantee, was the provision of additional carriage sidings and sheds at Willesden. The sidings were indeed completed, and the excavated material was taken to the site of new sidings to be laid out at Ripple Lane, thereby reducing the cost of the latter by nearly £13,000. The carriage-sheds programme, however, was suspended under war conditions.

In those last pre-war years, too, the British railway companies collectively were trying to secure better treatment from Government than they had previously enjoyed. They were common carriers; but whatever obligations road hauliers may have had, in respect, had become a dead letter during the years when the railways had had an absolute monopoly of heavy transport throughout the realm. The railways were severely restricted in many conditions, especially as to the fixing of rates, where as the road carrying industry, in the course of its motor renewal, had had things for a time very much its own way. Hauliers, and public service vehicle operators also, not to mention the coaching people who cashed-in with the touring and seasonal holiday traffic, put over a very plausible image of themselves as the new, *sporty*, modern *transporteurs*, who were at last breaking the monopoly of those stodgy old flannel-pants, the "railmen". Their public-relations methods were undoubtedly skilful, and, they managed to conjure a remarkable aura of conscious virtue, which, one believes, they were quite sure they possessed. To read the late Charles Rudy on railways in the *Coaching Journal* was like reading Colonel McCormick in the *Chicago Tribune* on the subject of the English, or one of the more crackpot Northern Irish Presbyterians criticising the Pope, only at least the American paper had a rather better prose style than the party first mentioned. Perhaps this conscious merit was most comparable to that of Benvenuto Cellini, incomparable artist and quite skilful murderer, who *knew* he was favoured of God because he had seen his own halo round the shadow of his head when he went walking out on a bright, dewy morning. One of the most masterly pieces of publicity, later on when the war was raging, was a simple slogan displayed in ticket offices: "Can't we go by *coach*?"

At that time, one could not, for we were down to essentials. It was too much to have expected Loftus Allen to have produced in advance: "*Must we go by coach?*" for it was a question that only began to be asked, years later, when many cross-country railway services were dying on us. By that time, most of us were making such journeys in private motor-cars, and the buses, as well as the trains, were feeling the draught.

But in the 1930s, any move towards easier terms for railway transport was greeted with indignation. The enemy was counter-attacking, and – who knew?—it might be a counter-offensive which would hamstring a new, young, admirable individualistic, *modern* industry! Granting to the railways of general power to operate road motor services in 1928, and Acts of 1930 and 1933 for the licensing and regulation of passenger and goods motor services respectively, occasioned much virtuous anger. Certainly, railways had run motor buses long before this, and so had anyone else who could buy one. In the 'thirties it led rather to the acquisition by railway companies of controlling interests in the more respectable bus companies such as, in the case of the LMS, Crosville, North Western Road Car, and Scottish Motor Traction. Then the railway companies, collectively, launched a campaign under the slogan: *Give the Railways a Square Deal*! It was based on the business of rate fixing, and it was naturally disapproved of by the haulage people, certain of whom riposted with *Give the Railways a Square Wheel*! (A piece of wit scarcely worthy even of the Modern Remove in a great school chiefly interested in Classical education, but which made people laugh.) However; the landslide of international politics was about to sweep over us all, and for a while these things would not matter.

In the war which was just about to break, necessity would bring to the British railway companies traffic which – had not Government made a pretty piece of slick dealing – might have brought them riches beyond their most Victorian dreams of avarice. With it came postponement of improvement, and reductions in maintenance, which were possibly beyond their nightmares.

CHAPTER FIVE

Stanier's Time

So FAR, the locomotive history of the London, Midland & Scottish Railway has been, in general, simply stodgy for the most part, which did not include such flights as that curious symposium which produced the Royal Scots, and that *demarche* which resulted in Beyer-Garratt patent locomotives which might have been better as double-Prairies than as back-to-back Moguls. (One has heard that Robert Whitelegg was much put-out by Fowler's insistence on the use of as few axles as possible, with no intermediate trucks.) For the rest there had been at first synthetic Crewe and synthetic-Horwich practice, to be quickly followed by synthetic Derby. For all his virtues and talents, Sir Henry Fowler does not seem to adorn mechanical history like a Gooch, a Stirling or a Churchard. As to the real drawing-office work which went into the locomotives he produced, that must remain for the present anonymous, and possibly always will. Sir Ernest Lemon's locomotive career, as noted, was very brief. His virtues in other directions have been noted already, those of a great administrator of abounding energy. The LMS Locomotive Department was still oppressed by old, conflicting loyalties, and among Scotsmen there was a smouldering resentment at English interference and domination: Midland on the Caledonian, Midland on the Glasgow and South Western, and plain neglect (or so it was regarded) on the Highland, which the Euston Establishment was by now apt to regard simply as a long and troublesome branch line which achieved some ephemeral importance once a year when the Tory went for relaxation in the form of potting grouse and stalking stags (the latter being certainly the only civilised way of killing deer). To blow away the mists of old bad-neighbourly feelings, a *foreigner* alone would do! Certainly not a Crewe man, nor yet a Derby man! Nor yet a St. Rollox man! Not, indeed, from Batignolles or Munich or Sampier-darena, nor yet from Altoona; but Swindon was sufficiently foreign! Further, he must be an outstanding locomotive man with the tough part of his career behind him, and a strong man able to sweep aside ancient prejudice. Centuries ago, Egbert, King of Wessex, had swept aside the invidious jealousies of Jute, Angle and Mercian to become the first King of England. Even the Scots, who had known those admirable Kings MacBeth and Robert Bruce, must have sighed for *anything-for-a-change*!

So to the LMS came a Man of Wessex, William Arthur Stanier, who had been born in Swindon in 1876 and was growing up ere the broad gauge

132

died. Oswald Nock has already produced a most competent and elegant
work on Sir William Stanier[1], as he was to become later, so if succeeding
passages seem here and there sketchy, let the present author recommend
another for more detailed intelligence of this remarkable man!

He was big, long-headed as a horse, with a bay like an excited hound,
and the mind of a scientist trained by the study of physics and conditioned
by long practical experience. To an apprentice-draughtsman he could be
most alarming (like Daniel Gooch). Over many years your author met
him simply as reporter and broadcaster (c. 1932 onwards) and therefore
found his sudden bark less formidable, though commanding. As the
Great Western's Works Manager at Swindon he was undoubtedly in the
running as future CME, and Swindon men had the reputation of staying
with the old establishment. How, then, did he come to that administrative
shambles, the London Midland & Scottish Railway's CME Department?
It was far from being a happy outfit. Everybody not of the Midland was
irked by Midland methods, which as far back as 1923 had involved the
transfer of Running from the Chief Mechanical Engineer's to the Operating
side, exacerbating that ancient Loco-Traffic feud which had agitated
internal railway loyalties since much earlier days. Mr. Nock has already
remarked that ex-North Western and ex-Caledonian locomotive people
tended to become partisans of the Operating side if only to spite the Midland locomotive people with their insistence on new compound locomotives. True, the Midland small-engine policy was beginning to crack.
Though Deeley's old design for a compound 4–6–0 engine never was
carried out, Derby had now begun to produce, and beyond the paper
stage, a giant Midland compound; a Pacific. Full drawings were prepared.
Even the main frames of the new prototype were cut. Then, through that
mysterious and unholy alliance, the West Coast Confederacy struck; on
the Operating side. In September 1926, the Great Western four-cylinder
4–6–0 engine No. 5000, *Launceston Castle*, slipped quietly up to Willesden
by the North & South Western Junction and thence to the old "Camden
Loco". She ran in regular trials, first between Euston and Crewe, and
then over the old Northern Division to and from Carlisle. On the whole
the engine did the work very well indeed, so much so that the LMS
Superintendent of Motive Power said he "would not mind" having
twenty Great Western Castles for the 1927 summer traffic. What followed
was about as outrageous a snub to a Chief Mechanical Engineer from his
Management as the railway world had known since the Highland had
banned F. G. Smith's River class and dismissed its designer. Sir Henry
Fowler was bidden to stop all work on the compound Pacific and to
borrow Castle drawings from Swindon. The Great Western was in no
mind to oblige to such an extent as that. We have already seen how the

[1] *William Stanier – An Engineering Biography*, by O. S. Nock. London: Ian Allan, 1964.

Royal Scot class took shape with Southern progeniture, but the first part of the story is quoted here to indicate how W. A. Stanier's connection with the LMS really began.

Sir Josiah Stamp was clearly fed-up with the old loyalties, which certainly were a confounded nuisance to any party trying to run a great railway as an undivided undertaking. He once remarked that if he made an old London & North Western man CME, Crewe would have a banquet with fireworks afterwards. To an outside observer, had there been one fully in the know, the situation would have been just as absurd as it appeared to outside observers not in the know. Like unto the mutual hatred of Hindu and Mussulman was the feeling between Crewe and Derby, though physical violence and slicings were scarcely to be expected in a British Railway Locomotive Department, however divided. For a while, the puissant – but in their original state scarcely perfect – Royal Scots had saved Fowler's bacon, though Stamp is reputed to have had a sweet way of sacking people in an emergency; that of most courteously and very regretfully accepting, by confidential letter, a resignation that had not, in fact, been tendered. It is not yet politic to give an instance, or to disclose sources of information. The first step, as we know, was to make Fowler a Vice-President with Ernest Lemon succeeding him as CME. But still Lemon was a Midland man. His great administrative ability certainly qualified him – one opines much more – for a Vice-Presidency, leaving a clear field for a real foreigner, with no troublesome pre-group loyalties, to succeed as Chief Mechanical Engineer.

Stamp was in a strong position for power politics, being at this time both Chairman of the company and President of the Executive. What followed was a result of successive luncheon parties by way of weaning William Stanier from that Great Western Railway which he had already served for just under 40 years. Lemon invited Stanier to lunch at the Athenaeum, ostensibly for a talk on water-softening, in which the Great Western company had had long experience. But at the same businesslike junketting, a second guest was Sir Harold Hartley. As an old ICI man, he doubtless knew much about water-softening, but Stanier had not expected this co-guest, and wondered what was afoot.

Then there was another luncheon, this time at the Travellers Club. Again Stanier was the guest, and this time Hartley, the Vice-President, was his host. Perhaps cautiously, but surely unequivocally, Hartley suggested to his guest that wouldn't-it-be-nice if he were Chief Mechanical Engineer of the greatest railway company in the world – America included – and that if he stayed on the Great Western, he would have a long time to wait for the retirement of Churchward's successor at Swindon, C. B. Collett. Stanier was not so very much younger than Collett. If he stayed at Swindon, his ultimate reign might be relatively brief.

Stanier's loyalty to his own company, with which he had grown up, was unquestionable. He was doubtless fully aware of the hole-and-corner methods not disdained by the bitterly divided London Midland & Scottish people, but the offer was a very handsome one, and if he accepted it, he would be in a position of strength to end for ever the Derby-Crewe nonsense that had plagued the undertaking so long.

Stanier very properly would not move without his own people's knowledge. He told Collett what was toward. At a meeting of the latter, at Stanier's instance, with their General Manager, Sir James Milne; their Chairman Viscount Churchill also looked in. He saw that Stanier's command on the Great Western would be short unless Collett died or retired untimely. With a cordial Great Western blessing, Stanier went to the LMS while his predecessor there, Lemon, moved into that Vice-Presidency made vacant by the retirement of J. H. Follows. His succession took effect from January 1, 1932. His assignment was to produce powerful modern locomotives, which would be standardised and built on a large scale. Only thus could the LMS company's extraordinarily varied inheritance of engines from its constituents be thinned out and as quickly as possible replaced. The first pre-grouping casualties were to be Glasgow and South Western. It was a massacre. From 1930 one remembers ancient Stirlings knocking around. From 1935 one recalls looking in vain for what, twelve years before, had seemed the "Sou' West's" pride and joy. The end was achieved as soon as new engines came and multiplied; a combined end in greater availability, reduced running costs through time-off for repair, and longer mileages run in consequence of these. The secondary stage would be a considerable reduction in the total locomotive stock. At the end of 1931 the company had 9,032 locomotives in public service. That was but a relatively small reduction on the 10,278 which all its constituents had brought to it in their capital stocks. Such reductions as we have known, consequent on the change-over from steam to diesel on non-electrified lines, plus total closure of lines through motor advance, were as yet unthinkable.

As one who has heard Sir William Stanier thunder the name "Gooch!" like a Cornish Revolutionary shouting "Trelawney!" in 1688, one can imagine that all was not happy among the turbulently feuding people he came to command. It is impossible not to feel for Captain Beames who had been, so briefly, CME of the London & North Western, and now knew himself to be irrevocably on the CME shelf with the now venerable Hughes and Sir Henry Fowler. The mournful expression on one of his official photographs, however, long antedates this late disappointment. Now, to Stanier, he wrote an extraordinarily decent declaration of loyalty, not concealing his disappointment, but remarking[1] that: "There is no one

[1] cf. O. S. Nock.

I would rather serve under than you." With those eleven words, maybe, were dissolved the last shreds of the ancient Crewe-Swindon feud. For the Crewe-Derby feud, the worst on the railway, let Stanier be the executioner. He made Beames his Deputy. He made a Midland man, S. J. Symes, his Personal Assistant. H. Chambers, also a Derby man, came next as Technical Assistant and Chief Locomotive Draughtsman. Next came two London & North Western men: F. A. Lemon, Works Superintendent, and R. A. Riddles as Assistant Works Superintendent. Works Superintendent, Derby, was H. G. Ivatt from the North Stafford. Another Midland man, R. C. Bond, went as Assistant Works Superintendent, Horwich, where his Chief Draughtsman was T. F. Coleman from the North Stafford. Scotland had as Divisional Mechanical Engineer, Locomotive, Carriage and Wagons David Urie, already commanding St. Rollox, and, as previously noted, briefly the last Locomotive Superintendent of the Highland Railway. On the whole it was as statesmanly a selection as one could have expected from a Great Western man, and much better than any of the by-now-boring warring parties.[1] Ivatt and Riddles were both ultimately to assume the purple in one place or another; the former on the LMS before it was done. D. C. Urie died untimely, though much later than this. He was the last of the old Scots CMEs, son of that Robert Urie who had put up with Dugald Drummond for so long, even following him from the Caledonian to the London & South Western to be his ultimate – and rather adequate – successor after many patient years: (they had one real stand-up row, which resolved things)[2]. Great names in the second generation were already emerging. Ivatt was to be the last LMS Chief Mechanical Engineer; he was already brother-in-law to the last of the Grand Originals in that calling.[3] Riddles was to be British Railways' man in the last years of steam, though his originality may have been stultified by that very democracy for which we were fighting in the 'forties, which could have a dead hand like any other ideal. Bulleid on the Southern foresaw this, which is why he went to Inchicore. These things, however, are a long way ahead; indeed outside this essay.

Midland influence on Running we have already seen, and J. E. Anderson, sometime Fowler's Deputy at Derby, had been in command of it since the Grouping. Late in 1932 he retired. Stanier placed Urie in succession. Ivatt went to St. Rollox. An interesting *coda* to the Derby-Crewe clash: Chambers, from Derby, went as noted to Crewe, and there his shoulder had to bear the main weight of carrying out the new chief's standardisation programme, involving what Crewe, Derby, St. Rollox and Horwich all regarded, at first, anyway, as synthetic Swindon designs. Yet these were

[1] Acknowledgement to O. S. Nock.
[2] Acknowledgement to Jock Urie, of Brighton.
[3] Oliver Bulleid, of Eastleigh and of Inchicore.

to be the first genuine LMS steam locomotives (unless one counts the Royal Scots, which were by Ashford out of Springburn). As these appeared, there was more heavy slaughter of the old stagers, and the heaviest casualties, to the surprise and dismay of those who loved them, were to be in the ranks of London & North Western engines. By 1943 there was to be but one Claughton class engine left, No. 6004 *Princess Louise*, rebuilt with the larger boiler, but this aged princess further survived to be taken into British Railways stock in 1948, when, to be sure, there were many other engines much more aged. Locomotives were not lightly demolished in the war years.

Both professional and amateur, outside the LMS organisation, had the liveliest curiosity as to what the new Chief would do in the way of design. We rather expected a strong Swindon flavour, just as our fathers had expected – and got – enhanced Caledonian locomotives on the London & South Western in the late 'nineties. The initial two new babies, however, were pretty clearly from an earlier sire. The first was as generally common-place a little pug – o–4–o shunting saddle tank engine – as one might see butting about ironworks or colliery. There were five such – 15½ by 20in, 3ft 10in, 160 lb – built by Kitsons of Leeds in 1932, and numbered 1540/4 (later 7000/4). The final engine had a gadget by the British Smoke Eliminator Company, which mixed boiler steam with pre-heated air from nozzles under the smokebox front and thence injected to the firebox. Walter Chalmers, sometime of the North British Railway, had, one is told, something to do with it. Two official photographs were sent out, one with the engine shrouded in black smoke and the other showing her as chaste-looking as you please; the "before and after use" sort of thing. The amateurs, however, were chiefly engaged by a very plain chimney suggestive of certain Indian State Railways, and foresaw the LMS under Stanier looking something like the GIP. The present author wrote a short anonymous piece in *The Railway Magazine* (February 1933), to which Mr. Consulting Editor added a remark on the shape of the "stovepipe" chimney with the posterior question: "A portent?"

Of course, the chimney was not a stovepipe. The Ashover Railway once had some – made in America, where the form was called quite properly *straight-stack* – but otherwise it was extremely rare in British locomotive design. The true stovepipe is absolutely cylindrical. In amateur circles there was a preoccupation with the shapes of locomotive chimneys so pronounced that one feels that Freud might have had some valuable things to say about it, though the only important concerns were those of efficiency and aesthetics. The same sort of chimney – only longer – distinguished the second locomotive design of Stanier's time – again in no way way "designed" by him, though some may have been misled by misprinted suggestions of a 30in stroke which indeed conveyed something

E*

of old Swindon. This design comprised ten o–4–4 tank engines, a sort of supplement to the old, and still numerous Midland type of S. W. Johnson, but combining 18in by 26in cylinders with 5ft 7in drivers. These rather nice-looking little locomotives (apart from much improved cabs they were not as comely as the more curvaceous Midland ones) were used chiefly on pull-and-push branch trains, and were to be seen as near to London as on the little Stanmore line from Harrow-and-Wealdstone.[1] Lemon's legacy?

Stanier's first original designs began with a useful 2–6–0 mixed-traffic to supplement the Hughes-Fowler 13000 class and numbered in the same series from 13245 upwards. Forty were built from 1933 onwards (later numbers 2945–2984), and, as people had expected, there was a very strong Great Western flavour about them, though the outside Walschaert gear was out of Swindon character. The tapered domeless boiler was there, and the horizontal cylinders. A few even had the safety-valves mounted between the top-feed clacks in true Swindon style, though the styling was much less florid. The chimney, for example, was distinctly Swindonian, but without the great copper cap; where the safety-valves were mounted amidships, there was a small dome-shaped casing with a big slot in the top instead of the Great Western's classic "milk-can". (Even this last made a very brief apparition, then was hurried out of sight.)

Most engines, however, followed existing LMS practice in having the Ross pop safety valves, uncased, over the firebox, with an even smaller dummy dome between the clacks. The tenders were pure Derby. Vital statistics of these rather plain maid-servants included 18in by 28in cylinders (compared with 21in by 26in in the Thirteen-hundreds), 225lb pressure compared with 180lb, the same 5ft 6in coupled wheels on 16ft 6in base, and markedly different boiler dimensions. For evaporative heating surface was 1,411 sq ft and superheating surface down to 193 sq ft, quite in Churchward tradition. High pressure and low superheat! The first ten were originally allocated to the Northern Division, the next twelve to the Midland, the next thirteen to the Western and the last five to the Central. The engines were classified 5F. They did not, like their Hughes-Fowler predecessors, haul express trains north of Perth; one remembers them chiefly in ordinary freight service, but also in slow passenger service, notably over and through the Pennines.

What so many of us awaited in 1933 was that by-now-legendary LMS Pacific, which we had first expected as a giant Midland compound, and then, after Stanier's succession, as a modern version of the Great Western engine *The Great Bear*, of 1908. Your author believes that he and his colleague the late J. Kenneth Taylor,[2] were among the very first to see

[1] This was slowly starved by the Metropolitan/London Transport Stanmore branch; a late instance of one railway killing another.

[2] Sometime Assistant Editor, *The Railway Gazette*, following the death of J. F. Gairns at the end of 1930.

this great engine enter London, for each morning we used the same
Dorking line train on the Southern Railway, and we conspired to play
truant from our irascible employer.[1] So we saw that great works-grey
engine limp apologetically into Euston with a hot box developed somewhere north of King's Langley, and later saw our more dutiful colleagues
turn up for an official view. As for the engine, she had no name yet,
though soon after she became *The Princess Royal*, which name had been
borne long ago by one of Ramsbottom's "Problems" on the London &
North Western. No: she was not *The Great Bear* warmed-up! As to her
machinery, one might have called her an elongated Great Western "King"
with more boiler and firebox supported on a massive supplementary frame
over a trailing axle. Her appearance was certainly of Great Western sort,
for all the severe finish, and like too many Great Western engines, it was
spoilt by what seemed a paltry tender; (but then I grew up with big bogie
tenders; whether British or German!). Later, the LMS Pacifics received
rather better ones, carrying 4,000 gallons and 10 tons; this, to be sure, was
simply a matter of increased bunker capacity to the extent of one ton on
top of the tank, which incidentally improved the appearance of the
general *ensemble*. Main dimensions of this very handsome design are given
in Table 3, though it may be remarked here that high pressure (250lb)
was combined with a low superheating surface – 370 sq ft – added to an
evaporative heating surface of 2,713 sq ft. Nominally, as suggested, *The
Princess Royal* was but equal in power to her father *King George V* on the
Great Western Railway, with four cylinders 16¼in by 88in; *ceteris* more-
or-less *paribus* apart from the considerably greater boiler dimensions.
Placing the outside cylinders over the second bogie axle and thus in rear
of the inside pair, with divided drive, followed the arrangement of the
successive Great Western four-cylinder designs and of the de Glehn-du
Bousquet compound engines of France, which Churchward had sampled
and closely studied, while afterwards sticking to simple expansion. A
feature not previously seen in British home practice was the combination
of a wide-grate firebox and ashpan overlapping supplementary outside
frames with the flat Belpaire top, an arrangement characteristic of the
Pennsylvania Railroad in the United States but generally rare. Alfred de
Belpaire, of course, had used it long ago in Belgium. On the Great
Western, *The Great Bear* had certainly had a wide Belpaire firebox, but with
inside frames and bearings throughout. Stanier did not perpetuate the
Churchward and Collett practice of using two sets of inside Walschaerts
gear to work four valves; there were inside and outside sets.

Minor features included one that was agreeable to many people. The
Princess mounted a deep-toned Caledonian type whistle instead of the

---

[1] John A. Kay, Managing Director and Editor-in-Chief, *The Railway Gazette*. He did not
officially notice the truancy, though neither truant was in great favour at the time.

usual English shrieking article. This may have been due to American derision at the Royal Scot's squealer on her memorable tour of the States and Canada. Sometime after that a range of available whistles had been connected up to a main steampipe at, I believe, Horwich, and given a critical audition by the company's important personages. It is most probable that David Urie favoured the deep Caledonian hoot, but it took Stanier to impose it on the railway as a standard form for all new engines. An even more alien, and admirable, feature was the use of Timken roller bearings for the tender axles. This form was already much liked in the States, where it was further pushed by the usual high-powered publicity.[1]

Two of these engines were built in 1933 and ten more in 1935. One number in the series 6200–6212 – 6202 – was abstracted for a turbine locomotive, of which more later. The Princess Royal class was exclusively named for royal ladies, including one queen (of Norway) but having already made some comment on, and a considerable list of, engine names, henceforward let the author list them separately (Appendix C). The original pair, after initial trials and running in, went straight to the West Coast expresses for which they had been designed, and the others were to follow them. They were adequate locomotives; double-heading could be cut down. They were not prone to ailments. Their suspension in particular gave very sweet riding at all speeds. On a basis of engine-weight only, these were the largest British express engines yet built.

Now many people of whose business it was none, from official point of view, were wondering what would be the result of Churchward ideas on superheating when applied to the Midlands and Scotland. The ratio of superheater to tube heating surface was 0·146 in a Princess, but 0·005 more than in a Great Western King, against 0·221 in a Royal Scot, and the LMS main line was not run exclusively on the best South Wales steam coal. The thing about Swindon's low degree of superheat was that it worked demonstrably well so long as the boiler made plenty of steam. Firing a box with softish coal, on a grate area of 45 sq ft, was no mean job. The trick was to fire heavily at the back of the box. Old London & North Western practice was even firing. The engines did well in steady running without prolonged heavy pulling. But Carlisle to Euston could be an ordeal, with steam enough, maybe, but none to spare; (one's remoter recollections of the London & North Western Railway include what seemed a perpetual roar of safety valves; only the London Brighton and South Coast was like it, and on one's own native railway under Dugald Drummond it was a bookable offence!)

Formidable as he might have been, Stanier was a statesmanly man. He

---

[1] A widely circulated photograph showed a few gentle girls, nicely got up in their best hats and coats, apparently pushing without unladylike effort an enormous Timken-fitted American locomotive.

had a different country to deal with, often different fuel, and different men from those of Wessex, and he studied these things carefully. Lesser men, thus migrated, had sometimes failed to do so in the past, and had fallen. A Princess behaved well on the West Coast main line when driven with a short cut-off and the regulator wide open. LMS enginemen learned how not to fire one as if she were a Claughton. But clearly a higher superheating surface was desirable, if all was to be well on such variety as Yorkshire and Midland coal at Camden, and Scots soft at Polmadie, as well as the familiar Welsh at Crewe. Further, the small superheater was found to be causing a positive stricture on the steam-flow. In a boiler mounted on the original engine in 1935, the number of flues was doubled, with a necessary reduction in the ordinary flues; at the same time the distance between tubeplates was considerably reduced. Combined heating surface went down, but the ratio of superheater to tube heating surface went up. Outwardly the boiler presented no different aspect; it was still domeless, though in this respect Stanier was to break farther away from Swindon practice. The second boiler was a great improvement on the original, although, in retrospect and from study of performance, it cannot be said to have been the last word, and of course quickly subsequent mechanical history of the LMS was to show that it was not. Nevertheless, the Princesses were now trustworthy, which is more than some princesses have been since the Maid of Norway died of seasickness before she could be married to the King of Scots; to mention a more respectable tragic example.

All was well for the present. The 1935 Princesses had the new boiler. The terrors of Shap and Beattock waned. As importantly, maintenance costs went down. The engines in this more or less final form enabled, in 1936, some acceleration of the "Mid-day Scott", with an additional stop at Penrith as well as the old one at Lancaster, 59 minutes being allowed for the 51·2 miles between the two places, which entailed the ascent of Grayrigg at rather more than 40 mph minimum speed, with at least fourteen coaches.

About this time there were changes in the CME's Department. R. A. Riddles became Stanier's Locomotive Assistant and then, Captain Beames having retired, his Principal Assistant (August 1935). In March of that year, Herbert Chambers became Stanier's Locomotive and Personal Assistant, but he was a sick man in the hour of his promotion, and had less influence than he could have hoped-for when younger and stronger. T. F. Coleman (from Stoke via Horwich) had succeeded him as Chief Draughtsman – that very significant office – and Riddles' place as Assistant Works Superintendent, Crewe, went to R. C. Bond. These made Stanier's top team in the middle 'thirties. It should be added that in 1936 Stanier himself was in India to serve on the Pacific Locomotive Committee, appointed in connection with certain very serious accidents with new standard Indian State locomotives.

The foregoing notes relate to the human background of the mechanical approach to much higher speeds which distinguished both the British northern lines during the late 1930s. Initial tests to this end were with the Princesses. The second engine of the class, No. 6201 *Princess Elizabeth*, was rebuilt with yet another modification of the original boiler, retaining the original length of tubes and flues, and firebox heating surface, but with the great superheater ratio (not identical with the second Princess boiler). All three sets of boiler dimensions are given in Appendix A. In this boiler a dome was mounted in rear of the top-feed, and this feature was to endure in Stanier's later practice. The Great Western attitude to domes had been that they were only necessary on boilers of very limited steam space, whereon they were quite logically made as large as possible; bigger than anybody else's.

Before we consider the later development of the standard LMS Pacific, let us recall what happened to that vacant space in the earlier one's numbers.

Since the pre-1914 years, steam turbine propulsion had attracted designers, whenever and wherever someone would put up the money to build an immensely expensive locomotive. In all the earlier attempts (apart from some primitive curiosities) arrangements for condensing the exhaust had been an essential part of the box-of-tricks, and electrical transmission a favourite adjunct also. An early visitor on the LMS network had been Ramsay's second turbine locomotive. Much work had been done in Germany and Switzerland, without lasting results and perhaps as notably as anywhere in Sweden by Ljungström. Beyer, Peacock and Company had built a Ljungström condensing turbine locomotive which had indeed worked regular passenger trains on the Midland main line between Manchester and London; but nobody bought it. But at the end of the 1920s there appeared in Sweden the non-condensing turbine locomotive. The Grängesberg–Oxelösund Railway, a most businesslike undertaking chiefly engaged in working heavy iron-ore trains from the Bergslag to the Baltic, and therefore, under its CME Harry Johnson, unlikely to fool-about with cranky things, had one built in 1929. Two followed in 1936. They were arranged 2–8–0, and at the time of writing are still in existence on the reserve, though the line has been electric for some time now. Transmission was unusually simple, through triple reduction gears to a jackshaft ahead of the coupled wheels. At the instance of Dr. (later Sir) Henry Guy of Metropolitan-Vickers, Stanier visited Harry Johnson at Eskilstuna – headquarters of the Grängesberg company – to see the first of these Swedish engines at work on 1,500 ton ore trains. A very marked reduction in maintenance owing to the lack of reciprocating parts, with well lubricated gears totally enclosed, was one great virtue of the design. The Swedish engine had been subjected to searching tests before taking its regular turn with the standard Johnson o–8–o ore engines, which probably explains why its date has often been given as 1932 instead of 1929. Dynamometer tests showed a 7¼ per cent saving in fuel and 15 per cent in water. The geared turbine drive gave no trouble. It is fortunate that such a prosperous company as the Grängesberg–Oxelösund undertook such experiments, but unfortunate that they were in a country already so deeply committed to expanding electric traction.

Derby Drawing Office, on Stanier's return, got to work on modifying the general design of the Princess Royal class, of which a spare set of frames had already been made, while Dr. Guy, Metrovick's turbine designer, took on that of the turbines, of which the engine was to have one large sixteen-stage one for forward running, on the left side, and a smaller one on the right for working in reverse, normally while running light to or from sheds. In practice, the lack of hammerblow in a "turbo-motive" permitted the raising of the maximum axle-loads from 22 tons 10cwt. to 24 tons. Transmission was through double helical triple-reduction gears, not to a jackshaft as in the Swedish engine, but to the leading coupled axle. To the uninstructed, No. 6202, as she became, looked like an inside-cylinder Pacific with some mysteriously cased apparatus on and below the platforms. Unlike every other turbine locomotive that had gone before – with the exception of the nearly symmetrical but very disappointing Reid-MacLeod engine in Scotland – this was a very handsome locomotive.

Originally there was a domeless boiler generally like that in the Princess Royal as modified, with a 32-element superheater, but with rather different arrangement of the small tubes and, further, a double blastpipe and a double chimney. Some modifications of the draught were needed to suit the continuous exhaust of a non-condensing turbine, and at first there was some trouble from exhaust clouds beating down, later rectified – as far as this problem ever was so with big smokeboxes and short chimneys – by the provision of side-deflectors of German sort, which the Southern Railway had taken up in England during the late 1920s.

In June 1935, the Turbomotive (horrid word, but everybody used it!) went into service, and showed herself capable of anything any other LMS express engine could do. One recalls with retrospective affection the rising hum – very brief – as she was given steam. Not yet had we come to associate a syren sound with less pleasant prospects than those of a journey up the West Coast. This was a very soft, gentle syren, bedded in the other noises of a big engine getting a massive train under way at the foot of a formidable gradient. Many people never noticed it, for tone-deafness, like colour-blindness, is a defect commoner than is generally realised; many a soldier has marched to drums alone, and loved them; many a traveller cannot understand why other travellers enthuse over Lochaber although they know the Bernese Oberland.

For the first four years of her existence, the turbine locomotive managed an annual average of 54,205 miles compared with some 80,000 from the Princess Royal class (73,268 miles in 1936)[1] which was very creditable indeed for a locomotive of isolated design, whose only near-prototypes were three smaller and markedly different engines hauling iron ore in Sweden. Mr. Nock remarks that lack of experience with turbine propulsion may have made the maintenance staff over cautious. After war had begun, No. 6202 was temporarily stored, but stored engines are an incubus in wartime. She returned and in the late 'forties was often to be seen – day after day – on the London–Merseyside trains; to the marked interest, one recalls, of some American soldiers. There were some bad failures, including an alarming breakage of the forward turbine spindle at full speed, but subject to the supply of spare parts by Metropolitan-Vickers – which naturally had many other things to do without copious staff – the engine was maintained and, all-in-all, fought a good war.

A later boiler had a 40-element superheater which at the same time slightly decreased the superheating surface (594 sq ft to 577 sq ft) and a third arrangement with triple elements brought it up to 823 sq ft.

The ultimate sad fate of this locomotive is too well-known for much comment. When the turbines were worn out she was rebuilt as an ordinary Princess by British Railways, with the name *Princess Anne*, and as such was almost immediately damaged beyond economic repair in the Harrow double-collision of October 8, 1952. One feels that but for the fortuity of mechanical history, the thing might have gone much farther and with advantage. No more successful turbine locomotive ever ran in express passenger service, and over many years at that.

Back in the 1920s, as noted, the LMS has stolen a march on the London & North Eastern by running non-stop to Edinburgh in an entirely exhibition-sort of run, truly in the old West Coast tradition. But in 1935, the East Coast company had certainly got-in-first with its "Silver Jubilee" streamlined steam service between Thames and Tyneside. Such services were clearly in the wind for both Anglo-Scottish services thereafter. Gresley on the LNER had a special engine ready-made and proved. Stanier had not, and that must be rectified. The outcome, as we know, was the running of the East Coast company's "Coronation" train between London and Edinburgh, and the LMS "Coronation Scot" between London and Glasgow, both in 1937. As to the runs of these two trains, the LMS one, on June 29, preceded that of the LNER by one day.

[1] R. C. Bond: *Journal Inst.Loco.E.,* 1946.

Both were in regular service on July 5. But one must go somewhat back to the origin of Stanier's contribution.

At the back-end of 1936, Stanier was in India, on the Wedgwood Committee appointed to inquire into the working of Indian State-owned railways, which had been showing what was for those days an alarming deficit. He had left S. J. Symes, the company's Chief Stores Super-intendent, in deputy-command, though his Principal Assistant, R. A. Riddles, and his Chief Locomotive Draughtsman, T. Coleman, were jointly responsible for the mechanical side. On November 15, *Princess Elizabeth*, and the dynamometer car (ex L&Y) were at Willesden, ready for a test to show what a Princess could do. At the last minute, she was found to be suffering from a leaking joint in the main steampipe. This engine *must* go! She was equipped for the test as none of the others. It was R. C. Bond who saved the situation, with the help of a bewildered guest at teatime in Crewe and a retired storekeeper, with whose blindly loyal help a spare ring was unearthed from one of Crewe's fearsome labyrinths (with the aid of a box of vestas) and, with a couple of minutes at most to spare, given to the driver of the 6.40 pm up train, to be delivered to the anxious Riddles on the platform at Euston, and to none other. It was done. Riddles and other devoted people sat up – or more properly, stood up – with the engine most of the night, and by morning Elizabeth had recovered from her self-operated tracheotomy. That day she ran from London Euston to Glasgow Central with 225 tons behind the tender, including the dynamometer car of course, in 5hr 53⅔min for the 401·4 miles, or at an average speed of 68·2 mph. There was a dinner in Glasgow, with Ernest Lemon presiding and the enginemen as guests of honour. Tom Clarke was the driver. During the dinner, Riddles had a note that the left outside crosshead slipper, having run hot, had lost its white metal. The engine was at Polmadie. Lemon told Riddles he was looking tired and sent him off to bed about ten o'clock. He (Riddles) had already sent a reply that the engine be got immediately to St. Rollox. Thither he went, when Lemon supposed him to be in his pyjamas, and there he spent the night with brief sleep, after the job was done, on a works bench. Gunmetal strips had saved the steel of the crosshead from touching, at very high piston speed, that of the slidebars, otherwise there would have been trouble indeed.

Next day, in very dirty weather, the engine ran with 255 tons (an extra coach) from Central to Euston at a start-to-stop average of 70 mph. Down at Crewe, Bond took Mrs. Bond out to Minshull Vernon to see her go by at 95 mph. He had no inkling of the laborious sport which had been going on at St. Rollox, but was made happy by the spectacle. At Euston, Lemon asked Riddles why he had been a minute down at Carstairs.

Having praised Lemon as an administrator and as a practical economist, perhaps one may read from that snappish inquiry the reason why he was not, nor ever might have been, a great locomotive man. For the present chronicle, its author has rarely been much stirred by speed for speed's sake, which, except when it comes to escaping from someone or something, seems basically a juvenile aspiration, especially pernicious since mass-produced motor cars became available to the Many. All the same, he finds this performance stimulating in retrospect. Very noteworthy were the summit speeds of 57 and 56 mph at Shap and Beattock Summits respectively, going north, and 70 mph at both going south. On the southbound run, *Princess Elizabeth* averaged 74·8 mph from Lamington to the Beattock Summit box (13·5 miles). These things seem much more impressive than the relatively facile *ton-up*.

Before going to India, Stanier had laid down the general design of an improved Pacific type locomotive for the regular high-speed Anglo-Scottish services to come, and the final design had been worked out by and under T. F. Coleman. Boiler dimensions showed a marked increase on those of the Princesses; though the distance between tube-plates remained the same, at 19 ft 3in. Heating surfaces rose from 1,272 to 1,545 sq ft (small tubes), from 825 to 1,032 sq ft (flues), from 217 to 230 sq ft (firebox), from 653 to 830 sq ft (superheating), giving a combined heating surface of 3,637 sq ft, an increase of 670 sq ft over that of a Princess with the later boiler. Grate area was up from 45 to 50 sq ft. Working pressure in both was 250lb per sq in.

There was a ring from Swindon in the coupled wheels' diameter, which was up to 6ft 9in. Important improvements were in the front-end which was designed on a very liberal plan for the free flow of steam (internal streamlining was the gimmick word of the time, and was not inapt for the steampipes and exhaust passages. The piston valves were increased from 8in to 9in diameter. Design of the exhaust ports resulted in a very marked reduction of resistance to steam flow, as much 23–37 per cent. Much was owed to the work of André Chapelon in France, as Stanier himself freely recorded.[1] Another Great Western feature resuscitated, though *inside-out*, was the use of two sets of Walschaert gear to work the four sets of valves. The outside cylinders were now ahead of the second bogie axle instead of directly above it. A good deal of care had been taken with the design of that bogie, not least in the control of sideplay. The flanges were made larger and *tighter* as to clearance between wheel and rail. Swindon practice in leading bogies, often archaic in earlier Great Western days, owed almost everything to Alfred George de Glehn, that Baltic-Scot generally regarded as a Frenchman, who was improbably born in Sydenham, Surrey. Churchward at Swindon, having purchased a de Glehn–du

---

[1] Presidential Address to the Institution of Locomotive Engineers, 1929.

Bousquet compound Atlantic engine (*La France*) had initiated her English career by carrying out a complete dismemberment of her to see what made her go.[1]

The result, on the LMS was an extraordinarily steady engine at very high speeds. Careful attention had been given to the design of the trailing-axle arrangement, again with thicker flanges, and to the design and dimensions of the axleboxes. Lateral oscillation at high speed was the enemy, as it had been from such long-ago bitter experience with Stephenson "long boilers" in the late 'forties and Crampton's 4-4-0 bogie engines on the London Chatham and Dover in the 'sixties, *inter alia pessima*. Already there was the Indian row about this very thing on the Indian State Pacific locomotives; following the issue of the first Report in the summer of 1937, there was a frightful smash (July 17) at Bihta on the East Indian Railway, a derailment on straight road with a deathroll exceeding 100. In 1938, following this, Stanier was again in India, on an independent Committee of Inquiry (English, French and Indian) appointed under Indian Government. Vernacular newspapers, incidentally, were fond of blaming the *diabolical Government*, whose object was supposed to be the annihilation of as many of the Indian poor as possible at the trifling expense of damage to Pacific locomotives and expendable gimcrack carriages. India's sorrows, however, must be passed by.

Between these events, the new LMS Pacific locomotive, not to be prone to such misfortunes and further favoured by a way somewhat more substantially permanent than that of the EIR, took real shape. Streamlining was much in the air. All sorts of vulgar essays were about, purporting to be "streamlining". The science has remote origins in shipbuilding (*head of a codfish, tail of a mackerel*) and made a logical advance centuries later with certain airships, beginning with that of the Brothers Renard and Captain Krebs during 1884-85, when their aircraft was the world's first to make a powered flight with return to starting point. Once one forgets commercial ballyhoo, how closely the branches of scientific transport knit together! It was the expanding aircraft industry, under the stimulant of war, that perfected and made the first proper use of the *wind-tunnel*, over half a century ago. And it was experiment with the wind-tunnel that determined the shape of the casing put over these new LMS Pacific locomotives. (No insult is intended to Gresley and Bulleid on the neighbouring London & North Eastern, who got the idea of an aerofoil which, of course, is something designed to give lift!) The object of streamlining is that of reducing to a minimum the resistance of inert air to an object passing through it.

So the *Coronation* took shape. One recalls one of her sisters on exhibition at Euston with the previous *Coronation* (a George the Fifth 4-4-0 of 1911)

[1] Re-erected, *La France* ran for many years.

and some much older veterans like *Cornwall* and *Coppernob*. Harking back once again to gas-sustained aircraft, the engine looked more like the original parallel Zeppelin airship than the more graceful great fish of the skies, such as the Parsifals, but the shape pleased those responsible for the wind-tunnel tests as well as the then ageing C. F. Dendy Marshall, learned author of *The Resistance of Express Trains*. While on the subject of appearances, let us recall that the entire "Coronation" train, with its smooth, aproned carriages, was painted in Prussian blue with silver streaks extending back in ruthless parallel from an inverted prow-point on the rounded casing over the smokebox door. The smokebox proper had a depressed top to fit into that nose, which, later, when casings werere moved, sadly spoiled the aspect of a singularly beautiful design. The design was at first called the Princess-Coronation Class, a cumbersome and preposterous title. The sixth, however, having been named *Duchess of Gloucester*, they ultimately became the Duchess class, so let us use that term henceforward.

The special rakes for the Coronation expresses generally followed what had been standard LMS practice from 1932 onwards, with flush sides including the end vestibules, these rakes had better be described now. Both side-corridor and open-aisle carriages were used, marshalled, from the tender going north, in this order: corridor brake-first-class, corridor first, first-class diner, kitchen car, open third, kitchen car, open third, corridor brake third, all except the kitchen cars having forced ventilation. The train was thus light, taring only 297 tons, which (in Kipling's words somewhere else) *was what the Mess intended*. In America, people hesitated to trust their persons in a train that did not tare under 80 tons per car, and had already remarked that the visiting Royal Scot would crumple up in a wreck. Furnishing of the usual LMS main line sort served the third-class passengers, which meant that each compartment seated three a side, with intermediate armrests, on well-sprung moquette overlay. Someone in *The New Statesman and Nation* remarked the discomfort of this company-owned train.[1] Visiting foreigners, as so often before or since, were captivated by the good seating which did not have to be quitted for meals. The first-class compartments seated but four each, one person per corner. Handsome veneers went into the generally plain decorative scheme; some, in a third-class car of each set, was made from Canadian silver elm cut from the original piles of Rennie's Waterloo Bridge, then lately demolished. The wood had been in the Thames mud from 1817 to 1936, and came up very nicely. Much use was made of tubular strip lighting, though not yet of the fluorescent sort. The general decoration was of that middle-1930s sort which your author still finds singularly obnoxious. It was, however, the sort of thing the majority was supposed to like, and

---

[1] A Dutt-Paukerism (acknowledgement to Peter Simple) which perhaps cast the first seed of doubt in the mental soil of a Third-Generation Radical.

British fashion in furnishing, just then, dwelt in the tents of the Philistines. Quite possibly it was really the *New Statesmanly* eye, rather than the limbs and back, that was offended, but if so, the criticism partook of a prevarication. The paper was generally good on aesthetics.

On June 29, there was a demonstration run with the "Coronation Scot" from London to Crewe and back. On the trains were numerous big guns of one sort and another, quite apart from competent reporters. Derek Barrie and Cecil J. Allen shared a compartment – with retrospectively funny results a little later – and S. P. W. Corbett was also timing the train, to compare notes after. Up in the leading brake coach was Oswald Nock, complete with clock. The present author was in Sweden at the time.[1]

With passengers, the load behind the tender was about 270 tons. T. J. Clarke was Driver, and J. Lewis, Fireman. Speed at the top of the Camden bank was a decorous 32 mph. Observers had been told in advance of a 95 mph maximum with the same engine, hauling 300-tons-plus, on the flat between Weedon and Blisworth. Nock has recorded that he expected something between Tring and Bletchley, and the engine averaged just over 80 mph from Harrow to Tring. But matters remained, for the present, decorous, with a maximum of 89 south of Cheddington. The Rugby and Stafford slacks were punctiliously observed, at 39 and 30 mph respectively; then the romp began. After Norton Bridge, which was passed at 60 mph, there was steady acceleration over the 17·1 miles to Milepost 156, on the descent from Madeley, and but 2·1 miles short of Crewe. At the top of the climb to Whitmore, speed was at 85 mph., at Madeley it was 94·5, at Betley Road it was 108. At Milepost 156 the three timers first noted, concurred on 113 mph. Just after that, with facing crossovers ahead, one of these devoted watchers shouted to another, with barrack-room emphasis, to get on the floor. The other was criticising his choice of adjectives when the train went through the crossover. Both, and some others, were then on the floor in a mixed-up heap. Kitchenwards was a crash as of ten dinner-services hitting the bottom of a lift shaft. On the engine the Hasler speed recorder touched 114 mph.

At Crewe, people awaited the end with alarm and dismay. The ambulance men went to action stations.

There was no disaster, probably thanks to the excellent design of the bogie and the trailing axle arrangements, already noted, for the engine stayed steady under circumstances which had upset other unfortunates, as in the unholy trinity at Salisbury, Grantham and Shrewsbury some thirty years before. At Crewe, the train rather overshot. Not much was said about it at the time, at any rate publicly. The last 10·6 miles to that abrupt halt had been covered in 7 minutes 6 seconds. Looking at the thing in cold blood, it was a fortunate escape from the business angle. A smash

[1] He wishes he could have recorded at first-hand some of the incidental happenings.

at that speed would have put back fast inter-city services for some years, long enough for war to overtake them and, when all that was over, to restart railway express services with a very severe handicap in their coming competition with internal airlines. Is it possible that, had there been derailment on that first crossover, electrification of the old London & North Western line would not have happened in the 1960s? Perhaps fancy? People soon forget. But such an accident would have come at the very worst time, as did the London & North Western derailment at Preston, so soon after the 1895 Race to Aberdeen, and the consequences would have been far more serious, for that race of the 'nineties had been of little importance save to company prestige and to the sporting element.

Brief details of this run: Euston to Crewe, 158·1 miles, the start-to-stop speed had been 73·1 mph; 158·1 miles in 129 min. 46 sec. Cecil J. Allen, whose figures these are, expressed himself with diplomatic mildness about the tumbling he had experienced, and as befitted an Inspector of Permanent Way Materials credited the excellence of the track on that facing crossover for the behaviour of the train at what he delicately called *higher than normal speed*. The train had averaged 100 mph for ten miles from Milepost 147 south of Whitmore. The return trip on the same day, with the same engine and train, was faster start-to-stop, without such a dizzy maximum. The 158·1 miles were covered in exactly 119 minutes. There was very striking acceleration up the Madeley Bank out of Crewe, with 74 mph up the three miles at 1 in 177. Speed on Whitmore Troughs was 80·5 mph. Thereafter, on level or on slight favourable gradients, speed was in the nineties again and again, with a maximum of 100 mph at Castlethorpe.

Too many trains had hit the Euston bufferstops in the past century for there to be any sort of a flying finish as at Crewe on the northbound run. But still the train was running at 96 through Harrow, 95 at Wembley and 85 (service slack) at Willesden, with 79 at Kilburn.

The summer timetable began on July 5, with the "Coronation Scot" times to and from Glasgow at 6½ hours with one stop at Carlisle. Start-to-stop speeds were 63·4 mph south of Carlisle and 58·5 north thereof. As might have been expected, there was some rearrangement of the "Mid-day Scot" – the old Corridor – still leaving at 2.0 pm and now a London–Edinburgh express with restaurant car throughout, to remind the East Coast outfit that it had no monopoly of capital cities. But the "Mid-day Scot's" Perth and Aberdeen portion now went out of Euston as an addition to the 1.35 (previously 1.30 pm) express to Barrow and Windermere and thus bridged a gap in that service between Oxenholme and Lockerbie. It reached Perth at 10.40 pm, at which time there was little to do in that charming city apart from going to bed, cheered perhaps by a dram of such whisky as one has not yet bought on a train, though this one liberally carried a restaurant car throughout. The LMS proudly offered a

whisky most auspiciously called *Royal Scot*, as does it successor under
State ownership, and that is very nice to be sure, even though it be not
malt. All is not beer that bitters, if it comes to that. Arrival in Aberdeen
at 3.0 am off the 11·0 pm from Glasgow (Buchanan Street), was not a sane
man's way of going to Aberdeen from London.

Much more important were improved Lancashire–Scotland services,
leaving Manchester (Exchange) at 4.45 pm and Liverpool (Lime Street) at
five o'clock, both with coaches for Edinburgh and Glasgow, which were
added to the "Mid-day Scot" at Wigan and Lancaster. From Liverpool to
Edinburgh there was now a saving of 53 minutes, with an overall time of
4hr 40min, the shortest yet. The Glasgow carriages were detached at
Carlisle, whence they followed the Edinburgh portion, without restaurant
car. Southbound, the "Mid-day Scot" was more in its old character;
its Aberdeen coaches were united with those from Glasgow at Law
Junction and with the Edinburgh–London portion at Symington.

A notable service was that of the retimed "Ulster Express", leaving
Euston at 7.0 pm instead of the previous time of 6.10, to run without a
stop to Morecambe, 234 miles in 4hr 12min, reaching Heysham 18 minutes
later at 11.30 pm for the night steamer to arrive at Belfast at 6.35 am. This
was one of the best of the very variable ways of going to and from Ireland
at that time; better than London–Stranraer Larne–Belfast; very much
better than the ghastly exchanges of Holyhead. In Scotland came – and
high time at that –two daily three-hour services between Glasgow and
Aberdeen, with two stops only, at Perth and Stonehaven (or Forfar in
the case of the morning up train).

The year 1937 was indeed a memorable one in Britain train times
generally. Though the LMS did not run the fastest trains, having none
which averaged 67 mph or over, it had 62 runs at 60 mph or more,
covering 6,145 miles, much in excess of the other companies' combined
total. Its fastest run was one at 65·1 mph, in just that distance and time,
from Rugby to Watford with the 6.20 pm Birmingham–London express.

A good feature of the 1937 summer timetables was the stopping of the
"Royal Scot", up and down, in Carlisle Citadel instead of outside King-
moor Shed for purely engine-changing purpose. It was useful for
North of England passengers, and on the up journey it gave Carlisle a
midday service to London 57 minutes faster than in previous summers.
As to other intermediate times, the Glasgow–Aberdeen three-hour
expresses were allowed 76 minutes for the 74½ miles from Perth to
Stonehaven.

Night trains were fairly fast, but not too much. Late starts and early
arrivals are a nuisance on overnight journeys. If one were using an
ordinary day compartment from Glasgow to London by the Night Scot,
the tea stop at Crewe gave a welcome refresher in the early morning, and

for the rest, one was as undisturbed as one's company would allow. A drunken or otherwise noisy party, as ever, was an unmitigated nuisance. In one's own experience soldiers were always well-behaved and sailors sometimes less so, though the real Yahoo was almost always civilian, and probably going to or from a ball game. Then there was a sort of intermediate user which might be delicately described as curious, and was to be seen on the "Royal Highlander". The main train left London at 7.20 pm, reaching Inverness at 8.45 am, to be followed in summer by its second portion at 7.40 pm. This second part made its first northbound intermediate stop at Bletchley, at 8.41 (to pick up grouse-shooting dons off the seven-o'clock from Oxford?) But it also set some people down. One warm summer evening in 1937 your author, peering from an ordinary coach, saw two elegant girls alight from the adjacent first-class sleeper and march briskly away together, without luggage. Later, a famous officer told him: "Oh, yes. They go straight back on the 8.50 to Euston".

Reverting to the very respectable Duchesses: Five were built in 1937, and ten more in 1938. The last five were without the streamlined casing, a deprivation which, in your author's opinion, greatly enhanced their aspect, showing for the first time what a beautiful engine, in terms of visible mechanical balance, this design could be. All three fives differed in appearance, for the second lot had red casings instead of blue, with golden bands and lines. From youthful memories of the blue Caledonian engines, one recalls that where these had much lead-white mixed with the Prussian blue, the colour weathered far better, never blackening as did the supposed standard shade. The blue "Coronation Scot", in the words of a lady whose house overlooked the line, became "dirty-looking" in a sadly short time, though more care was taken of it than with some other equipment. In this middle 1930s, be it told, many of the LMS locomotives and vehicles were in a really shocking state of grubby dowdiness. Even the London & North Eastern shone by comparison, while the Great Western and the Southern fairly sparkled. The LMS red streamliners, however, one remembers as having maintained their splendours quite well. There was some pride left.

As suggested, many of us liked best a Duchess *undraped*. To outside observers that covering seemed to make little if any difference to ability in handling a train, while its absence greatly improved accessibility. Doubtless the engines were cooler too.

The front of the streamlined casing necessitated a depressed top to the smokebox, ahead of the double chimney. When, some years later, casings were removed, the effect was singularly ugly. The Many, however, had been impressed by the train in its fashionably streamlined form of 1937. At that time, designers were streamlining perambulators and gramophones; the Wells film *Things to Come* even showed a streamlined tank crawling like some horrible mechanical mollusc into the midst of some undefined enemy lines. Thirty-six Duchesses were ultimately built to Stanier's designs, and two more, with certain detail alterations and most importantly, roller bearings, under H. G. Ivatt: (Nos. 6256 *Sir William Stanier, FRS* and No. 6257 *City of Salford*). Naming after cities had begun with No. 46235 *City of Birmingham*, with the exception noted above and with No. 6244 which was *King George VI*. The 1948 list, the first after British Railways had taken over, showed but two streamlined engines, Nos (B.R.) 46226 *Duchess of Norfolk* and a later one, No. 46243 *City of Lancaster*. Be it remarked that under wartime-maintenance standards of cleanliness, the streamlined locomotives looked about as slatternly as the noble steam engine could look. Norman Wilkinson painted a sad picture of girls rubbing the grimy shell of one at Camden. It needed more than the best of girls with a hunk of cottonwaste!

Once again, with the "Coronation Scot", the company decided to place a train on exhibition in the United States, to make also a goodwill tour with it, at and in connection with the New York World's Fair of 1939. It was not composed of the original locomotive and carriages. The engine was in fact No. 6229 *Duchess of Hamilton*, she having swapped nameplates with the real *Coronation*. The supposed *Coronation*, like the train that went with her, was red with gold. The supposed *Duchess of Hamilton* puzzled some people by appearing in a blue coat that was not quite new. As might have been expected, the train was made representative of British express passenger practice generally, and therefore included a first-class sleeping car; twelve berths to it, and mounted on six-wheel bogies, a design of 1936. The complete make-up of the exhibition train, in order from tender, was thus: corridor brake-first, corridor first-class, first-class "buffet lounge", first-class diner, kitchen car, third-class diner, the sleeper just noted, and club saloon at the rear. The last-mentioned had the usual enormous leather chairs, but of rather better, and more varied, design from those of 1930. Certain of the vehicles were articulated in pairs, on the Gresley plan, as had been some earlier LMS excursion stock. All carriages had Stone's controllable pressure heating and ventilation with oil filters, giving a complete change of air throughout within six minutes, continuously. Further, there were telephones for summoning the dining car attendants. Weight was cut down by the use of high-tensile steels, and much use was made of welding in body construction. The tare of the train was 263 tons, about that of three Pullman Standard cars and thus quite frivolous to American ideas: equal perhaps to that of the nice little Red Bird on the Chicago Great Western (which also was hauled by a suitably nice little red Pacific).[1]

Under her alias, *Duchess of Hamilton* was equipped for American move-

[1] cf. Norman Thompson in *The Railway Magazine*, September 1930.

ment much better than had been the Royal Scot class engine previously sent out. No longer did it appear as if an old motor headlamp had been shoved up with a cats-cradle of cables; the powerful headlamp required by American law was very neatly housed into an extension of the locomotive casing. The bell, similarly required, was not quite so happily disposed on the curve of the casing above it, for it was too high, but all things being considered, this version of the Coronation Scot had little of the makeshift look which the Royal Scot had exhibited in North America – generally getting away with it – some years earlier. The standard American automatic couplers, being at a lower level than the European buffing gear, were fairly easily imposed on the equipment. The engine's whistle, though still quite unlike an American chime, did not excite merriment this time, with its fine Caledonian hoot. All the same, an American whistle was presented through a fund organised by *The Model Railroader*. A further addition to fulfil American requirements was a special internal spark arrester, for goodness knew what sort of fuel the engine might have to eat. Side floodlights were installed for publicity purposes and on this account and because of long exhibition sessions without benefit of dynamo, special arrangements had to be made in respect of the carriage accumulators. Decoration was somewhat elaborate, in the flat style of the 'thirties. The Stephensons' *Rocket* rampaged up one bulkhead adjacent to the bar.

R. A. Riddles accompanied the train to and around the American East and Middle-West. It was shipped on the *Belpamela* (Christen Smith) from Southampton late in January, having arrived there (with the benevolent help of the Southern Railway) on the 19th. The goodwill tour began at Philadelphia and opened with a trip to Washington and back over the Pennsylvania and the Baltimore and Ohio Railroad. At that time Robert M. Van Sant was the B&O Vice-President in command of publicity, a most sympathetic character in your author's experience of him, and something of an anglophile in days when not all Americans were so. He put a strong railway police guard on the train, having heard of depredations made on the Royal Scot during that earlier visit. Leaving Philadelphia again by the Pennsylvania Railroad, the train ran to Altoona and then back on to the Baltimore and Ohio at Pittsburgh for the run to Columbus. The Big Four (the Cleveland, Columbus, Cincinnati and St. Louis Railroad) was then used as far as Cincinnati, the Louisville and Nashville to Louisville, the Pennsylvania (Lines West) from Louisville to St. Louis via Indianapolis, the Chicago and Alton to Chicago, the Michigan Central to Detroit with a call at Kalamazoo, and the New York Central to Albany, apart from a Pennsylvania detour from Cleveland to Youngstown. East of Albany the train went over the noble Berkshires to Boston by the Boston and Albany Railroad, and finally it headed south-west to New York by the New Haven company's line.

Bear with a personal thing at this point! Hungry for requisite guineas in that year – though for him it was a fairly good one – your chronicler painted a rather hurried picture called *The Scot Abroad* for *The Railway Magazine* (July 1939). It was not a bad picture, but it agitated some people by showing a left-hand semaphore on an American railroad. The thing was that this signal was copied from some at Boston South Station, which had such things. Brickbats arrived from people on both sides of the ocean. Then Ward Lock and Company kindly bought the picture outright, with the request that it be reverse-printed and would-I-please reverse the lettering and numerals on the engine to this end. So I did, and the picture made a jacket design for the next *Wonder Book of Railways* (that splendid thing that taught one so much from Christmas 1912 onwards). Nobody complained this time, the semaphore having become right-hand! Ward Lock's old offices had a sad end, fairly soon after, from German bombing. One wonders whether *The Scot Abroad* perished in the flames. If not, it ought to have curiosity value by now!

War struck in Europe at the beginning of September. The LMS engine was safely shipped home, in spite of active submarine hunters. The carriages stayed in the States until all was over, serving as an officers' club for the United States Forces at home. In Great Britain, engines were requisite and necessary: carriages of exhibition sort were less so, though the solitary third-class one would have been useful when many of its kind were shortly to be blown to bits or burnt-out. There had been no adventurings, this time, to the Pacific Coast and back by Canada.

Stanier's Pacifics have taken up quite some space, as they did on turntable. Let us go back to sketch the advent and use of some other engines, some of them very important, which began to arrive in vast numbers from the early 1930s onwards. Far from least in this practice was the rebuilding of the Royal Scot class which, as noted, stemmed from the apotheosis of the Schmidt-boilered compound engine *Fury*. Her perfectly sound frames, wheels, tender and so forth had been waiting rather a long time for something useful to be done with them. Late in 1935 came from these bare bones a Royal Scot with a taper boiler; tube heating surface down from 1,892 to 1,669 sq ft, firebox up from 189 to 195 sq ft, superheating elements down from 399 to 360 sq ft and grate area just up at 21·25 sq ft. Pressure was unchanged at 250lb/sq in. Such troubles as there were in *British Legion* were in the front end, as in the ports and the valves. Following experiment and alteration, designs were prepared for the rebuilding of the Royal Scots, with double blastpipe and chimney. Again, as with *Fury/British Legion*, little was to survive beyond the *bare bones*.

By that time Stanier had been seconded under Government as Scientific Advisor to the Minister of Production (1942). His railway office was officially under C. E. Fairburn, as Acting Chief Mechanical and Electrical Engineer in his absence, but more actually in the hands of H. G. Ivatt, who was more of a steam man, son of H. A. Ivatt, sometime of the Great Northern, and brother-in-law of Oliver Bulleid who was by then well established on the Southern Railway. It was the younger Ivatt who seems to have made the final transformation of the Royal Scots on the lines practically suggested by the rebuilding of *Fury* into *British Legion*. The first of the taper-boilered Scots, apart from the last-named, was No. 6103 *Royal Scots Fusilier* (April 1943).

As in the metamorphosed *Fury*, the boiler barrel was tapered, with a working pressure of 250lb. Double blast-pipe and chimney were used. The grate area was 31·25 sq ft, evaporative heating surface was 1,850 sq ft (195 sq ft firebox) and superheater elements brought the combined heating surface to 2,270 sq ft. General engine dimensions were unchanged Piston valves were of 9in diameter. Stanier's bogies, stemming via Swindon from de Glehn's, and new suspension to the coupled axles, were innovations, and the smokebox saddles, inside cylinders and smokeboxes were integrally cast. Improvement was marked in several respects. The engines did much good work in their new form, notably on the old Midland/Glasgow and South Western route. The rebuilding reduced engine weight by about two tons. By the end of LMS ownership, 45 of the 71 Royal Scots had bene thus treated, excluding No. 6170 *British Legion*. Those which carried their old, vast smokeboxes (and other things) to the end of company ownership were the original *Royal Scot* and Nos. 6102, 6106/7, 6110, 6113, 6123, 6130, 6134, 6136/7, 6140/3, 6148, 6151, 6153, 6155/6, 6158, 6163/5 and 6167.

What the company urgently needed, quite apart from prodigious Pacifics and rejuvenated Scots, was a large number of adequate standard-ised locomotives for main-line service and of as few types as possible. Hence the advent of very many 2–8–0 engines equally capable with heavy coal or reasonably fast freight, of a 4–6–0 equivalent to the Patriot or Baby Scot class, and of a general-service 4–6–0, capable of going anywhere from Bournemouth to Wick and of hauling anything from fast passenger to fast freight. These last were to become the famous and ubiquitous Black Fives.

Both the 4–6–0 classes came out in 1934, and both were markedly Great Western in certain important respects. Of the express engines, 113 were built straight off, with tapered domeless boilers having a low degree of superheat. Crewe built Nos. 5552–5556 and 5607–5654. The intermediate fifty were built by North British and the last ten, 5655–5664, at Derby Works. The rest, turned out during the middle and later 1930s, brought the class total up to 191, numbered in unbroken sequence up to 5742. These were the Jubilees, so called from the naming of No. 5552 as *Silver Jubilee* in 1935, the twenty-fifth of George V's. At the same time the engine was painted in what was intended to remain all glossy-black, and certain metal parts, including the flat cap over the top-feed connections, were nickel-plated.

One does not remember this as a very happy piece of adornment or even naming, though people had quite an affection for *Old George*. To those of us who were in our middle-twenties or under, the King had always been The King. Your author can just remember having seen flags out, from his perambulator, and that would have been the Coronation of 1911. But the name *Silver Jubilee* had the Public and its Press often mixed-up. It was the name of a train on the London & North Eastern and of an engine on the LMS. Really one had no time to sort these things out! Then; all that black and silver! One thought of Oscar Wilde's terrible description of an execution: (*And the Governor all in shiny black, With the yellow face of Doom.*)[1] Well, perhaps not as bad as that! But somewhere in Tennyson, surely, was the line . . . *Had never seen a costlier funeral.* Brass-on-black could look very well for a locomotive, but silver-on-black? No, it was not entirely happy![2]

Nor was initial experience with the Jubilees, though it was but passing, and consequent upon the building of so many engines straight-off before the design got over its baby-troubles. Improvement of the blast-pipe put their initially doubtful steaming qualities right, and the later form of boiler, with a higher superheating surface, improved them still more. But initially the men felt that they could have done with lots more Baby Scots instead. Mechanical points in a minute! Names for the moment! Ultimately all of this class had names. To begin with, the company worked its way from *Silver Jubilee* through the Dominions, the Empire of India, the Colonies and Protectorates. That got the list as far as *Zanzibar* (No. 5638). Now it was the turn of the Admirals, whose names ran from *Raleigh* to *De Robeck* (5678) including such personages as *Keyes*, *Kempenfelt*, *Jellicoe* and *Prince Rupert* in no particularly chronological order. Then there was *Armada* (5679) followed by a long line of famous warships, which one found admirable. How happy was *Express*! The list wound up with famous locomotive names, which had formerly belonged to Royal Scots, and the former Irish Kingdoms, to conclude with No. 5742 *Connaught*. It had its absurdities, this naming sequence; tragic in the case of No. 5637 *Windward Islands*, whose battered cadaver was removed from the Harrow wreckage of 1952 on $5\frac{1}{2}$ wheels. Class-naming has ever achieved the ultimate ridiculous, if the class be sufficiently successful to become really numerous. Such conventions were all right with fleets. The old Cunard

---

[1] *The Ballad of Reading Gaol*. Wilde was *inside* at the time, and the Governor he thought of was doubtless the unpleasant Mr. Nelson.
[2] George V died in the following year.

and White Star Lines were unlikely to run out of worthy names ending
either in -ia or -ic; the Booth Line was welcome to its Hs and the
Orient Line to its Os. But locomotives in a class were more numerous
than ships in a fleet. *Gibraltar* was all right; *nice* town! But, with all respect
to Government; *Gilbert and Ellice Islands?*

Enough of all that! The Jubilee class, having three cylinders 17in by
26in and 225lb pressure, had at first a combined heating surface of
1,852·4 sq ft whereof the firebox contributed 162·4 sq ft and the superheater 22·5 sq ft. The grate area was 29·5 sq ft. In the later boiler, which
was domed, the respective figures were 1,941, 181 and 300 sq ft and the
grate area 31 sq ft. Later still, in 1942, Nos. 5735 *Comet* and 5736 *Phoenix*
received still more powerful boilers carrying 250lb pressure, which
brought their tractive effort at 85 per cent up from 26,610 to 29,570lb
and advanced their running rating from 5XP to 6P. These ultimately
admirable (and very nice-looking) engines did much of their most
important work on the old Midland system and its connections. There
were some remarkable test runs with No. 5660 *Rooke*, over much of the
Midland and the Glasgow and South Western main lines, late in 1937,
with a train of 305 tons including the ex-L&Y dynamometer car, including
a startling climb from Carlisle to the summit at Aisgill in 48·5 minutes for
the 48·4 miles.[1] (Driver W. North and Fireman H. George of Leeds
Whitehall.)

Engines of such a numerous class had their misadventures. This same
Rooke was in an accident at Dumfries during the war. Another is shown in
Norman Wilkinson's painting of a train being bombed and shot-up from
the air near Bletchley in October 1940.[2]

Now for those most useful things, the Black Fives, whose name,
though universal, was not official; doubtless based on the fact that they
were classified 5 and, although outwardly rather like Jubilees on fast
glance, were always painted black instead of red. To use one more
generalisation, they were Stanier's LMS variation on the Great Western
Railway's Hall class, with which he had had so much to do, though the
Walschaert gear was outside, a feature which the Great Western avoided
making whenever possible. By the end of LMS ownership, there were
802 of them, and delivery from works was not complete. They were
numbered thus far from 4698–5459. Four were given names for Scottish
regiments; Nos. 5154 *Lanarkshire Yeomanry*, 5156 *Ayrshire Yeomanry*,
5157 *The Glasgow Highlander* and 5158 *Glasgow Yeomanry*. As far as one
recalls, No. 5157 was the first to receive plates, and one remembers also
a faint pang that there was not an engine called *The Gorbals Diehard*,

---

[1] Tables for the four days of running, October 12–15, Bristol–Leeds–Glasgow and back,
appear in Nock's *Sir William Stanier.*
[2] George C. Nash's *The LMS at War.*

though that were a body invented by the late Lord Tweedsmuir (John Buchan).[1]

The GWR Hall comparison has been made, and is surely a fair one. That class had stemmed from a Great Western express engine, *St. Martin* being rebuilt for general service after the arrival of the Castle class in 1923. The first new engines had arrived in 1928. The LMS had not got such a thing, unless one counted London & North Western Princes and some variety of engines – none numerous – in Scotland. The former, though very good engines, were already old-fashioned, and *so* full of Crewe! As remarked, proper standardisation was the thing for which the company had been waiting for so long, and in vain. With all respect to Derby's old-favourites-warmed-up-for-supper, it had taken about a decade! So now the LMS had Halls of its own, and much more useful than some marble ones.

This class was an immediate success, as its numbers will have shown already. Basic dimensions included 18½ by 28in cylinders (two), 6ft coupled wheels and 6ft driving wheels, which gave a tractive effort at 85 per cent boiler pressure of 25,455lb. In the Hall class the stroke was 30in, with pressure and driving wheels diameter the same. The Black Fives had "French" (de Glehn) bogies and Stanier's much improved axleboxes and big-end brasses. The first twenty of the class were built at Crewe and the next – or almost simultaneous – fifty by Vulcan Foundry at Newton, taking the running numbers from 5000 to 5069. In these, to begin with, there were 14-element superheaters, giving 227·5 sq ft heating surface, to which the tubes and flues added 1,460 sq ft and the firebox 156 sq ft, giving a combined heating surface of 1,843·5 sq ft. The grate area was 27·8 sq ft. These were finished by 1935, when the second batch was begun (5070–5451) with a 24-element superheater of 307 sq ft heating surface and the firebox expanded to give 171·3 sq ft with a grate area of 28·65 sq ft. Combined heating surface was now 1,938·3 sq ft. There was a dome to the boiler with a grid-type regulator. In 1938, the last entirely pre-war year, work was begun on the final series, numbered from 5452 up to 5499 and ultimately from 4999 downwards. In these the boiler had a superheater of 28 elements (359 sq ft heating surface) and 1,479 sq ft in tubes and flues. The firebox heating surface was very slightly reduced to 171 sq ft so that the combined heating surface was 2,009 sq ft. Grate area remained unchanged from that of the second series, which had been built at Crewe (5070–5074), by Vulcan Foundry (5075–5124) and by Armstrong Whitworth (5125–5451).

These engines, as noted, spread all over the country where the LMS was concerned, and as was only to be expected, some changes were rung as the years advanced. There were 500 in service at the end of the first half-

[1] *Huntingtower* (Hodder and Stoughton).

year of war. Nock has called them *everybody's friends*, a good term in one's own experience of punctuality north of Stanley Junction and consequent good temper of one's acquaintances in Inverness and relatives in Caithness, which last did not, on the whole, love their train for herself. Apart from the northern migrants in particular, the Black Fives in general were made guinea-pigs now and then, in the interests of the advancement of the expansive use of steam in reciprocating locomotive engines. For a long time now, the LMS had been quite kindly interested in the Caprotti valve gear and in the use of revolving bearings, for which Italy, Sweden and America had done so much. These sturdy locomotives, unlikely to daunt inexperience, and proof – as far as any engine can be – against the mismanagement of fools, were natural subjects for experiment. They seem to have been better than either Bowen Cooke's or Hughes' 4–6–0 types at real express duties for which those classes had been designed while the Black Fives were not. Eleven were equipped, in later LMS days, with Caprotti valve gear and roller bearings (Nos. 4747–4757), four (Nos. 4738–4741) had the Caprotti gear though they retained ordinary bearings. Further, roller bearings were applied on nine (4758–4766) with Walschaert gear and to No. 4767 which had Stephenson gear. The outside steampipe casings of the Caprotti engines gave them rather the face of an aged orang-utan (a very decent ape, but not beautiful in old age). Just after the war, when the oil companies were preparing, while coal was short, to crash every opening in order to run the country, several were equipped for oil burning, viz. Nos. 4827, 4829, 4830 and 4844. All-in-all, the Black Fives were one of the best locomotive investments ever made. One recalls an enthusiast of the more fanatical sort, too, whose ambition was to photograph every one of them with the same sort of dedication as that with which dear Tom Perkins set out to travel over every public railway line in the British Isles, though one cannot imagine that it was quite such an instructive employment, however much it pleased him if and when he had bagged the lot.

That the LMS was so late, among haulers of coal and heavy minerals, in adopting the 2–8–0 type of locomotive, remains what the King of Siam might have called a puzzlement, especially since such engines, so full of the practice of Derby, had been working for years on the Somerset and Dorset Joint Railway. The West Country seemed to be a favoured habitat, for the Great Western Railway had pioneered the type with Churchward's design when the century was yet very young. It was to be expected that Stanier would break the freeze, and so he did in 1935. First of the class, classified 8F, was No. 8000, with a domeless boiler. Basic dimensions included 18½in by 28in cylinders (2), 4ft 8½in coupled wheels with a maximum axle-load of 16 tons only – less than the 18·6 tons maximum in the tender. Long valve-travel and long laps bespoke classic Churchward

Suburban electric multiple units.
ABOVE: Liverpool-Ormskirk, 1927, in
BR days. BELOW: Wirral lines, 1938.
FOOT OF PAGE: Southport line. 1939,

Sir William Guy Granet.

Lord Stamp.

Sir Henry Fowler.

Sir Ernest Lemon.

Sir William Stanier.

Ashton Davies.

T. W. Royle.

H. G. Ivatt.

Baby Scot; the tail.

Eric Treacy

tradition, as did, at first, the low degree of superheat. Later boilers had
larger fireboxes in boilers almost identical, apart from superheater, with
those of the later Black Fives. Main boiler dimensions (later version in
brackets) included the following items: Evaporative heating surface,
tubes and flues, 1,308 (1,479) and firebox, 155 sq ft (171); superheater,
235 sq ft (245); grate area, 27·8 sq ft (28·5); pressure, 225 sq ft. Here was
a freight engine that could be useful in most places, powerful and with
more flexibility than the older types.

Still, initial construction was less massive than one might have expected,
or in retrospect supposed. There had been much less mortality among the
earlier freight engines than among pre-grouping passenger types, and
some of them were in considerable numbers. Even in the first post-
company figures, of 1948, the Midland standard goods, including those
built by the LMS under Fowler (580) came to 772 engines (about the total
of all classes on the London & South Western, one of the ten major
systems of 1914). Of the London & North Western o–8–o type there were
588 engines (98 G1, 60 G2 and 430 G2a) and there were 175 of the LMS
Fowler standard o–8–o (not, perhaps, a distinguished engine, but fairly
recent and in good order). Of older engines there were immense numbers
of Midland and Caledonian origin, not to mention London & North
Western, mostly ancient. Of the new 2–8–o engines, but 126 were built
down to the end of 1939, but in December of that year the Ministry of
Supply chose for this new class the mission which the Robinson 2–8–o of
the Great Central had served in the previous war. In the mind of professional Government, this war was doubtless going to be much like the
Kaiser's adventure with two armies bogged down in the West for years,
facing each other in anger, but with the magical Maginot Line instead of
the ultimately busted Hindenburg Line. Anyway, the BEF would bring,
its own railway equipment for use on French lines when the French
locomotives and rolling stock were, by planned withdrawal, elsewhere.
The British Government engines had Westinghouse brake equipment and
French tyre profiles; they lacked roller bearings in the motion; they were
even intended at first to have Flaman speed recorders and French automatic warning equipment. Of course, the war worked out quite differently,
as wars usually have done, but of this, more later.

At the end of 1939 the Ministry of Supply ordered 240 engines of this
class. Delivery began in May 1940, but none went to France for by June
the Germans were arriving there, to capture various "Jinties" and Great
Western goods engines, but nothing very new.

Of the Stanier 2–8–o, there were ultimately 624 in the LMS stock,
including ex-Government engines that had escaped the hazards of Egypt,
Palestine, Iraq, Persia and some other places then collectively called the
Middle East (the Near East being presumably confined to Turkey, which

F

was neutral with British and German Ambassadors as neighbours, though not quite on calling terms). Not only Crewe and Horwich (though not Derby) but Swindon, Darlington, Doncaster, Eastleigh, Ashford, Brighton, Vulcan Foundry, North British and Beyer Peacock had built them, whether for the LMS or for Government. Further, 68 built by the Southern Railway at Brighton had been allotted to the London & North Eastern, which numbered them 3500–3567, and then lent them back to the LMS which gave them Nos. 8705–8729 in 1947. The LNER classified them O6. No. 8293, an engine built for the Government by Beyer Peacock in 1940 and on loan to the Great Western, struck that company's *Dudley Castle* head-on at a diamond crossing near Slough early in the morning of July 2, 1941 while hauling a down freight from Old Oak Common to Severn Tunnel Junction. The train struck was an alleged express from Plymouth (it had taken over $8\frac{1}{2}$ hours to get as far as Slough) crossing over from the up-main to the up-relief lines. Five passengers were killed. The collision was spectacular. Its cause was partly in a signalling fault, though had the borrowed engine been equipped with the Great Western's automatic warning system, that might have saved the situation.

The first British Railways list (1948) contained the following engines taken over under the heading "2-8-0 Class 8F", the initial forty-thousand being the extra digit added in BR renumbering: Nos. 48000/11, 48017, 48024, 48026/7, 48029, 48033, 48035/7, 48050, 48053/7, 48060, 48062/7, 48069/70, 48073/6, 48078/85, 48088/90, 48092/3, 48095/48225, 48264/85, 48293, 48301/99, 48400/79, 48490/5, 48500/59, 48600/68772. That made 624 engines, though not all had belonged to the LMS, though stemming from them. Of the last series, those from 48705 onwards had been allotted to the London & North Eastern Railway, which classified them as O6, and lent them back to the LMS which renumbered them in its own series in 1947, the unitial 26 having been built by the Southern for LNE use, as noted. These – and other running numbers – may be queried, though without much profit. As we have seen, they could be swapped; not necessarily for American visits and (in the case of the Great Western) for royal funerals, but even in the course of renewals after accident or – horrid word – cannibalisation. One has heard evidence from all four of the British companies from the 1930s onwards.

The LMS Class 8F was a finely versatile engine. It could work a British semi-fast; it could work all it was intended for, of course and it could work troops back to the Western Desert front after a spell of Cairo leave. (The service was called The Blue Train because most of the passengers were suffering from crapula.) Twenty years after the end of the LMS, and very much towards the end of steam itself, the class was still to be seen in many places from Crewe to Carlisle. British Railways had 719 of this class, even in the early 1960s.

That William Stanier would build for the LMS a 2-6-2 tank engine, coming as he did from Swindon, was expected by many. That he would build a bigger tank engine, 2-6-4, was considered probable, in view of the success which had attended *The Prince* and others in Fowler's days. A 2-8-0 tank engine – or 2-8-2 – of the South Wales sort, was expected by some, but did not materialise. Short heavy hauls were less in the LMS programme than in that of the Great Western, for the South Welsh valleys were unique.

Urgently needed were competent tank engines for snappy passenger haulage over shorter distances, for breadwinning by steam conveyance was as yet far from its decline except south of the Thames and about Lancashire and the Tyne. Birmingham's morning and evening railway crowds were steam-hauled, and so were Glasgow's. (One likes to recall the four-times-daily trips to and from Dundee over the Tay Bridge, but that is London & North Eastern lore!) During 1934-35, Stanier brought out thirty-seven three-cylinder 2-6-4 tank engines, initially for the London, Tilbury and Southend line, where the Adams-Whitelegg 4-4-2 type, in its time so efficient and also so handsome, was near the end of its tether. The new engines had the pseudo-Great Western domeless boiler, and were numbered 2500-2536. Pressure was 200 lb, as in the Derby 2-6-4T, as was the driving wheel diameter of 5ft 9in, which last remained constant in this type on the LMS. The three cylinders were 16in by 26in, with long laps and long valve-travel. The engines were thus slightly and nominally more powerful than those of Fowler's time: 24,600 lb tractive effort compared with 23,125 sq ft. The original boilers stuck to Swindonian low superheat; 160 sq ft against 266·25 sq ft.

Be it added that three-cylinder engines were *not* in the Swindon tradition, though one doubts that Stanier cared much for this, once he had gone to another place. On the LMS, experience was the thing that mattered, whether it came from Swindon or whether it were based on observation in the new country. It was not an act of faith to Old Swindon, but the ideal of having a more simply-arranged locomotive for general service, that caused him in the following year of 1935 to present his company with an outwardly similar 2-6-4 tank engine but with two cylinders only, of 19⅝in diameter, stroke remaining the same. Nominal tractive effort rose slightly to 24,670lb. Seventy engines were built, and numbered 2425-2494; then followed 136 numbered 2537-2672, making 206 engines in all. Further, and it is opportune to mention them here, after Stanier's departure, C. E. Fairburn brought out a very similar class which continued to be built by British Railways from 1948 onwards. Fairburn's engines were slightly lighter, and shorter in the coupled wheelbase, though leading dimensions and tractive effort remained unchanged. They first appeared in 1945 with No. 2147, and the series continued in consecutive numbering to 2299, after which there was a jump to 2673–2699. In 1948 the Fairburn variety numbered about 180 engines, and was still being built in the series 2147–2299. By that time, British Railways were adding four thousand to the LMS numbers. As with other Stanier or Stanier-inspired designs, changes were rung on the boilers and superheater equipment.

In 1941 there was coaching construction under Stanier that was not at all proclaimed from the housetops. It was the building of three new royal carriages, the first since the Midland Railway had built one to David Bain's design in 1912. One evening during the war, the present writer happened like so many people to be passing through Euston. In the mirk of the blacked-out station he saw the familiar rear of one of the London & North Western royal brake-first carriages with, beyond it, the equally familiar lines of a Wolverton "semi-royal". But beyond that loomed something not so much rich and strange as strange and solid-looking. It was, incidentally, the first time I had seen the royal train in red instead of in the old London & North Western colours. Naturally, nobody was talking about the presence of the royal train, which had thus been disguised to look like something more ordinary. No information even leaked out at the time about any changes in its aspect of make-up. I simply knew that something *was up*.

As for the solid-looking *somethings*, we learned officially after the war that they consisted of three twelve-wheel cars. Two were living carriages, 69 ft long by 9 ft wide and weighing 57 tons tare, which was very heavy for the generally very light LMS stock. Each of these contained a day-room, a bedroom, a bathroom and servants' quarters. As in the old royal saloons, the end vestibules had recessed double doors. This was the only traditional feature to be retained from C. A. Park's most elegant designs for Edward VII. In that last rather vinegary sentence lies one's criticism. Park's train had been a work of art, of a sort already outmoded when it appeared. The new train – or set of three carriages – was admirable as a set of rolling-stock. Domestically, it was expensive-Grand-Hotel; in short, the best that Philistine England could produce when her artists were either dying like Rex Whistler or holed-up.

One hopes that the arrangements did not too much irk the highest household in the land. They were physically comfortable, more so than Mr. Park's, perhaps. Now and then our monarchy has produced royal aesthetes, such as some of the Tudors, and the second and fourth of the Four Georges. It would be impertinent to specify personages since the latter. The plumbing was excellent, whereas in Park's famous carriages it had been very old fashioned; (metal baths had been put in for George V and pottery ones for George VI, with no change in the archaic water-closets). These twin royal saloons were accompanied by a power car, also twelve-wheeled, and taring 52 tons. This vehicle contained, as its title suggested, lighting, heating and ventilation plant, together with a twenty-five-line automatic telephone exchange, also fourteen staff berths in 3½ compartments, two lavatories, brake and luggage compartments, so that, at a pinch, the three new cars made a self-contained rake.

There was forced ventilation with steam and electric heaters, and wet ice for cooling. Six temperatures were arranged for. The set was of all-steel construction with welded joints and asbestos insulation between the steel plates. Against the hazards of war, all windows had steel shutters. Pullman diaphragms were used instead of the old-style bellows which had distinguished the London & North Western carriages, and to which the LMS had long continued to be partial, whatever some people might be doing at Doncaster, Swindon and Lancing. Thus, for the first time in the history of British railways, an entirely new royal train arrived without fanfares, even under a blanket of secrecy.

Ordinary stock in the latter years of the LMS showed little change from that of the 1930s, even in post-war replacement, and was closely copied in the first standard coaches of British Railways, which the *Architectural Review* damned with faint praise, remarking that the style was "curiously dated". The fitting of upper berths in first-class sleeping compartments, to give a more economic load in wartime, furnished a prototype for the second-class sleepers of British Railways. No new electric stock was built; the business people of Lancashire rocked and rolled along in the two (Southport and Bury) varieties of L&Y cars; those in and out of London had the alternatives of London & North Western vestibuled stock (which ran uncommonly well even in old age) and the adequate but scarcely distinguished LMS side-door compartment carriages, which sometimes indeed merited the Australian term of *rattler*.

In the administrative sense, the LMS diesel locomotives were Stanier's, though he was essentially a steam man where engines were concerned, and his lieutenant for oil engines was to a great extent C. E. Fairburn. In any case, the design of these was to a great extent in the hands of outside makers. LMS early essays in oil traction have been noted, and the first diesel locomotive had been No. 1831, the converted Midland tank engine with a Davey Paxman 400bhp engine and a hydraulic transmission by Haslam and Newtons of Derby. The work was doubtless done in 1932, and the official appearance followed early in 1933.

In the following year came the solitary No. 7058, with an Armstrong-Whitworth 250hp engine and electrical transmission, also with jackshaft drive to six coupled wheels. Again, it was a solitary; (it became British Railways No. 13000, which at least suggests that it was very useful to some people, even if not repeated).

In 1936 came an oil-electric shunting locomotive on six 4ft 0½in wheels, the joint product of English Electric and Hawthorn Leslie. Transmission included two nose-suspended electric motors and drive through a single-reduction gear. With a rated tractive effort of 33,000lb from a 350hp engine, it was a useful shunter, if slow. Two more were built, the last one somewhat lighter; 47 tons compared with 51 tons. These three bore LMS numbers 7074, 7076 and 7079. Twelve years later they became British Railways Nos. 12000/2.

Largest series of the diesel shunters built under Stanier's order were Nos. 7080–7119, introduced in 1939. They were 0–6–0 with side rods and jackshaft drive with long connecting rods from the shaft between the first and second coupled axles to the trailing one (the front being assumed as the cab-end of the locomotive). These were an English Electric product. There was a 350hp diesel engine and a single electric motor. Coupled wheels' diameter was 4ft 3in, and the rated tractive effort 33,000lb. Weight was 54¾ tons. These were highly successful locomotives. They became BR Nos. 12003–12032. Later diesels belong to the post-Stanier years.

From George Stephenson, Sir William Stanier was the twelfth locomotive engineer to preside over the Institution of Mechanical Engineers, and his Presidential Address was delivered on October 24, 1941, with the title *The Position of the Locomotive in Mechanical Engineering*. Among many things, the Address showed an intense preoccupation with recent French steam practice, as of André Chapelon and his practical insistence on the importance of giving greater area to valves, ports and passages, and of internal streamlining to give a freer flow of steam. Those of his hearers not already aware were interested to hear that the outbreak of war had held up designs, already on the board, for a modified LMS Pacific locomotive, much on the lines of a Coronation or Duchess, but with 300lb pressure. Much was to have been drawn from Chapelon's work in front-end design, though simple expansion was still to have been employed. With a compound engine, the centre-to-centre distances between inside low-pressure cylinders would have restricted the length of the driving axle bearings, while placing the high-pressure cylinders inside and the low-pressure outside, as in the South Eastern (PLM) Region of French National Railways, would have been impossible within the limits of the unfortunate British loading gauge unless, for one thing alone, all our high platforms were to be cut back *a l'Hollandaise* (the French did not go in for real platforms).

Shortly before the war, the Rugby Testing Station for locomotives had been begun under the joint enterprise of the LMS and the London & North Eastern Railway, with R. C. Bond as Superintendent Engineer, responsible to both Stanier and Gresley. Neither of the latter were to see it completed while in office, for Gresley died, while Stanier, in the second half of 1942, was seconded to the Ministry of Production as one of a triumvirate of full-time Scientific Advisers. He continued nominally to be CME to the company until the early part of 1943, when he was succeeded by C. E. Fairburn who had already held the office in an Acting Capacity, having been Deputy CME and Electrical Engineer since 1937. Stanier received his knighthood from George VI on February 9, 1943. In March 1944, he became a Fellow of the Royal Society.

Only two other locomotive engineers had ever become FRS; Robert Stephenson, who doubtless considered it his due, and rather surprisingly Edward Bury. Stanier was a giant among mechanical engineers, not merely of the steam era but in the wider sense.

A Fellow of that august body, however, had been Sir Herbert Jackson, KBE., FRS., who served as one of the original members of the company's Advisory Committee on Scientific Research from 1930 to his death in 1936. The Board instituted the annual award of a medal and prize in his memory. First recipient was A. S. Davidson of the Crewe Chemical Laboratory, in 1938, for a paper entitled *Chemical and Biological Examination of Water Supplies*. The medal bore a fine likeness of Jackson on the obverse, and the LMS badge on the reverse sides.

TABLE 3

Stanier Locomotives from 1933-1937, as originally built

	Date of first engine	Wheel-type	Cylinders (inches) and number	Coupled wheels diameter (ft ins)	Heating surface (tubes and flues) in sq ft	Heating surface (Firebox) in sq ft	Evaporative heating surface sq ft	Superheating surface, sq ft	Combined heating surface in sq ft	Grate area in sq ft	Working pressure in lb per sq in	Weight of engine in working order (tons cwt)
1.	1933	4-6-2	16¼ × 28 (4)	6 6	2523	190	2713	370	3083	45	250	104 10
2.	1937	4-6-2	16½ × 28 (4)	6 9	2577	230	2807	856	3663	50	250	108 2
3.	1934	4-6-0	17 × 26 (3)	6 9	1462.5	162.4	1624.9	227.5	1852.4	29.5	225	79 11
4.	1934	4-6-0	18½ × 28 (2)	6 0	1460	156	1616	227.5	1843.5	27.8	225	72
5.	1933	2-6-0	18 × 28 (2)	5 6	1256	155	1411	193	1604	27.8	225	65
6.	1934	2-6-4T	16 × 26 (3)	5 9	1011	137	1148	160	1308	25	200	92 10
7.	1937	2-6-4T	19¼ × 26 (2)	5 9	1186	139	1265	185	1450	25	200	91 6
8.	1935	2-8-0	18½ × 28 (2)	4 8½	1302	155	1463	235	1698	27.8	225	70 10

NOTES: 1, *Princess Royal*; 2, *Coronation*; 3, Jubilees; 4, Black Fives; 5, Mogul with original domeless boiler. *Princess Royal's* tender, 4,000 gall and 9 tons, weighed 54T 3c; *Coronation's* tender, 4,000 gall and 10 tons, weighed 56T 7c; 3,500 gall tenders weighed 42T 4c.

CHAPTER SIX

The Vortex, 1939-1945

IN THE late 1930s, even while the Coronation Scot was galloping up and down the West Coast main line, British railways generally were preparing for work under war conditions; indeed it can be said that the industry was far better prepared than were British politicians and their hangers-on. Nearly two decades had passed since that war-to-end-all-wars, and clearly the thing was going to happen again.

With war blowing up irrevocably, under generally disgraceful circumstances, those responsible for British tranport knew more cr less from previous experience of German strategy what would happen. Submarines would hunt merchant ships, especially tankers, with the added advantage of Irish hide-outs. There would be sudden, stringent control of everything dependent on oil fuel, which meant the motors with which we were playing so happily. The nation would have to depend more exclusively than for many years on its railway system for heavy inland transport, and back would come our old friends the Railway Executive Committee, with Government control.

So it was. On September 1, 1939, the Minister of Transport made an Order taking control of the four main-line British railways with their joint undertakings, the lines of the London Passenger Transport Board, the Mersey Railway and several others, and the Railway Executive Committee was set up under the Chairmanship of Sir Ralph Wedgwood, General Manager of the London & North Eastern, and including heads from each of the other main lines, the LMS Member being Sir William Wood. The Germans were suddenly in Poland, but Great Britain had not yet declared war. That came on September 3, but the first war emergency movement, that of city children, teachers and expectant mothers, was made at once, to be completed in the four days September 1-4. Preparations had been made for the city-to-country transport of three million women and children, but in fact only 1,220,496 actually moved to railheads in supposedly safe areas, whence they were further dispersed by buses. Many of these places were in the Midlands and the North of England. On the LMS 1,450 special train movements were made to fifteen distribution centres. To ease congestion on the ex-London & North Western lines out of the metropolis, the children, ranging in age from three to thirteen years, were taken out by suburban electric trains at eight-minute intervals during the peak, for transfer to steam trains at

Watford. The London children included not only Cockneys, but Jews from Berlin, who had got out in time, and one young solitary who had been got out of Danzig even as the German tanks smashed down the gay red-and-white frontier barriers and rolled into the Polish Corridor.

All these children were treble-labelled, and each carried a change of clothes (or was supposed to), a meal for the journey, and one of those tragi-comic civilian gas-masks which had been doled out nearly a year before, when war had seemed imminent over Czecho-Slovakia. Some of the destinations were as much as 200 miles from the dispatching cities. Not all the rolling stock thus hurriedly pressed into service was suitable for taking large numbers of small children over considerable distances – in some cases their first experience of travel by railway – but there were no serious casualties, no falling out of suddenly-open doors, and certain trains made what American bus companies call "comfort stops". As George C. Nash[1] delicately put it, "bachelor stationmasters in country towns were soon facing the most embarrassing domestic situations, but – to give them their due – with a lack of bashfulness that must have suprised even themselves". My old colleague John F. Parke, for many years of *Modern Transport*, summed things up thus succinctly: "The children were all right, but – *the expectant mothers* . . . !"

Not only were these to be handled. Aerial bombing was expected to be imminent, probably without any declaration of war, from September 1 onwards, and food stocks had to be very seriously considered, especially those stored at the docks. Amongst the first such removals were those of meat and butter from the London Docks. Between August 31 and September 4 the LMS ran or originated thirty-two special trains (twelve went to Great Western destinations) and these were followed by seven more carrying 1,600 tons of tea. With the children and the foodstuffs dealt with, there followed treasures from the art galleries and museums, and relics from Westminster Abbey. Ere war broke out, the staff, records and equipment of the Bank of England had gone, in two special trains.

In the previous war, much fighting equipment had been made in railway workshops, as well as military rolling stock ranging from immense railway gun carriages to ambulance trains. But as far back as 1937 the LMS Chief Mechanical Engineer's Department had undertaken the design of a medium tank, which doubtless would have excited Dr. Goebbels, had he heard of it, into fresh charges of war-mongering, whatever the great works of Essen, Kassel and other places might have been doing at the time. After the Czech crisis, but before the Polish explosion, the LMS had taken over a great empty mansion in Hertfordshire, adding hutments in the park, for use as Headquarters in the event of war. This was done after the Italian invasion of Albania at Easter, 1939. On

[1] *The LMS at War*, published by the company in 1946.

September 1, the Headquarters staff from Euston moved in. By Zero Hour on September 4, a Monday, three thousand of them were at work there.

Timetables had to be instantly revised – away went the summer train services, and a good deal more besides. The most stringent blackout against night air attack was at once improvised, and after a few days, in the passenger trains, absolute darkness had been alleviated by the use of blued-over electric bulbs, providing an effect like that of blue night lamps in sleeping cars, only even more sepulchral. As to special traffic, there was at once a strong echo from the 1914–18 war, with the Fleet at Scapa. To us who remembered the old war, it seemed as if this was where we had first come in.

Yet the massive aerial bombing of railway connections which had been expected, and as far as possible provided for, having regard to the immense increase in the striking power of bombing aircraft, seemed to hang fire. Apart from some highly unpleasant things at sea, it was what some American, with some reason, called the *Phoney War*. The city evacuees in large measure drifted back to their unbombed parents. The soldiers, apart from those lucky enough to take their appendixes and things into nice warm hospitals, shivered in squalor, boredom and bitter cold, whether it were at home or abroad. The railwaymen – and this was more to the good, learned how to work trains under conditions of blackout. Signal lamps were hooded to make them invisible from above; the lot of passengers was made much more tolerable by the provision of hoods to ordinary carriage lamps, once the windows had been bordered to make the roller-blinds chinkless. Driving a tarpaulined locomotive, however, was no joke. When there was no moon, landmarks were barely perceptible. At running sheds, frost fires had to be screened. Even a heap of glowing ash and clinker could tell an approaching enemy that here was a place worthy of a stick of bombs. Yet still the bombs came not.[1]

Not the enemy, but nature, brought the worst times to the railways during this phase. Dense fog descended on the blacked-out systems in December 1939, followed by heavy snow, which was at its worst in the last week of January 1940. On the London Midland & Scottish, there were 313 snow-blocks, and 500 miles of telegraph and telephone wires were dead through breakage. Signals went out of action, points were jammed by snow and packed ice; on locomotives even injectors were frozen. One up West Coast express left Glasgow Central on a Saturday and reached Euston on Tuesday. The LMS, having a relatively small electrified mileage, suffered less from iced-up conductor rails than such a

---

[1] At that time, diverse and powerful classes in Germany were still convinced that so imperial a nation as the British would never come to grips with such strong potential allies against Soviet Communism as themselves.

railway as the Southern, but then and at all times – particularly in frosty weather – the greatest care had to be taken in respect of blackout to avoid arcing at points and crossovers, and trains were required to coast over these.

Then came the successive German invasions of Norway and the Low Countries, the turning of the Maginot Line and the fall of France. With the irony of history the British railways, all geared to the support of armed forces on a vast extra-insular front, from the North Atlantic and the Orkneys to the Channel connections, were suddenly called upon to bear the retreat of those forces from Continental Europe, and to transform themselves, in a few weeks, from a system of supply lines in the rear to one of urgent transport and communications within a beleaguered fortress threatened with imminent invasion.

The heaviest brunt of evacuation, in the Channel area, fell of course on the Southern Railway, but dispersal was all about the country. The four railway companies, at short notice, formed a carriage pool, to which the LMS contributed 44 sets in a total of 186. In 16 days, 319,116 troops were moved from the reception ports in 620 train movements. Twelve days after completion of the Dunkirk evacuation came the arrival of those who had retreated through France to Breton and Biscayan ports, with 200 more trains to which the LMS contributed 123. The old west-to-north movement from such places as Plymouth and Falmouth was extremely useful. Three of the trains handled by the LMS carried French munition workers exclusively.

Of the company's fleet at sea, 41 ships had been requisitioned for Government service. The *Scotia* (Capt. W. H. Hughes) which had been on the Holyhead Royal Mail run, made a trip to Dunkirk, was struck by a torpedo which failed to explode against the bilge keel on one side, and came back with 3,000 troops. On her next trip she took off 2,000 French soldiers from Dunkirk. Under attack from the air she received several direct hits including two lethal ones, on the stern and straight down the after funnel. A destroyer and other ships managed to reach her and stand by, picking up survivors, but losses were very heavy. Captain Hughes survived. He and his crew received one DSC and three DSMs.

A Belfast–Heysham ship, the *Duke of York*, evacuating mixed allied troops from St. Valery, was bombarded by shore batteries but survived. Chief Officer B. Williams picked up one unexploded shell and hove it over the rail. The *Princess Maud* from the Stranraer–Larne run was likewise shelled off Dunkirk, but managed to evacuate troops both there and later at St. Valery. All this time the trains were pouring away from the Kent Coast, with the enemy too busy on the French side to attend to them in the ways that hostile airmen could attend to a train in open country. The wearied and disarmed soldiers slumped and slept in quite incredible variety of rolling stock – West Coast stuff of the gaslit-flat sort, massive old Midland clerestories, all the old main-line carriages which, just before the war, one had seen stored away in quiet Scottish sidings – and away they rumbled into the heart of England, successively behind Maunsell moguls of the Southern and Stanier Black Fives – and anything else which would move a heavy troop train without trouble.[1] So far the company's war-losses in locomotives had been negligible. Some standard 0-6-0 tank shunters had been left in France, like some coaches, one of which the author encountered at Longmoor in Hampshire, whither it had come back by way, soldiers said, of the Hamburg neighbourhood in 1946. Ere that, Stanier 2-8-0 freight engines were to find their way far south-east into the Elburz Mountains of Persia.

Following the disaster in the field, the railway came, with the rest of the nation, under heavy fire. Things really began with London, where the docks were the main target and the scarifying of the civilian population an important issue. Considering what was subsequently done, before counter invasion, to the German State Railway, one believes that there was an error of judgement in the German High Command, for much worse might have been done to the LMS, as to the others. From our own view-point, though we did not talk much about it at the time, it was fortunate that the egregious Corporal Hitler was in a position to overrule the shrewd Captain Goering.[2] Not that the latter is known to have had important knowledge of railways, for all his handsome Gauge O layout (Marklin?) at Schloss Karen. All the same, what was done was, if not fairly adequate, at least workmanlike, from the enemy point of view. After many years, one finds oneself looking back, as it were, to a chess-board on which one's opponent had bungled, as a change from one's own bungling. Still looking back, one feels that there was least bungling where civil transport, by land or water, was concerned, whatever may have gone on among politicians and the General Staff. In the words of Sir John Elliot:[3] "Once a railwayman, always a railwayman" and in the much earlier words of Rudyard Kipling: "We came well and cleanly out of it".[4]

In early September, the real fireworks began at home. Dock warehouses blazed. High explosives came down on junctions and railway yards. Trains were dive-bombed and machine-gunned. The city of Coventry burned as an example, the late William Joyce told us over the wireless, of what was going to happen to all our other cities. That night 122 bombs came down on the LMS in the Coventry area, 40 of them on one track,

---

[1] These things are from hearsay and other people's written words. The author also was busy getting away from the German Army, but under the chances of war his successive companions were first French and then Czech soldiers.

[2] Substantive ranks given, as before formation of the Third Realm.

[3] *The Daily Telegraph* (February 21, 1966).

[4] *In the Presence* (1912).

and the main London–Birmingham line was blocked for four days. In the London area, during that autumn, Euston was damaged (the Great Hall was set on fire, and saved), St. Pancras was hit and put out of action for five days and West Ham received such a pasting that it was out for eleven weeks; (one casualty there was a fortunately empty District Line train). During the 9½ months from August 24, 1940 to May 10, 1941, there were 170 attacks on the London Midland & Scottish Railway, 97 of them described as *heavy*.

Other people's bomb stories became a crashing bore then, and it would be idle to trot them all out again a quarter of a century later, but some instances yet should be recalled. Damage to signals and communications were often extremely serious. One of the worst things was the destruction of the Divisional Control Office and the simultaneous flooding of the Emergency Control Office in Manchester on the night of December 23, 1940, when a large portion of Victoria Station was blown up by a close stick of bombs. Temporary Control was installed in some convenient cellars. The great signalbox at Birmingham New Street was struck in April. It had a 152-lever frame. Some forty levers were disrupted with the instrument shelf and block instruments, the telephones, batteries and relays. The structure surrounding these was virtually demolished. Next morning necessitated complete possession of all running lines – for once Birmingham had to depend on the Great Western – while the wreckage was carried away and a lineman's room was hastily equipped as a temporary block-post. Two emergency signalboxes were brought in by train and erected, forty new levers were fitted and the frame relocked.

Just before Christmas 1940, Merseyside had visitations on three nights in succession. Lime Street and Exchange were both damaged, but the worst incident blew out the arches of the bottleneck approach roads to the latter station. By way of tragi-comic relief, one recalls the escape of the former Furness Railway's ancient Bury locomotive *Coppernob* during severe bombing in the spring of '41. At the old Barrow Central Station, this relic had been preserved since FR days in a glass pavilion. This, and much of the station, flew into flinders, but the old engine stood proudly upright amongst the sea of broken glass and iron. The moral effect, without exaggeration, was prodigious. It was like finding a grandmother, scratched but healthily angry, amongst the wreckage of her home.

In Scotland, the worst damage was at or about Greenock, as far as the LMS company was concerned, but on the Northern Counties line in Ireland, much of York Road Station, Belfast, was destroyed, together with the goods sheds and the carriage and wagon shops, on May 4, 1941. The Station Hotel was gutted. Rolling stock casualties came to 20 coaches and 270 wagons, a serious item on a small railway system.

Back in London, St. Pancras had a bad time. In the autumn of 1940 it had been struck three times in a month, with one closure of five days. On May 10 of '41, it had it again, and this time suffered closure for a week. Damage on these occasions included an awful mess made of the Somers Town goods station, which coughed some of its grim red facade out into the Euston Road, further severe damage to signalling and to the approach roads, and during the attack of May 10–11, something that came straight through Barlow's great parabolic roof, then through the platform level to explode in the catacombs, making an immense cavity full of all sorts of human and material wreckage with a bizarre border of ripped carriage bodies, amputated bogies and odd pairs of wheels.

Recalling this scene, it is odd to reflect on the relative immunity of LMS rolling stock under the impact of what somebody – was it Hitler? – called total war. During the 46 months from June 1940 to December 1944, the company lost on the home system, by enemy action, but one locomotive, with 254 carriages of all sorts, 1,230 common-user wagons on its lines, 37 road motors and 46 trailers. Of horse-drawn drays, 439 were lost. In retrospect, being a lover of them, the author feels saddest about the horses, though indeed they fared better than the things they pulled. Thirty-four were killed and 75 injured but saved. To people who have to do with horses, *they* are people, and better than some. In London late in 1940, although a stable of 99 stalls was burnt, all the horses were safely got out.

As for the LMS staff, over 44,000 went into the forces or into full-time civil defence; over 1,500 died thus, not counting those who still were working their railway and, doing so, were bombed and shot up, or simply were killed in the way of working trains amid outrageous darkness. One of the casualties was the President of the Executive, the Old Man himself, and at that when he was off duty, which was rarely. Someone had once permitted himself a tasteless sneer at Lord Stamp's substantial Victorian residence down in London Chatham and Dover country, in Bomb-Alley as some people called it. The distinguished householder had retorted that he liked his *Tantallon*, and would stay in it until he was blown out of it. On April 16, 1941, a direct hit blew the house to pieces and with it the First Baron Stamp of Shortlands, his lady, and their eldest son who was legally presumed to have survived his sire by a grace note of time.

Josiah Charles Stamp, born on June 21, 1880, was a perfect example of the good puritan boy who made better, while having a geniality about him that was not generally associated with this type. His way to success was to develop his mind as a cerebral filing system, and to condition himself to maintaining a capacity for continual work. He was naturally endowed for both, combining encyclopaedic memory with prodigious energy, and once said that the royal road to success was the systematic accumu-

lation of an immense number of facts. That sounds rather like Dickens'
Mr. Gradgrind.[1] But Stamp had a brilliant intelligence, whereas Gradgrind's idea of facts was in the compulsion of children to remember that a
horse was a graminiverous quadruped.

Stamp's upbringing was frugal and his academic career was bought
with hard toil: consequently he was thirty-one before he could take his
first degree. At London University he took a First in Economics and
Political Science in 1911. He was a Cobden Prizeman in 1912, DSc in 1916
and a Hutchinson Medallist in the same year. He was Newmarch Lecturer
on Statistics from 1919 to 1921 and again in 1923. Of the Royal Statistical
Society he was a Council Member from 1916, Joint Secretary of the Society
and Editor of its *Proceedings*. He was President during 1930–32 and
Honorary Vice-President thereafter. In 1920 he had become a Council
member of the Royal Economics Society. His official honours went in this
sequence: CBE, 1918; KBE, 1920; GBE, 1924; GCB, 1935; created Baron
Stamp of Shortlands, 1938, in the Birthday Honours of that year. He was a
Knight Grand Cross of the Order of St. John of Jerusalem and a Knight
Grand Cross with Star of the Austrian Order of Merit. From 1929 to
1930 he was President of the Institute of Transport. Many other offices,
honours and publications were his. As noted earlier, he was a strongly
evangelical Christian, being a Sunday-School teacher as well as a don and
an economist. The foundation for all these things, as one has implied,
was long and uncomplaining drudgery of the sort that mortifies less alert
minds.

Lord Stamp was thus killed when he was at the summit of his prodigious
career, but such was the organisation he had created on the LMS that
there was nothing in the way of anarchic interregnum. Sir William Wood,
his Senior Vice-President, succeeded him as President of the Executive.

William Valentine Wood was an Ulsterman, born on February 14,
1883, and had entered the railway service as a boy in the Accounts
Department of the old Belfast and Northern Counties Railway in 1898.
He thus became an LMS man through the long-ago acquisition of the
BNCR by the Midland Railway. On the rather late imposition of Government Control on the Irish railways, Wood was appointed Secretary, and
later became a Member of the Railway Accountants' Committee set up by
the Irish Railway Executive Committee. This late imposition of State
control on the railways of Ireland seems odd to us, in the light of history.
All Ireland was then a component of the United Kingdom, and whether
everybody liked it or no, they were at war with the Central Powers. Some
of the more substantial farmers there, as elsewhere, liked it very much
indeed. ("And what about the war, Father? Do ye think it will hold,
now?") Conscription was not imposed. The real soldiers, such as Ireland

[1] *Hard Times,*

would always produce, could be expected anyway, and the others were important food-producers.[1] But in 1916 the Easter Rising, with Dublin blazing more fiercely than any English city under German bombs of those days, had given the British Government a real fright. Hence control of railways, and the beginning of William Valentine Wood's quiet rise to eventual power.

On the formation of the Ministry of Transport under Sir Eric Geddes, Wood left the Railway Service in Ireland to join him, and became Director of Transport (Accounting). He became Accountant to the Ministry of Transport in 1921. But – *once a railwayman always a railwayman* – he returned to his old industry and, the London Midland & Scottish company having been formed, he became Assistant to the Accountant General. He became Controller of Costs and Statistics in 1927, in which year he was knighted in the Birthday Honours. In 1930 he was Vice-President, Finance and Service Department. He was a man of Stamp's sort and after Stamp's heart.

Amid destruction, whether through acts of war or by accident, construction had to be carried on under the continual threat of the former: London Midland & Scottish shops staff just before the war numbered little less than 25,000. During the war years this total increased to 29,900 excluding 4,000 directed under Government, and Crewe alone had about 7,500. As remarked, the making of war machinery had begun before the war itself. The War Office approach over tanks was made in 1937, and the making of wings for aircraft was initiated in 1938.

On the outbreak of war, new construction of locomotives and vehicles was to a great extent suspended, in readiness for the other things. Yet during the first eight months we had an example of British Government obtuseness at its worst. Very few Government orders were received, and both skilled and unskilled workers were consequently drained off. Neither weapons nor railway equipment were being built in any quantity when the Prime Minister (Neville Chamberlain) endeavoured to assure the British public that Hitler had *missed the bus* in Norway, which, in fact, he occupied in record time. The events of that spring fortunately gave Government a shock, and spurred response to the urgent representations of senior railway officers. It was at their insistence that a committee was formed from members of the Ministries of Transport, Supply, Aircraft Production, Labour, the Admiralty and the Railway Executive Committee. It was *to agree on the type and quantity of manufacture to be undertaken in the shops and how much reserve capacity could be allocated to the various supply departments.* One wonders sometimes whether many of the members, apart from the REC, had a clue.

[1] The position was much the same during 1939-45 with Southern Ireland neutral but with more Irish soldiers abroad,

There were three successive Ministers of Transport during 1940: Captain Euan Wallace; Sir John Reith, who as founder of the BBC presumably knew something about communications; and the sporting Colonel J. T. C. Moore-Brabazon, who certainly had a pioneer's experience of aeroplanes, liked motor cars and locomotives for their own sake, and was to continue in office until the following year. Certainly, under him, there was *some* realism in the office, but things were not properly resolved until the conversion of the outfit into the Ministry of War Transport in 1941, and the appointment of F. J. Leathers as Minister. Now Leathers was a coal and shipping magnate; he really knew something about heavy transport business whether by land or water. He was not a Member of Parliament, so he was speedily made a Peer so that he could sit as well as direct. At last the Government, now fortunately under Churchill, had shown some real wisdom in regard to the transport situation. Lord Leathers remained in office until 1945. No better man had ever headed that much abused Ministry.

By the late summer of 1940, when high-speed production of aircraft was requisite for the survival of the nation, LMS works were turning out, and had already turned out many, wings for fighter aircraft – Hawker Hurricanes. Really heavy production had begun in May; eventually that of aircraft components alone included some 3,500 pairs of wings. Repairs were undertaken to both bomber and fighter aircraft in great numbers and the careful breaking up of those too heavily damaged in order to recover spares. The first tank to be produced in LMS locomotive shops was ready in the first month of the war, so those at the receiving end had no excuse for doubts that such things could be properly done in such places. Later, the output of armoured vehicles was about fourteen a month. Not only locomotive shops were engaged on this sort of thing. As the tide of war slowly turned from expected invasion to preparation for assault on the Continent, carriage shops were engaged in the production of troop-carrying gliders.

At length, so tremendous was the output of armaments, even to millions of shells, that even allowing for the near suspension of new construction, the company's primary business of furnishing itself with its own transport equipment showed ominous signs of incipient breakdown. By the time of the fall of France, 66 locomotives had been released and 16 of these lost across the Channel. The Stanier 2–8–0 goods engine was made, for the time being, a standard locomotive for war service. There was a Government demand for 150 locomotives for the conveyance of supplies to Russia via Persia. Now the Persian line across the mountains was already built, and being worked by a curious collection of locomotives, some of them new from Sweden, and some of them worn-out warriors sometime displaced by electrification, also from Sweden and from Austria.

Fifty more engines went from the LMS, having been hurriedly converted to burn oil. But at home, maintenance was going down even while stock was depleted; the proportion of engines awaiting general overhaul became alarming. Now Government had to be induced to ease railway production of military equipment in order to better the locomotive situation.

In 1942, things were somewhat easier on the locomotive side. As already noted, some engines had been borrowed from the Southern Railway which, much electrified in the London and South Coast areas, could spare an allowance of its older specimens. One recalls unlikely encounters; a veteran Stirling 7ft express, sometime South Eastern, in the Nottingham neighbourhood and a South Western 0–4–4 tank engine in Central Scotland, where men were still used to the Drummond style anyway. The sight of a Stoudley D1 tank engine, bound for Caithness, may or may not have reminded someone that about 70 years before, its designer had commanded Lochgorm Works, Inverness. Interested Naval men, ashore from northern waters, sometimes noticed and recounted these things.

In the working of the LMS at this stage, the coaching position was not easy, although, particularly under the influence of Ernest Lemon, much had been done in the standardisation and mass-production of vehicles. At the outbreak of war, the company had about 17,500 carriages of all kinds. New construction practically ceased. At first, over three thousand were idle owing to the drastic reduction of train services, but by 1943, before the invasion of France, passenger traffic had increased 7 per cent over the pre-war figure, while carriages by then numbered about 1,350 less. Some of course had been destroyed by bombing in the meantime, but there had been heavy calls on stock for the improvisation of ambulance trains. Theft and wanton damage became widespread, so movable equipment was as far as possible withdrawn, and no wonder; in 1941 the company had 400,000 hand-towels stolen.

With, maybe, no more guilty secret than memory of an illicit apple when one was eleven, stealing things, especially in times of war shortage, is a crime most people can understand. Wanton damage for its own sake, one hopes, is not, but the minority is a considerable and active one. In that war, with so much of what might have been called businesslike damage being done by opposed peoples, the amount of wanton slashing and hacking was prodigious, and this was odd, with so much destruction going on already and the enemy as target for general resentment. Looting, by the way, was a capital offence at the time, though nobody in fact swung for it. Pilferage became alarming. The worst of it seemed to be at the Docks.

As far as passenger travel was concerned, whether Service or Civil, overcrowding at night was the most unpleasant thing short of enemy action. One recalls stepping over two men, both asleep and even snoring on the floor, though one had his head in one coach and his feet in another. That, too, was on the LMS which still clung to the old-style bellows while the LNER and the Southern generally used the American type invented by Sessions in the late 'eighties, usually termed the Pullman vestibule and forming with its close-prest friction-plates a much steadier gangway between vehicles. In fairness to our present subject, the writer would remark that the East Coast expresses by night were in his own experience the most fearsome. If his recollections of an execrable French train in 1940, and of the best that devastated Germany could muster immediately after the war, are anything to go by, the British wartime traveller did fairly well even by ordinary conveyance.

All four British railways were carrying more passengers in fewer trains, and were earning more passenger ill-will for their pains than for some time previously. The German would growl: "*Krieg ist Krieg!*" The Frenchman would grunt: "*C'est la guerre!*" The Unknown Political Prisoner was taken for rides more frightful than anything in the previous history of railways. But the Anglo-Saxon, less patiently than the Spartan Gael, endured his night's sprawl on the floor of a draughty corridor. Understandable was the angry disgust of a woman obliged to assuage her needs with one foot braced against a door with a broken lock. Both, in many cases, took such a scunner at riding in a train that they promised themselves never to do so again, once the unrestricted private motor reappeared. The writer has publicly noticed this aspect before, even a long time ago, but having-told-you-so is poor comfort as a rule. One railway PRO was most upset, but tacitly agreed that one's article (anonymous as it happened) "had something". The war was then just over, but still, north of Carstairs, the train had no proper lamps, while the return (East Coast) was unspeakable except by a man having a remarkable command of the English language enriched by William Shakespeare, Robert Burns, Jonathan Swift, and some other masters of invective. To be fair, the Royal Scot of the period was surprisingly good, if slower than formerly. The day trains were generally better because, leave being what it was, most people preferred to travel by night to save time all too short.

Most of the extras, of course, had gone, and almost all of the strictly limited sleeping berths were reserved in advance for people on Government business. As briefly noted already, to make the most of the sleeping cars, upper berths were put into what formerly had been single berth first-class compartments. Thus they furnished the sort of first-class sleeper still provided by certain Continental undertakings at about double the price exacted today, for the good old single-berth arrangement, by our much-maligned British Railways. This wartime expedient was, however,

a good thing. It was to form the prototype of the British second-class
sleeper to come, a thing very superior to the four-berth third-class British
sleeper of 1928 and after, and infinitely better than the Continental six-
berth second-class travelling-family-vault of the present. If one of his
stories is to be construed as a real-life experience, Edgar Allen Poe once
believed himself prematurely coffined on an American canal boat.
Continental couchettes can be like that, too!

People of the armed forces were guided and looked after as far as
possible, and not only by RTOs, who themselves were in close liaison
with the welfare societies. There was always a Church Army man on duty
at Crewe, as well as British and American military men, to quote one
example. Then one recalls a very weary and very hungry soldier truly
counting his pennies at Preston, and the way his face lit up when a nice
WVS lady told him he could have what he liked; there was nothing to pay
there. At the same time, the free canteens could be abused. Men in much
less need would sometimes stuff themselves at Preston and then throw
their official rations under the carriages at Crewe, to the great encourage-
ment of the numerous rats in that ancient caravanserai.

Impressions of allies were variable and sometimes quaint. One American
soldier, asked what he thought of British trains, gloomily replied that he
couldn't say; before he had crossed the ocean, he had never bin in a
goddam railroad! But another said: "My! what a wonderful system of
transportation you have in this country! We were landed at some Scotch
place with mountains by the ocean and to hell from anywhere, but there
warn't only a train every day; there war two! And, oh boy! Your day
coaches are swell!" Not everybody would have agreed with him after a
packed night journey north or south, with its choice of fearsome fug or
freezing draught, the horrible cold stenches of abused necessaria, and the
detestable blue glimmer of the night lamps over the slumped forms of
faceless men and women. But, faced by a common enemy, total strangers
seemed to be much more friendly to one another than in more fortunate
days. It was the next generation that looked back in anger.

An occasional awful journey could be endured fairly enough. Unless
the train were bombed and shot up, even the sort of journey just described
was quite tolerable compared with ordinary ones in occupied country, for
"awful" is a purely relative term, applicable to anything from nuclear
fission to an after-dinner speech. But Head of State and Head of Government both had to spend many days a-rail, sometimes, as did other
important personages. They had to live in their trains, these being moved
about from one place to another. The LMS Royal Train, which of course
was fully equipped for use as living quarters for many days, made 57
tours, covering over 31,000 miles, on its parent system from September
1939, to the end of 1944. Its three new carriages we have noted already.

This same train made additionally 44 tours on the London & North Eastern, 13 on the Great Western and six on the Southern Railways. Its movements were never bruited, and to make it inconspicuous it was at last painted in the standard red with grey roofs, instead of in the London & North Western colours retained to please George V. It thus looked, from the air, like any other LMS train save that some of the carriages were noticeably more old-fashioned than the standard article. The company provided too the special living train for the Prime Minister, and this might have been described as a mobile "No. 10" with an old London & North Western "semi-royal" for one of its most important components. These trains were staffed by the LMS wherever they went, and the catering was always in its hands. Railwaymen – and now and then the passing amateur – knew the trains well enough when they saw them, and kept their mouths shut. Churchill is said to have become much attached to his train. One of his virtues was that he knew how to live, under whatever circumstances.

The LMS had been pre-eminent in the construction and provision of carriages, a tradition going back to the long-ago lead set by the Midland company. In some ways the carriages were old-fashioned. As remarked, the old-style bellows persisted. The bodies were lighter than those of other companies, but in this there was virtue when it came to furnishing extremely long trains for special purposes. Even before the war, the company had produced fully detailed drawings for ambulance trains, assembled essential components at Derby and set aside suitable vehicles for conversion. The order arrived on September 2, 1939. Some were prepared in the company's shops; for the rest, the material and the convertible vehicles were sent off to works of the other three main-line railways.

A train for home service consisted at first of nine and later of eleven carriages, of seven different types. Trains for foreign service were in rakes of 16 vehicles of nine types, with Continental couplings and drawgear, and steam-heat connections suitable for those of French locomotives. Early in 1940, 344 LMS carriages of various sorts had been converted, making 12 trains for home service and 13 for overseas. Nine of the latter were lost on the evacuation, soon after; the others were retained until they were called for in the late summer of 1942. Thereafter, each of the railways in Great Britain converted their own stock to the same ends. Of the 925 ultimately dealt with, 343 – the highest single contribution, came from Derby and Wolverton. Derby further provided 80 mobile battery-charging sets. Provision of rolling-stock for foreign service was be-devilled by the difference of vacuum and air brakes; one more thing for which we had to thank the obtuseness of Francis Webb, long ago on the London & North Western Railway.

One wonders, in this coaching connection, how much was owed to Sir Ernest Lemon, and that takes us from equipment to personalities again for it had been he who had taken over the traditions of Derby Carriage and Wagon Works from Reid, who was the successor of Bain, who was the successor of Clayton, all mighty coach-builders.

There was something rocket-like in Lemon's later career; a soaring, a display of differently coloured stars, and then darkness. He was indeed a man who burned himself out, like Robert Stephenson and Isambard Brunel nearly a century before. Just over a year before the war, in June 1938, the Prime Minister had asked Stamp for Lemon to become Director General of Aircraft Production, with a seat on the Air Council. How strange superficially, yet on scrutiny how obvious, was the connection between the old Derby C. and W. Works, with its mastery of mass-produced vehicles, and the assembly of military aircraft!

So Lemon left the LMS. Having completed in time the programme set before him by April 1940, and one may well dare say, made ready the panic-stations production of fighter aircraft in that year, he went back to the LMS, and to his office of Vice-President (Operating and Commercial). His services to the Air Ministry brought him a knighthood in the New Year honours of 1941. Though he had returned to the railway, he was retained the on Air Ministry's Industrial Panel and (in the properly guarded language of *The Railway Gazette*) "was engaged for a period on behalf of the Minister of Production in connection with the output of certain types of aircraft . . ." One thinks of that memorable wooden aeroplane, the Mosquito, then back to the mass production, in wood, of tumblehome doors for railway carriages, and one goes on wondering.

Lemon was a rare type of railway officer, one who was at once an able mechanical engineer and a brilliant traffic man. Then he over-loaded his own circuit. Late in 1942 he was ill, indeed very ill. In February 1943 he was retired from the LMS, to be succeeded as Chairman of the Railway Companies' Commission and as a Vice-President of the London Midland & Scottish Railway's Executive Committee by Ashton Davies. One of those under him bitterly commented: "69 years of age compared with his 58!" This same man wrote, in private correspondence to Sir Ernest Lemon's son, Major R. M. L. Lemon:[1] "Briefly the reason given him for being compensated is that he did not fit in with the Watford organisation. The real reason behind it is, however, the fact that the Railway Companies' Commission, of which he was appointed Chairman twelve months or more ago, has never been given a real chance of working in a practical way. We [the Commission] have been subjected to all kinds of restrictions on the part of the General Managers . . . and your father has been in a continual state of frustration and mental irritation as he realised how

[1] Later Chief Operating Superintendent, East African Railways and Harbours.

impossible it was to get a proper job done as was intended in the first place."

At the beginning of February 1943, the LMS Executive Committee also suffered by the death of C. S. Harrison, who had held that office since June 1941. He was an old London & North Western man who had joined at Broad Street in 1901, gone to Euston in 1903 and had served under six of the old company's General Managers. The Executive Committee, with Sir William Wood at its head, faced the war traffic and the company's twilight that was to follow. In it was that massive old Lancastrian, Ashton Davies; senior to him was Sir Harold Hartley, and with them was G. L. Darbyshire.

WARTIME ACCIDENTS

In this time the company had some severe misfortunes in its working, apart from war save in the fact that the detestable blackout was accessory to many accidents. Combined with moonless fog, it made the working of a railway something that Dante and Milton might have failed to describe, even in sympathetic collaboration. Troubles began early in the war, when there was a spectacular smash in the middle of Bletchley station. The night of October 13, 1939, was dark with a vicious wet east wind blowing, when the down Royal Highlander, preceding a down Irish express via Stranraer, stopped at Bletchley. There an old London & North Western 0–8–0 locomotive, tender first, was adding a van to this Inverness train when it was struck at some speed by the Stranraer train, headed by Class 5 No. 5025 (leading) and Royal Scot class No. 6130 *The West Yorkshire Regiment*. The Black Five and the shunting engine thus met smokebox to smokebox, and were very severely damaged. Still the impact of these heavy engines in the middle of the collision, with the buffing of the van behind one and a Royal Scot behind the other, absorbed forces which might have been more terribly loosed, especially on the Inverness train. The death-roll of four was thus a lenient visitation. But for that shunting movement the two engines of the Stranraer train would have made shocking havoc amongst the Inverness carriages. Alternatively, had the shunting engine been moving out again, the Inverness train would have been saved, or at most slightly damaged by rebound, but the consequences for the Stranraer train would have been worse.

Scotland had several troubles in unusual places. On January 13, 1940, the first of two freight trains to the Kyle of Lochalsh was divided by a broken coupling on the 1 in 50 climb to Raven Rock. It ran back, but was timeously smashed-up in the trap siding on the Dingwall side of Achterneed, before it could strike the following train. The line was blocked for two days. There were no casualties, however; the goods guard had jumped when he found he could do no more with his skidding brake van.

Worse happened on March 5. Part of a northbound freight train broke away on the down loop at Slochd, through failure of an iron coupling hook on a private owner's wagon. (A deep crystalline flaw was afterwards found in the offending hook.) The 20-ton goods brake and 21 wagons began to run back, and the goods guard, a man of limited experience, failed to notice this in time. Otherwise he had easily held the runaway. He then jumped, but instead of warning at once the Slochd signalman, who could have taken quick action, he began with misplaced fortitude to tramp back towards Carr-Bridge, in the wake of the runaway. God alone knows what good he thought he was doing! Further, the Slochd signalman, who might have noticed the breakaway at once, wasted some eight minutes before he telephoned Carr-Bridge about it.

It was thus too late, to derail these careering wagons as they approached Carr-Bridge, where the signalman had by then accepted, and had in section, the following goods train which was double-headed like the first. The Carr-Bridge man acted quickly in warning his colleague at Aviemore, but there the tablet had already passed to the leading driver of the second train, which had at once started up the bank. The Aviemore signalman tried desperately to intercept it. This *might* have been done by letting it crash closed level-crossing gates north of Aviemore, but now there was no time, owing to those eight minutes lost by bungling at Slochd.

Climbing at about 35 mph, $2\frac{1}{2}$ miles north of Aviemore the second train struck the descending runaway at very high combined speed. The leading engine of the second train was thrown over at right-angles to the track, and both enginemen were killed. The brake van on the runaway, an old Highland Railway 20-ton six-wheel type, was without sanding gear, so mechanical obsolescence contributed to human foolishness in causing this deplorable accident. The signalmen at Carr-Bridge and Aviemore were both to be commended for their quick but unrewarded action in trying to save the situation. Single-track approach from the south ruled out the installation of ordinary catch-points.

At that time, the official reports on railway accidents were being issued as duplicated sheets, and were sometimes less detailed than the former blue books. Summaries of them record that both trains were hauled by Black Fives, but by another account, an old Highland Loch class was overthrown. One of these last, indeed, ended its days as a moving target for the training of airmen in the business of *train-busting*.

There are other stories of this rather adequate accident, for which the writer is indebted to Mr. Gavin Wilson. One is that coal trains were involved, and that with all this scatteration of good fuel in the heather, country people about Aviemore had no need to buy coal for a year; even, by one version, for the duration of the war. The other yarn is that some lumbermen from Newfoundland had lately arrived for forestry work in the neighbourhood. Carr-Bridge did not offer much in the way of entertainment to either exiles or returned natives, but its platforms had seats for storytelling, smoking and watching a small portion of the world go by; indeed there were more trains than were usual in Newfoundland, and sometimes they stopped with news, or a girl's face at a window.

Suddenly out of the cutting, and over the Dulnain bridge, shot these runaway wagons, headed by the wretched goods-brake, its blocks screaming murder-with-fireworks. Over the facing loop points they rushed, through the station at about 70 mph, and away out at the south end. The men went back to camp. Doubtless they took the distant mighty bang for Highland thunder. For they told their friends what they had seen, and that they had never known a train travel so fast; *so fast you couldn't even see the locomotive*! Next evening, Carr-Bridge station had quite a company to watch these fast trains go through. The line being very badly blocked, they were disappointed. There were not even ordinary trains.

Well; so the story goes! It belongs with that of the Out-Back Australian who, seeing a remotely approaching train, remarked with enthusiasm that she was right bang on the day. Back to serious Scotland; and passing by a train derailed without casualties at Tain on the following day, there were two more serious Scottish accidents during the autumn of 1940, on the Caledonian main line between Carlisle and Carstairs.

On September 10, owing to enemy action, the regular driver and fireman of the 10.0 am express from Glasgow to London via the West Coast Route were delayed and unable to take their train. A passed fireman and a passed cleaner took the engine, streamlined Pacific No. 6224 *Princess Alexandra*, three minutes before starting time. The fire was reported good at the time. Near Carstairs, even with this big engine and a well prepared fire, they lost their steam and the train came to a stand through their inability to maintain vacuum. Restarting, they staggered on, but a combination of low water and increasing gradient against the engine uncovered the firebox crown. Near Cleghorn the crownplate collapsed. Both enginemen were scalded and the acting fireman died. Anything in the nature of a boiler explosion was rare on a British railway. As noted, war conditions were a contributory cause in this case. The train remained on the rails and no other persons were hurt.

On November 5 there was a bad collision at Gretna Junction. At 6.9 in the evening, which was wet and nearly dark, a goods train from Shawfield to Carlisle, headed by ex Caledonian 4-6-0 locomotive No. 14650, was moving very slowly from the up Glasgow and South Western to the up West Coast line at the junction when the tender and leading wagons were struck on the diamond crossing of the down line by the

10.5 am express from Euston to Perth, headed by three-cylinder compound 4-4-0 engine No. 1141 and consisting of ten carriages. Speed on impact was about 45 mph. The express engine was thrown over on her left side. Driver Martin of this, and two passengers, were killed, half the express having been derailed, with much damage to the leading coaches. The tender of the goods train engine was derailed by impact and fifteen wagons smashed up.

Circumstances were unusually mysterious, and there was a whiff of perplexity in the Report of Colonel A. C. Trench who inquired for the Ministry of Transport. The fireman of the express, who survived, was sure he and his driver had both seen the down main distant at *clear*. He had seen no other signals, felt no brake application, and saw nothing of the goods until his engine hit it. Of the goods train, driver, fireman and guard all concurred in describing what might have been called peculiar behaviour of semaphores. Gretna Green box was switched out, and the six miles from Eastriggs to Gretna Junction thus formed a block section. The driver of the goods said he found both the Gretna Junction up branch distant signals at *caution*, and therefore reduced speed to about 15 mph to be ready to stop at the outer home, to which drivers off the branch were quite used. The train was an ordinary British loose-coupled goods of the period, unbraked except for engine and van.

The Junction inner distant was on the same post as the Gretna Green advance stop signal, which of course was at *clear*, the box being switched out. Both arms had repeaters, consequently there were four arms one above each other, on the same post. The goods driver said that the inner distant came off before he reached it, at which he released the engine brake. As noted, his fireman and guard agreed to this, and Colonel Trench remarked that the unlikely aspect of four green lights on the same post was not a thing liable to be mistaken, or more correctly, mis-identified. Rounding the curve to the junction, the driver said he saw the outer home off, then, unexpectedly, the inner home at danger. He made a full application of the engine's Westinghouse brake but could not stop clear of the Junction.

Colonel Trench remarked that if the evidence of the three men on this train were true, it was possible that the Junction signalman had originally intended to pass the goods to the main line before the express arrived and had pulled-off for it when it was occupying a track circuit at Gretna Green, which sounded a buzzer in his box when the outer home was on. He had accepted the goods from Eastriggs at 5.50 and received "train in section" five minutes later. Then, the Colonel suggested, this man might have realised the imminence of the express and decided to pass it through first, putting back the signals in the face of the goods and resetting the junction, not realising the closeness of the slower train. He accepted the express at six o'clock, offered it to Quintinshill at 6.5, and pulled-off for it at 6.7 on receiving "entering section". The trains struck two minutes later. The Junction signalman denied that he had put back signals and reset the road. The less probable alternative was that the driver of the goods, expecting a clear road to and through the junction, had not sufficient control over his train until it was too close to the outer home, which he overran by 600 yd., and that he immediately "arranged" agreement with his fireman and guard on his story of the inner distant being pulled off in his face. It seemed unlikely; he was used to the road and to being stopped at the junction. The conflicting witnesses were all men of long service, good record and local experience. Colonel Trench reported that he could only base his opinion on apparent possibilities, an unusual conclusion. This accident, though involving an important West Coast express, aroused less public attention than some, and has thus deserved, more than some worse but simpler cases, our attention.

On October 14, 1940, there was at Wembley, on the London approach, a derailment strangely recalling that at Wellingborough on the Midland Railway just over 42 years earlier. The train involved was the 11.50 midday Liverpool–London express, of eleven carriages and two wagons, headed by Patriot class engine No. 5529. At 7.10 in the evening (*express* was in wartime a courtesy title) while passing through Wembley at speed, this train struck a heavily loaded, four-wheeled platform trolley which had got out of control and had run down the north end of the platform ramp between the up-fast and down-slow roads, fouling the former. The thing had got away from three not-very-robust men who had been handling it as best they could in the blackout, and one of its frail axles seems to have been nevertheless sufficient to derail one of the engine's pairs of bogie wheels. More serious derailment ensued at a crossing beyond. The engine turned over on her right side, with the tender partly jacknifed, killing both enginemen. Nine passengers died, with most casualties in the leading coach.

In his Annual Report on Railway Accidents in 1940, the Chief Inspecting Officer of Railways, Lieut. Colonel Sir Alan Mount, suggested that risks through blackout might have contributed to 10 per cent of casualties, and he paid tribute to the splendid work of railwaymen in very trying circumstances. "The way in which all departments met the situation," he wrote, "was beyond praise, and justified confidence for the future that services will be maintained and repairs to bomb damage will continue to be effected with equal promptitude."

There were more troubles to come, but none was such a bad year as 1915 in the previous war. Apart from enemy action and train accidents, there was an oddly nasty thing at Blackpool on August 27, 1941. Two aeroplanes collided over the town and one fell upon Central Station. There were fifteen deaths, consequences having been rather similar to those of a bombing, or "incident" as it was delicately called in official language at the time. Of train accidents, that at Holmes Chapel, on September 14, 1941, gave a case of two trains in one block section, through signalling faults of either or both of two men. The 12.50 am passenger train from Crewe to Manchester ran into the back of the 12.35 am from Crewe to Leeds. The Manchester engine, 2–6–4T No. 2395, at about 35 mph, went right through the rear steel van of the Leeds train, splitting it into fairly large pieces, before overturning to the right. Nine persons were killed or fatally hurt.

Much worse was the collision of the two six-fifty-threes at Eccles on December 30, 1941, which killed 23 passengers including three railway people travelling. It was at 8.18 am of a dark morning in dense fog when the 6.53 train from Kenyon Junction to Manchester, crossing from up-slow to up-fast roads was struck, just in rear of its engine, on the diamond crossing, by 2–6–4 tank engine No. 2406, heading the 6.53 train from Rochdale to Pennington and running about 30 mph, rapidly accelerating from its just-previous stop at Eccles. The second and third Manchester coaches, and the leading one of the Pennington train, were demolished, and two more Manchester coaches split open along the sides. The signalman at Eccles had suspended block working some time before, erroneously believing that he had a fogman on duty at the down-slow distant. This signal, and the two homes also, were badly placed. The Pennington driver did not see the distant, but the fireman said it was at *clear*, so he relied on this statement and on the absence of a detonator. As for the outer home, which he did not see, he said he had caught a green hand signal, and had heard no detonator. That was vehemently denied by the fogman on duty at this signal. Major G. R. S. Wilson, who inquired for the Ministry of War Transport, held the signalman responsible, while accepting his expressed belief that there was a fogman at the down-slow distant. The Pennington driver, he considered, had not take sufficient care under such conditions. Recalling the unholy combination of winter fog and blackout, one cannot help feeling some sympathy for those who had so fatally blundered.

Just before the German capitulation, on April 19, 1945, there was a collision at Dale Lane No. 1 signalbox, Kirkby, between the 6.15 am train from Bradford to Liverpool and an engine with goods brake. Both locomotives were overturned and five railwaymen killed, including both drivers and the fireman of the passenger train. The passenger guard, Mrs. G. Barnett, though severely shocked, showed much devotion in accounting for all her passengers.

Here, though technically it belongs to the post-war period, may be described the last of this sad group of troubles. On September 30, 1945, with the war just over in the East, came the worst accident to a passenger train in the history of the London Midland & Scottish company, though not of its constituents. In some ways its circumstances resembled those at Leighton Buzzard, back in 1930, but its consequences were more severe. The train involved was the 8.20 pm night express from Perth, consisting of fifteen carriages of various sorts. One was all-steel, most of the others were composite and some were all-wooden as to the bodies. They were well filled with passengers. The engine was Royal Scot No. 6157 *The Royal Artilleryman*. This train, under clear signals, approached and went through the facing crossover from up-fast to up-slow at full speed (which it should not have done) at three-to-four minutes past nine o'clock of the morning after its overnight rumble from Central Scotland. The morning was cloudless.

On the crossover, *The Royal Artilleryman* recovered from the initial (right-hand) roll but was careened to the left on the second, to the up-slow road. The engine went out into the adjacent field, 9ft below track level and well away from the line, lying down on her left side. The tender finished up at right-angles to the engine, but still upright. Six of the first seven carriages were destroyed by piling up, the train having covered its own length after the engine turned over, and only the last three, two sleeping cars and a van, remained on the rails. Forty-three persons were killed by this shocking smash. They included both the enginemen, so none could find out why, fully warned of diversion from up-fast to up-slow, the train had gone through this at an estimated speed of at least 60 mph when there was a speed restriction of 20 mph on the crossover. Visible warning of the diversion, displayed 2,000 yd north of it, must have been missed. Such diversions were far from uncommon with night Scotch expresses approaching London. Driver Swaby, who died, had a good record and temperate habits. He was a Crewe man. There was the question of early visibility as in seeing, or not seeing, both fixed and warning signals against the mounting morning sun at the autumn equinox, and therein, one believes, lies the explanation.

Of the others dead, five were English royal-train staff returning home after going north on duty. Fortunately there was a doctor on the train, and after his devoted kind he was instantly at work. There were also soldiers, quick to emergency, and the local services backed-up admirably. The first casualty was in the West Hertfordshire Hospital 25 minutes later.

Quite fascinating was the clearing of the damaged equipment. Breaking-up the remains of gutted carriages, though it may be abruptly gruesome, is simple. Less so was the recovery of a relatively large overturned steam locomotive far out in a field of mangold. The smash had blocked all four roads at Bourne End. The down-fast was cleared by 10.55 am, less than two hours after the accident. The up-fast road was clear by 4.0 pm of the

30th. All roads were clear in the early hours of October 2. There remained the engine lying on her side amongst the mangold-wurzels.

First, *The Royal Artilleryman* was stripped down, everything that could be removed being so. The motion was cut up by oxy-acetylene flame as if it were already on the scrap road, and thrown into waiting wagons. By the time all was done, there was a shell on wheels and frames, within the scope of two 50 ton cranes, to bring upright and get on to temporary track, and thus back to its proper place. A similar operation with a larger engine was to distinguish – if that be quite the word – the clearing operations at Weedon under British Railways in September 1951. The writer saw by chance the remains of both wrecks which transcended his first such sight (collision at Munich East, Whitsun 1926) and he believes that the breakdown gangs at Weedon must have profited from the experiences of those at Bourne End.[1] The Weedon engine not only was bigger but seemed to have gone farther out amongst root vegetables.

Both accidents took place on what one must regard, historically, as unfortunate sections of the old London & North Western main line, they having seen repeated disaster down the years. The London & North Western had wrecked the Irish Mail at Weedon on August 14, 1915. There is much curious coincidence in such things. Even the safe and virtuous Great Western Railway had smashed up two expresses at Norton-Fitzwarren, with half a century between them, and every proper South Western man knew that it was unlucky for trains to pass Salisbury without stopping, though only one really spilled itself (1906).

Bourne End did not provide the last instance of an accident to an LMS train, but it is enough at this stage. The company's time was running out, not economically but socially. Great Britain was among the last countries in Europe to have no State Railways.[2] Your author was brought up to believe that a railway was a public service rather than a commercial undertaking, so his sighs were purely emotional at the falling dusk of the last companies. Tory, Whig and Jacobin alike, we knew that the day of the railway company was done, at any rate in our country. Opinions on what was to be done with the railways themselves widely varied between Right-Wing-destructive to Left-Wing-constructive policies. The latter tended to regard the railway as a provider of employment. The former had already realised that, indefinitely, the country would be run by the oil industry, and that any other which did not toe the line must be squashed. Government had already made an extremely sharp deal with the railway companies for their hire in wartime, based on their rather disappointing receipts for the year 1938. Government, especially in wartime, may be

---

[1] By comparision, the Munich thing was easy; the big Maffei engine remained upright and scarcely scarred amongst the mischief she had made.

[2] Except such special examples as Longmoor Military Railway.

expected to do things like that, even though it be less corrupt than government in more eastern or more western countries. For railways under government, the outlook was bleak. For railways under private enterprise, it was fairly ruinous. Two great birds hovered above; the eagle of mechanical change and the vulture of big business.

In the meantime, all the British railways – indeed all railways at that time concerned in keeping their respective countries going – had been working as they had never worked before. With the exception of an ignoble minority in the big goods stations, who competed with comparable minorities in docks and harbours in the business of black-market commerce, railway people had come out of their war well. They could walk, without diffidence, with sailors. Nobody had sung for them Whiting's *Eternal Father strong to save*. Kipling's *Recessional* might have been more appropriate under the circumstances.

CHAPTER SEVEN

Götterdämmerung

WERE THEY indeed gods, those who faced the twilight of the most substantial railway company in the world-history of the industry? Or at least demi-gods, as some of them undoubtedly thought they were? Or were they just withdrawing businessmen, quietly gentlemanly like most of the Chairmen, or noisy like one Councillor Wilson who used to raise such merry hell at some of the last Annual General Meetings? Or were they various sorts of railway officer, some already believing that theirs was a public service, others still thinking in terms of the London & North Western competing with the Midland, apparently in blissful unawareness of the existence of the motor, let alone the aircraft, and ignoring any such heresy as the idea that a system of public transport could be anything but a commercial undertaking? Or were they people who, as noted before, thought of their railway as a provider of employment even more than as a public service?

They were of all these sorts, apart from the supposed Gods.

With war ended, some war conditions persisted. The Railway Executive Committee was to continue in more or less of action until it was succeeded by the British Transport Commission on January 1, 1948. War with Germany ended on May 8, 1945, and with both America and Russia claiming to have won it, we were rather pleased that the unconditional surrender was made to a British general, that strange and wondrous Irishman Bernard Montgomery. On August 15, the Emperor of Japan surrendered to America, naming as his principal reason the use of a new and terrible bomb. The war was over, and on both sides some people were more afraid than ever. Meanwhile, there had been domestic changes which both allies and enemies, unused to the peculiarities of British democracy, found inexplicable. Churchill's Administration fell and Attlee's came to power with war still in full bloody blast, though nearly burnt out. All knew what to expect from the first Socialist Government since 1931. On November 19, 1945, it announced its proposals for the nationalisation of certain industries, including railways, canals and long-distance road haulage. What became the Transport Act received the Royal Assent by George VI on August 6, 1947. The impending transfer of ownership was received with rejoicings on the Government side of the House, on the floor of which the Honourable Member for Liverpool Exchange did a little dance all on her own. It was at least more graceful than the notorious "poor bag of assets" sneer of that eminent Socialist, the Honourable Member for Swindon.

Certainly, the antics of the former were funny, and the present writer believes, even more than did his Radical forebears, that it was a very good thing, that Transport Act, 1947; that the old companies would have retrenched, and retrenched, to the point of extinction rather than provide any public service that was not commercially viable. What Lord Royden, penultimate Chairman of the LMS, really thought cannot be stated at this stage in history, even if one knew. One remembers him as an adroit master of a noisy Annual General Meeting, not least in dealing with the vociferous Right Wing. That included such parties as one of the company's motor drivers, who was also a stockholder, who sought to show how dividends were lost by the nefarious practices of his colleagues, and was just about to read out a sort of *dossier* when he was sharply told to sit down. It came with a splendid crackle; Sir Richard Moon, sixty years before, could not have bettered it. Stockholders even more awkward, but correct, were courteously answered.

Royden's last Annual General Meeting was the company's twenty-third, in 1946. With the nation itself, the railway had emerged undefeated from years of war, but battered and exhausted. Country and railway both looked very shabby. Though fighting had ceased and there was some relief in home conditions, the shortage of experienced staff was heavy. Passenger traffic was very heavy, for new motor cars were as yet scarce, and motor fuel still somewhat severely rationed. It was indeed three per cent above that of 1944, the last full year of war in Europe, and as much as 78 per cent more than it had been in 1938, that unlucky year on which Government's rent to the railways had been determined. With this huge increase in passenger bookings – people had naturally flocked on long-delayed holidays – was a 25 per cent reduction in loaded passenger train miles, so the trains were often horribly crowded still, thus accumulating extra loads of unpopularity. 1946 freights were down, though still much above pre-war level. Net ton-miles for 1945 came to 9,593 million, that was 38 per cent above those of twelve months before the war. General merchandise was 25 per cent up, coal 11 per cent and other minerals 16 per cent.

At the same time, equipment was in a poor way. Track maintenance was even more difficult than in the middle of the war. Some new locomotives had been built but no new carriages until a few came in the last autumn.

At his last meeting, Lord Royden asked rhetorically what was the case for retaining company ownership. The implication (one is not quoting now) seems to have been that when the railway was doing record business, it was Government that pocketed the proceeds. What he went on to say was that his company had passed through tests most severe since 1939, with complete success, and still under limitations on profit as laid down by Parliament in 1921, the year of the Railways Act. The nation, and not the stockholders, had reaped a rich harvest.

Lord Leathers, when Minister of War Transport, had said: "The railways are still the mainstay of the inland transport system . . . an indispensable part of the military machine. . . . Few people seem to realise what the extent of the railways' achievement is." There had been other tributes from eminent statesmen, including Winston Churchill.

One might suggest now that while Government had always been ready to make use of the railways (and to screw them as hard as possible), it was Parliament, not quite the same thing, that had all along regarded railway managements as natural enemies. Those on the Left had ever considered them grinders of the faces of the poor, being at once harsh and skinflint with their servants in the business of keeping up dividends for the idle rich. The Tories had never forgiven the industry for being the first to invade landed property and privacy from without, to the benefit of rich Whig Townees in the earlier part of the nineteenth century. So on either side of the House, the railway companies had ever had plenty of enemies. Answering his own question at his last AGM, Lord Royden simply said that the Government had not shown what advantage would accrue to the user of the railways by the transfer of the stockholders' property to itself. One cannot say that Government – or rather the Party supporting that Government – had done so. One has already indicated one's opinion on the other side of the prospect. Either way, the nation was bedevilled by politicians.

A valedictory note: Thomas Royden, Second Baronet (1917) and first Baron Royden of Frankby, had been born on May 22, 1871, which was just before the fall of the Second Commune of Paris, which took his infancy back some way. He was a Wykehamist and a Magdalen man – a combination that had produced from last century both great Tories and great Radicals – and he had become a Director of the Lancashire & Yorkshire Railway in 1909. In the first amalgamation year of 1922 he came to the board of the enlarged London & North Western company and thus, practically automatically, to that of the London Midland & Scottish Railway, in 1923. Of the last-named he became Deputy Chairman in that rather anxious year of 1940, and Chairman in the following year. Sir Thomas Royden, as he then was, became a Baron in the New Year's Honours List of 1944, when he had chaired his railway through the most trying phase in its history. From personal recollections: Though not a large man, even when astrakhaned and befrogged against the chill of Euston's great Shareholders' Room under the austerities of wartime heating, he was a dominant figure, as much so in his snappish, schoolmasterly way as was the impeccably gentlemanly Eric Gore-Browne on the Southern Railway.

Lord Royden's successor to the Chair of the LMS knew, when he assumed it, that his time was short, but like his predecessor, Sir Robert Burrows had been a Deputy Chairman since 1940. His roots were in collieries. He was nearly thirteen years younger than Royden, having been born on March 17, 1884. He had been a Director of the LMS since the end of 1937 and thus had not what some of us then called Pre-Grouping Seniority.

Last days of the railway as a company-owned entity were chiefly distinguished by recovery from wartime dilapidations and by its final mechanical developments. Brave ideas about rebuilding Euston Station in London had gone by the board. Its Propylaeum still stood foursquare to the cold winds of North London. Its superb Great Hall still excited the admiration of the few while giving shelter to the mutable rank-scented many and giving little inkling of the rot in its hidden rafters. Blackout screens were removed from Euston, as from Liverpool Lime Street, Glasgow Central, and of other big stations. Some lesser places recovered more quickly. Stoke-on-Trent remained its grim self, the station presenting its face to the North Stafford Hotel and its rump to what some American wartime visitor most politely called the city-centre of Stoke proper. Stoke Station was, under the North Stafford, intended to acquire four through platforms and four bays, and access to the town on the west side towards Copeland Street, but the LMS never carried out its admirable constituent's intentions, based on the removal of the old goods yard and diversion of heavy local freight traffic from the main line. It must be admitted that several of the old companies' great ideas perished under the Railways Act, 1921, and not exclusively in LMS territory.[1] The LMS company certainly kept alive some lines which might have been closed on the grounds of unviability, and never, to one's knowledge, cooked statistics to give grounds for the closing of some marginal line that happened to be an operating nuisance.[2] Right to the end of its existence, the LMS more-or-less cheerfully ran trains to places like Dornoch, though how long it would have continued to do so with the revival of private motoring one dare not suggest.

Just now we noted the North Stafford, whence came H. G. Ivatt, the last C.M.E. of the London Midland & Scottish Railway. He was also the last of the LMS company's big *steam men*, though mechanical history being at the stage in question he had not much scope. Stanier had preceded him in LMS steam. Fairburn had been busy with the emergent

[1] *eg* The North Eastern's electrification on 1,500 V. dc from York to Newcastle.
[2] The technique is to exclude all traffics from terminals and junctions on a connecting line between two main routes, though at least one important town be intermediate. But this is *modern*.

Diesel. His brother-in-law Bulleid, in steam again, was making the last English fight for it on the Southern Railway, with great ideas which put him in the company of Giesl-Geislingen in Austria and the *entourage* of André Chapelon in France. The younger Ivatt had a thankless task, which possibly may make him less memorable than his sire on the Great Northern. People will remember – or at least recognise – Ivatt 4-4-2 engines on the GNR when they have long forgotten variations by Ivatt on a theme by Stanier. They were very beautiful variations, quite apart from their mechanical virtues, when it came to Pacific-type express engines. When it came to original design – and God knew what that meant in the last years of the LMS, and many other companies – one cannot conclude that there was much art. All the same, the last of the Stanier-Ivatt Pacific-type express engines was as beautiful as any.

In the late Pacifics – and in such other late Stanier types as the 2-6-4 tank engines which British Railways continued to build, outward appearances were changed by a cut between the upper and lower platforms at the front, giving them a more Continental – or even American – look. "Foreign-ness" was emphasised in many of the later big engines by the forward top-feed mounting which, from the front, looked like a small extra dome. This party considers that appearances would have been improved if there had been such a thing indeed, instead of something that looked thick from the front and thin from the side. A *fin-de-la-guerre* alteration had been in livery; a combination of black with black-banded, yellow-lined furbelows of maroon. At last the company was being honest about that maroon! It was no longer pretended that dark reddish-brown was the same as the old Midland crimson-lake. It had become browner in the meantime, anyway. It applied to the carriages too.

More importantly, to a mechanical historian, was the application of roller bearings to the last two Pacifics, already mentioned (6256 *Sir William Stanier, FRS* and 6257 *City of Salford*). Be it remarked that by the first year of British Railways, 1948, there remained two Stanier Pacifics *with the lid on*; Nos. 46226 *Duchess of Norfolk* and 46243 *City of Lancaster*. Streamlined steam was already far out of favour, and if some eyes were wet, many more were dry.

The last of LMS steam locomotives were less-and-less streamlined – externally at any rate. The first of some more Moguls – light for mixed traffic on secondary lines – appeared in 1946 with No. 6400. There was something vaguely – very remotely – familiar about her apparent dimensions and outline. One's Editor of that time noted this and one concurred, for once in a while. We both thought of a Midland-American of 1899. I *think* we disagreed as to whether it were Baldwin or Schenectady. I know I liked Baldwins best; they were honest Americans, not trying to look like something else.

The critical locomotives had 5ft coupled wheels and 16in by 24in cylinders – modest enough – but the pressure was 200lb, which made something of a difference. There were the expected features of a taper boiler with superheater and outside piston valves worked by Walschaert's gear. The engines were still being built in 1948, by the middle of which year there were about 35. They went far afield. One, surely, was late on the Dornoch Light Railway, which hitherto had usually known only archaic-Stroudley, and Drummond, tank engines. Long ago there had been a brief, and scarcely fortunate Webb visitation. The geographical history of steam locomotives was sometimes like that, as previous instances have shown. This was one of the first instances in Great Britain, over a long time, of a new locomotive with separate tender that could go anywhere. The engine weighed only 47 tons 2 cwt. The tractive effort at usual rating was 17,410lb. Contemporary with these light branch-line engines (which were classified 2F) was a set of 2–6–2 passenger tank engines (2P) of similar dimensions and with most parts interchangeable. All-up weight was naturally higher, at $63\frac{1}{4}$ tons, and numbering began at 1200. About thirty were completed to the end of LMS ownership, and they were still being delivered.

A propos of certain remote Scottish branch lines, served right at the end by such locomotives, one recalls also meeting a man who, a few years earlier in the Army, sought and was given the office of RTO at Strathpeffer. It is splendid country. There was about one train a week, with extras.

Altogether more massive, and to conventionally-conditioned eyes hideous, were the last of the LMS Mogul mixed-traffic engines. The boiler was tapered, with a Belpaire firebox, and of course the engines were superheated. Cylinders were $17\frac{1}{2}$in by 26in, with the usual piston valves and Walschaert's gear. Blastpipe and chimney were doubled. A working pressure of 225lb/sq in brought the tractive effort to 24,170lb, which was handsome for an engine with 5ft 3in coupled wheels, weighing only 59 tons 2 cwt – about the only handsome thing involved, though it was a useful little engine, bigger than the Fairburn Moguls and well suited to such lines as those across country from Bletchley. The platforms were very high – first-quarter-up from the bottom of the very highly-pitched boiler – making them the most American-looking locomotives ever seen in the English Midlands, apart from true American ones.

With these useful mucky-ducks, numbered from 3000 upwards and still being delivered when the State took over in 1948, we come to the end of original designs in steam for the London Midland & Scottish Railway. Contemporary with the first deliveries came the rebuilding of certain Patriot class 4–6–0 express engines with double blastpipes and chimneys, tapered boilers carrying 250lb/sq in and cylinder-diameter reduced to

17in. The process resulted in the power classification being changed from 5 XP to 6P. It made a very fine engine.

But even on the LMS the pointer, pushed somewhat by Mr. Fairburn, was towards internal-combustion of oil by compression-ignition, and although British Railways were yet to build steam on a briefly grand scale (with quite some of R. A. Riddles' influence) the diesel was on its way in. The company, as we have seen, had been one of the British pioneers of such traction, and had found it useful and reasonably reliable, at any rate in shunting service. America had long been using it in long and fast hauls, though the war had given steam a reprieve in the States. The *Steam Debacle* was not-quite-yet.

Two designs were brought out at the end of H. G. Ivatt's tenure, and built as the company's own history drew to its close. One was for an express passenger engine, paired, so that it could work either singly or in double unit, and the other for a general mixed-traffic locomotive. To take the express design first; the idea behind this was to have something which, with two units worked as one, could handle the fastest, heaviest West Coast expresses at timings which might become tighter yet, while a single unit might be the equivalent to a 2–6–4 tank engine, in steam. Whether it were so, except as to availability, may be scouted (it could work an express). The diesel had a flying start on availability.

The separable double-unit consisted of a pair arranged Co-Co, each with a driver's cab at either end; each therefore a complete locomotive. This couple was numbered 10000 and 10001. Each unit, weighing 110 tons, contained a sixteen-cylinder 1,600hp engine (10in bore by 12in stroke) with the electric generator directly coupled to the engine crank-shaft. On the two motor bogies there were six axle-hung nose-suspended motors driving through single-reduction spur gears. The motors were connected in three parallel groups, each comprising two motors per-manently connected in series. There were roller bearings to the armatures and sleeve bearings to the nose-suspension units.

Placing of six motors to six axles in two motor bogies presented certain problems, which had nothing to do with each pair of motors working in series. At the middle axle of each bogie came the rub. With an ordinary bolster arrangement there was no room for an intermediate axle-hung motor. The bogies on these twin locomotives were therefore of what was called *novel* design. In each, the weight of half the engine-generator set, and of half the superstructure, was born on the axles of the two bolsters themselves through sliding surfaces at four points. The central pivot was subject only to forces of traction and location. The connecting member for the two bolsters, in other schemes a massive, heavy thing, could now be made much lighter in section than usual, giving sufficient clearance for the middle motor on each bogie. Laminated springs were used for the bolsters, and the axleboxes had roller bearings.

All this was worked out and made at Derby; the engine-generator-traction-motor equipment was English Electric. As to auxiliary equipment, this included an auxiliary generator, overhung on the main generator, supplying current for the control circuits, for battery-charging, operation of motor-driven compressors, exhausters, traction motor blowers, and lighting. There were tanks for water and oil to supply a Clarkson thimble-tube boiler for train heating in a compartment which also contained a small but sufficient latrine. The two locomotives in double-unit exerted a nominal combined tractive effort of 41,000lb. The work of these engines belongs to more recent history, and so, of course, do the lessons they taught in service. They lasted upwards of twenty years. No. 10001 was the first to go, when, very early in 1968, she was seen being broken up in a scrapper's yard at Acton.

The second LMS diesel design was for a general-service, mixed-traffic locomotive, and was prepared simultaneously. It was a Bo-Bo (that is double-motor-bogie) design, with a single cab at one end and a narrower bonnet, corresponding to the boiler-part of a steam engine, to house the engine-generator set. The engine was an 800hp sixteen-cylinder job by Davey-Paxman, and the electrical equipment was by British Thomson-Houston. Again, we are coming to post-company history. One remembers a first encounter with this locomotive on the North London line about 1950, not with much retrospective enthusiasm though doubtless it was useful and *erfolgreich*. Oneself was more busy with ships at the time, and in the course of that was entertained by two very engaging stories, English and German respectively, about the watery end of the late Rudolf Diesel overboard a Harwich steamship. The Germans said our Secret Service did it, my friends said the Germans' Secret Service did it. But that is not, save indirectly, a railway story.

With these admirable, if nasty, locomotives, one comes to the end of London Midland & Scottish motive-power history. Your author is neither an engineer nor a business-man; his attitude to life remains that of John Ruskin (who, for all the *Seven Lamps of Architecture*, could see no beauty in the train). Enough of that! Save that Ruskin said we were children of a noble race, trained by surrounding art.

Lord! What a hope!

From the last-constructive to the last-destructive: As some will have opined already, the LMS was not always a fortunate railway as to accidents. Nor, for that matter, had been its three major constituents. All, at one time and another, had first smashed-up and then burnt their trains. Burnings had subsided with the decline of gaslight, but the smashes were not yet done.

On New Year's Day of 1946 there was a very serious collision at

Lichfield on the Trent Valley line, where there were two through roads and two against down and up platforms. About 6.58 pm the 2.50 pm fish train from Fleetwood to London – seven vehicles and brake, headed by Class 5 4–6–0 engine No. 5495 – was wrongly diverted from up-fast to up-slow. At the up platform stood the 6.8 pm ordinary passenger train from Stafford to Nuneaton (Prince of Wales class 4–6–0 engine with four carriages). The Class 5 engine on the "fish" went right through three of the four Midland wooden carriages, smashing the last three to bits and driving the old London & North Western engine 280ft forward. Thirteen persons were killed and seven more died, making a deathroll of twenty.

Evidence conflicted on the position of the up-fast signal. The up colour-light distant was at *clear*. The driver of the fish train may have heaved a sigh of relief at this, for he had had maddening delays over 17 miles, and have taken the home for granted in the *off* position inner distant being at *clear*. But there had been serious mechanical failure. Lieut.-Colonel E. Woodhouse reported that contributory factors had been the failure of a facing-points bolt to disengage from the stretcher, buckling of the down rod under the signalbox, alleged failure of the detector to prevent No. 4 home signal from responding to its lever, as of non-observance of that signal, assuming it to have been at *danger*. Ballast movement might have prevented full movement of the rocking shaft lever.

Colonel Woodhouse reported that he was not surprised that the signalman had not noticed that the bolt had failed by about 1½in to complete its stroke, thus remaining foul of the notch in the stretcher by about half an inch. That could, or would, have been concealed by spring in the rodding. He hesitated to criticise this signalman for not having noticed unusual resistence when he brought the critical lever back to normal. The worst fault was in the arrangement of the down rod, with no intermediate guide in a length exceeding 10ft. It was thus inadequate for an eccentric thrust on it, caused by an offset of five or even seven inches at its lower end. Woodhouse's Report was voluminous, with admirable drawings.

The accident was spectacular. Of the local passenger train there remained a neatly amputated piece of coach body, sufficiently intact to have made a good garden shed, deposited right-way-up on the platform. In 1946, people were still used to much more gory things. The collision has attracted less attention than it might have done in quieter times.

In the summer there were two accidents in Scotland, neither of them through railway fault. One showed severe casualties; the other had none serious, but was somewhat startling. On July 25, a decrepit local motor bus, with additional kitchen chairs in the gangway, had its brakes fail on the hill descending to Balmuckety Crossing on the Kirriemuir branch. This bus went through the closed gates and was instantly struck by the

G*

branch train, a modest ex-Caledonian assembly, which smashed it to pieces. The train was scarcely damaged, but ten persons in the bus were killed. The accident could not happen again, the Kirriemuir branch – forbye much else – being no more. Alas, poor Thrums!

The other accident, in the Pass of Brander on August 8, 1946, was of the sort legally described as an Act of God. The line through this steep defile of the Awe, as is well known, has long been protected by wire barriers which set to danger frequently-placed automatic semaphores if and when a boulder comes rolling down the side of Ben Cruachan. On this occasion, however, a large boulder not only came down but bounced so high that it cleared the wires, being thus at least 7ft clear of the mountainside. It landed on the track – at that point about 100ft almost sheer above the River Awe, and derailed the 6.5 am train from Oban to Glasgow, a fairly light one headed by the usual Black Five. Luckily engine and carriages, though somewhat canted over, remained on that perilous shelf, and none was much hurt. Had they gone over, the result might have resembled old-time horrors in the North American Rockies.

Of sadly disgraceful sort was the derailment near Polesworth on July 21, 1947, involving the 8.30 am London–Liverpool express, having sixteen carriages headed by 4-6-2 engine No. 6244, *King George VI*. Following derailment of leading-bogie wheels, the coaches went off the road, pulling the engine, which then went over. The two leading coaches were broken up. Five persons were killed, four of them instantly.

No; there was no burking it! The cause was decrepit track. Sleepers were 18 years old, and the screw fastenings were found loose. What a sorry thing for those who recalled the old London & North Western company's pride in its permanent way! One wonders what old E. F. C. Trench thought about it, for he was still around then, lively and alert at that. *C'etait la guerre!* One likes to think so, anyway. The former Midland company, too, had had very fine tracks, and even the Caledonian company (which had not, as a rule), had not had an accident like this, anyway within living memory.

Right at the end of the company's history, on December 10, 1947, something really terrifying happened in Manchester, on the old Miles Platting bank. In darkness and dense fog, the 6.50 pm special goods train from Neville Hill to Eccles was descending this unholy slide. It consisted of twenty tank wagons with petrol, two runner wagons and a goods-brake, and was headed by ex-London & North Western 0-8-0 locomotive No. 8903, making a total descending weight of 593 tons when the train ran away with the engine. The last-named had vacuum brakes. Company's Rules did not allow handbrakes to be pinned-down on petrol wagons for fear of danger from sparks.

With the train pushing the engine down the bank, the driver made urgent whistle signals which were most fortunately picked up and understood. The signalman at Millgate Signalbox warned his colleague at Turntable Box of the runaway. There was a stationary freight train fouling its path in the through part of Manchester Victoria, leading to Exchange. The man at Turntable acted quickly and very adroitly. He turned the careering train into Victoria's No. 7 (terminal) platform, where it hit and destroyed substantial hydraulic buffers. The engine rushed the concourse beyond, and her driver was caught against the tender and killed. Everybody else acted quickly. Fire was quickly dowsed on the engine, which had struck the buffers at about 25 mph. The first runner-wagon was smashed up; the first three tankers were derailed and leaking. There was petrol all over the place. But more quick work prevented fire and explosion which might otherwise have blown the frontier between the cities of Manchester and Salford.

It was not as big a bang as well it might have been. Paraphrasing T. S. Eliot, as well as inverting him, one might say that the London Midland & Scottish Railway ended not with a whimper but a bang. For with that particular bang at Manchester Victoria, the company had just three weeks to run through the great schedule of history, and there was no whimper on New Year's Eve.

Biggest of the four British main-line railways, it went out like its companion companies, with neither heroics nor fuss. It bequeathed to its successors many able and eminent men. Its last President of the Executive, Sir William Wood, had under him as Vice Presidents G. L. Darbyshire, CBE, T. W. Royle, CVO, MBE (whose wife, it will be remembered, was spanked as a little girl for impertinence to F. W. Webb at a tea party), F. A. Pape, and R. A. Riddles, who was to have considerable influence in the successive last days of steam on British Railways. Last Manager of the Northern Counties Committee in Ireland was J. W. Hutton.

The company's sands were run out, after the glass had been upright for exactly twenty-four years. The railway and its equipment were still shabby from war that had ceased over two years before. It had fought its war well, with little thanks from politicians, whether Left, Right or Centre. Its officers had collected some Orders and Medals more merited than some awarded to other parties. Government had driven a hard bargain before it drove a compulsory one.

Was the London Midland & Scottish Railway a *good line*? On the whole yes, especially when one considered its wildly various components, some of them antagonistic for years. Let us leave it at that, without making individous comparisons with the Great Western, the London & North Eastern and the Southern, in alphabetical order. All four looked very much the same as they had done in 1939, as to their equipment. On the LMS, the great stations of Euston and St. Pancras stood as they had done, for so many years, in London. So did splendid, grubby Huddersfield. So did the absurd Siamese twin of Birmingham New Street. So did the great joint stations of Carlisle, Aberdeen and Perth General. (Perth Princes Street, now an abandoned ruin but with, ironically, West Coast expresses passing through it on single track, remained vintage Caledonian.) The trains were the same, only a decade older and often much the worse for wear. Of those who had worked for the railway, some had deep regrets and some received the new dawn with idealistic rejoicings. To a fanfare of whistles – Caledonian and Stanier hooters, Midland mezzo-soprani, London & North Western shrieks and even yet, perhaps, a couple of North London squeals, the LMS took its last bow at midnight, December 31, 1947.

Next morning, its old railway looked exactly the same. But a railway era was ended. Were they indeed gods, those men who commanded the old railway companies? No, they were not gods. Josiah Stamp would have been horrified at the suggestion, so pagan in its implication! Horace had some words for it: *Dis te minorem quod geris imperas.* Because you hold yourself lower than the Gods, you command!

The Irish Enclave

IRISH COMPLICATIONS on the formation of the London Midland and Scottish company were not as involved as might have been expected. There was one thing which caused some bother when, under an Act of the Irish Free State, 1924, all railways wholly within that state – with the exception of the Listowel and Ballybunion monorail – were amalgamated to form the Great Southern Railways. One of those, of course, was the Dublin and South Eastern, to which the London & North Western had advanced £100,000 in 1902 to help with the construction of its Waterford extension. The LMS claimed the statutory right to have one of its Directors on the Great Southern Board pending repayment. It was, however, unwilling to continue a subsidy of some £20,000 annually, which it had been paying to the Dublin & South Eastern. The Irish point of view, scarcely unexpectedly, was that the Great Southern wanted no LMS Director, but that the Great Southern was natural heir to the Dublin and South Eastern's subsidy, which had been a voluntary payment. With neither side approving of the other's ideas, the case had to be referred to the Railway Tribunal. The other three Irish undertakings which formed the Great Southern constituents – the Great Southern and Western, the Midland Great Western, and the Cork, Bandon and South Coast, scarcely felt up to making good the subsidy hitherto paid from England to the fourth constituent. None of them owned goldmines, in any sense of the term, and the Cork company had particular cause, already, to be anxious.

The position of the Northern Counties Railway was much simpler, for it had been an appendage of the Midland for many years, and the only trouble was that what the Midland had once been so eager to acquire, was not now quite so promising a source of revenue as it had been, even in old-time competition with the Great Northern Railway (Ireland). Certainly it still had prestige value. The LMS still could claim with pride that it served the three components of the United Kingdom, even though the Six Counties were but the rump of one. Whether it really wanted to do so was quite another matter.

"Our Northern Counties Railway", as it was called in LMS language at the Annual General Meetings in Euston, had 201 miles of route on the Irish broad gauge of 5ft 3in, and 64 miles on the 3ft gauge. Its main line ran from Belfast to Derry via Ballymena and Coleraine, with a short but still remunerative branch to Portstewart and Portrush; a very important one up to Larne with, at first, a ridiculous connection to the main line at Greenisland, whereby the main-line trains had to reverse there; a long devious loop line striking west from Cookstown Junction, skirting the northern shores of Lough Neagh, and eventually rejoining the main line at Macfin Junction, still between Antrim and Coleraine, but having in the meantime thrown out two branches of its own from near Magherafelt, one south to Cookstown where it connected with the Great Northern, and one to Draperstown. From Limavady Junction beside Lough Foyle, it had a lone branch to Dungiven. The narrow-gauge branches – or appendages – included that to Strabane from the right bank of the Foyle at Derry, and worked by the County Donegal Railways Joint Committee, to which the NCC was a party, and others originally built by quite distinct companies; that from Larne to Ballymena, with a branch to Doagh and an extension to Retreat, and the very picturesque – indeed in one's experience delightful – Ballycastle Railway north-east from Ballymoney. One of the curiosities of the last-named was that the terminus at Bally-castle was the nearest railway station (unless one counted Machrihanish) to the Scottish town of Port Ellen in Islay, which exported such good malt whisky. The two stations in Derry, Waterside (broad-gauge) and Victoria Road (narrow-gauge) were end-on to each other, but not properly in the city, which had the Great Northern company's Foyle Road opposite Victoria Road. There was no physical connection until mixed gauge was laid on the lower deck of the Craigavon Bridge, for the transfer of wagons to the Londonderry dock lines. This remarkable bridge was opened as recently as July 18, 1933, replacing the old Carlisle Bridge. It does not count as having been a part of the NCC system.

An important enterprise, however, and the last major piece of civil engineering to have been carried out on a railway in Northern Ireland, was the improvement of the junction at Greenisland. As remarked, for many years every train by the Northern Counties main line, out of Belfast, had needed reversal at Greenisland. In the early 1930s this anachronism was cut out. Between White Abbey and Jordanstown, new up and down lines were built, to east and west respectively of the old formation connecting Belfast and Larne. Between them from White Abbey a new spur was built, curving to the west and joining a short new connection from the old line from Greenisland Junction to the West, about a mile east of Mossley station, about five furlongs of the old Greenisland–Mossley section being cut out. The most imposing feature was that of the viaducts. The smaller of these was made to curve to the right, carrying the down Larne line under a skew girder span of the larger viaduct curving westwards with the new spur to the Derry line. Both viaducts carried their respective lines over the valley of Valentine's Glen, and both comprised ferro-concrete arches, those of the Derry line viaduct being the largest such spans yet built in the British Isles. Double track was used – or divided double track in the case of the Whiteabbey–Jordanstown section – except for the spur from Greenisland to the new junction near Mossley. The Greenisland–Mossley section thus lost its importance in passenger traffic. All trains from Belfast to Antrim, Ballymoney, Coleraine, Portrush and Derry now could and did run out over the new high viaduct. Through carriages from Larne to Derry and Portrush, on the Stranraer boat trains, were now generally worked into and out of Belfast, though of course through goods from Larne passed over the old spur.

Completion of the scheme was much delayed by the strike of Irish locomotive men in 1933, for ballast engines were not available at a critical time in the making of the earthworks. It was not until January 17, 1934, that the Duke of Abercorn, Governor of Northern Ireland, formally opened the Greenisland Loop, with Major J. A. W. Torrens, D.L., Chairman of the NCC, Sir Josiah Stamp and senior railway officers as hosts. The Viceregal train was hauled by a new 2–6–0 express engine, to be described later, and named *Duke of Abercorn*. It steamed out from York Road, Belfast, to a decorated stand which had been erected on the up road of the new greater viaduct, where the ceremony took place. Thereafter, with splendid inevitability, train, hosts and guests proceeded to Portrush, where there was suitable junketing in the Northern Counties Hotel. On January 22, regular services were begun over the new line. The distance saved was but two miles, but the time saved came to 10–13 minutes, owing to the elimination of that silly reversal at Greenisland. Accelerations of main-line trains throughout their journeys ranged from 15 to as much as 25 minutes thanks to the incidence of new, more powerful locomotives on the best trains, and faster running between stations west of Antrim.

Part of the programme, as carried out, was the resignalling with colour lights by the Westinghouse company of the lines between Belfast York Road, Greenisland and Ballyclare Junction, embracing the triangle which had been formed by the new loop. A new signalbox was built at Greenisland, with train describers and an illuminated track diagram, to control all movements in the triangle. West of Ballymena on the main line, track was single except at stations, but there was a programme of resignalling and the relaying of crossing loops so that the latter should provide one completely straight road at each place for the passage of expresses in either direction. Whatever the merits of the Virgin City of Londonderry, from the NCC point of view, with that flank attack by the Great Northern, Portrush was a very important place indeed. It had very considerable seasonal holiday traffic; further, like such English towns as Brighton, Scarborough, Blackpool, Herne Bay and even Bognor, it had an important business-residential traffic. With the beginning of the 1934 summer service, there were morning and evening fast residential trains covering the $65\frac{1}{4}$ miles in 80 minutes, some without a stop and some, more creditably, with an intermediate stop. Even the Larne trains were accelerated, with an average speed of 30 mph on some fourteen trains daily, with six intermediate stops for the business trains, which was not discreditable and much better than some comparable services in Great Britain, especially in the North and in Scotland where, to be sure, there was considerably more congestion. Between Belfast and Carrickfergus, at this time, a Leyland railcar was doing useful service on purely local traffic. Be it remembered that Ireland was a pioneer country in the use of diesel traction for regular passenger services.

The lines of the Northern Counties Committee at this time had a peculiar aspect. They were, as from early days, quite substantial-looking, and with a splendid stretch along from Coleraine to Derry under the imposing formation of Binevenagh and beside Loch Foyle. The semaphores on lines beyond the Westinghouse electrical system north of Belfast, were of French's balanced type, and suggested certain parts of South Wales as well as the Great Northern Railway (England). The passenger rolling stock, like many of the engines, was redolent of Derby in its less inspired moments, which is to say that exteriorly the carriages followed the conventions of R. W. Reid, though the furnishing of the third-class compartments was more akin to that of the South Eastern and Chatham Railway. The second-class carriages, for which one paid extra, were, one regrets to recall, identical with the third. (The South Eastern, by contrast, had rather sumptuous "seconds".) Then there were some open carriages which externally resembled LMS mainland vehicles of the same sort, but which, inside, were furnished like an ordinary American day-car save that the apparently reversible seats had their backs fixed to face in pairs. They were by no means bad, though the prospect on entering the coach was less than luscious. At night, such a carriage would have been a caution, but people did not normally occupy the hours between dinner and breakfast on an NCC express, as they did on trains between London and Glasgow, or Würzburg and Amsterdam, or wherever of that kind. Indeed, because of the total lack of real night trains in these parts, the propping-up of passengers' heads was much less important than in other places. A showy North Atlantic Express, between Portrush and Belfast, still would not have passed the basic standards of European International services as to its passenger arrangements in first and second class, though, to be fair, its third class was much superior to anything of the kind running straight through from Ostend to Budapest. Also, again to be fair, second class was already a dead-letter in Northern Ireland, whereas between Ostend and Budapest, for example, it was very important indeed to many people traversing great distances for the most they could afford to pay. The North Atlantic Express, however, was claimed to be very luxurious, and so, of its kind, it was. Its luxury was that of the plush bar, in which people are encouraged to be happy, but not to go to sleep. One recalls its sea-green velvets with curious affection, and also its large windows. Unfortunately, it did not wend its way round the coast of Antrim, where they could have been used to full advantage, while the private motorist – and the touring motor coach – did just that. The Government of Northern Ireland, sponsor of the improvement, to its present state, of that splendid road, is more understandable though by no means forgivable in its later shabby attitude towards the railways serving its portion of the Realm.

From the railway point of view Northern Ireland formed, in those days, a proconsulate, and in the Roman sense of the word, too. The Midland Railway had allowed the NCC, very properly, to pursue the course of an independent railway. When it had taken over the old Belfast and Northern Counties Railway, that undertaking was quite self-sufficient. It had as its Locomotive Superintendent, then, a most remarkable man, Bowman Malcolm. He achieved seniority in his early twenties – 22, I believe – and Sir Daniel Gooch, as he was to become later, was possibly the only man in British and Irish locomotive engineering to beat that record. Malcolm, like all good Ulstermen of his time, watched more than the Plain Shrewd Briton[1] what people were doing abroad, and he noticed what Von Borries was doing in Germany. The von Borries two-cylinder compound engine had done well on express passenger trains in Prussia. Thomas Worsdell took it up in England, first on the Great Eastern and then on the North Eastern Railway. Malcolm took it to Ireland, and built it for both broad- and narrow-gauge lines of the Belfast and Northern Counties Railway. Some examples lasted right through the LMS period, perhaps most notably in the narrow-gauge 2–4–2 tank engines which had served the Ballymena and Larne direct line over the mountains which was killed (as was not remarked at the time) by the building of the Greenisland Loop on the broad-gauge route. These were to end their days on the Ballycastle line, together with some rather handsome carriages – true LMS-NCC stock – which had also belonged to the Ballymena and Larne service and had constituted the only really-truly corridor passenger coaches, fully vestibuled, to run on any narrow-gauge railway in the British Isles.

Bowman Malcolm retired at the end of 1922, he having been quite independent of, successively, Johnson, Deeley and Fowler commanding the Midland outfit at Derby. He was succeded by one of his sometime young men, W. K. Wallace, who, however, made his name as a civil, rather than as a mechanical, engineer. From the time of his appointment,

[1] The late Lord Beaverbrook? The late Lord Rothermere? It might have been either.

the influence of Derby became more and more apparent in the NCC Locomotive Department. In September 1930, he became Chief Stores Superintendent (Euston) on the LMS and was succeeded by H. P. Stewart as Engineer and Locomotive Superintendent, NCC.

As suggested, the existing stock in 1923 still abounded with Malcolm engines, many of them two-cylinder compounds with that strange beat – charming to an artist – of two to a revolution. There were "Light Compounds" and "Heavy Compounds"; the former included little 2–4–0 engines looking as if they had been chopped off-short, especially when Mr. Wallace had rebuilt them with small high-pitched boilers. The pride of the old stagers were two large-wheeled 4–4–0 express engines named *Jubilee* and *Parkmount*, two-cylinder compounds designed by Malcolm, whereof the former was rebuilt by Wallace with a Midland style boiler, and converted to two-cylinder simple expansion.[1]

Under Wallace, as suggested, the Committee's equipment became steadily more Midland[2] in appearance, emphasised by the Deeley cutaway chimney which became the standard form on the NCC for many years to come. The LMS red livery, too, was used for all sorts of engines and remained so for years after black had become general on the mainland except for the most modern express engines. Stray examples of the old "invisible green" had lingered into the early 1930s for the real Midland red had not been used under Midland company auspices. My picture of *Binevenagh* was taken as late as 1947, and she was still in the shabby remains of LMS red. This engine was a simplified rebuild of a Malcolm compound, and had 200lb pressure. At the time of the photograph, she and a sister called *Ben Madigan* were Portrush branch engines, taking on the carriages of express trains divided at Coleraine where the express engine from Belfast continued to Derry.

The NCC system, as suggested, was a railway in itself, and its locomotive history cannot be detailed here except for certain classes which appeared under Wallace's and Stewart's direction. Of these, in 1924, the North British Locomotive Company built a set of 4–4–0 passenger engines which were pure Derby, and generally describable as Midland Class 2 except for 6ft coupled wheels and, of course, the 5ft 3in gauge. Cylinders were 19in by 24in and pressure 170lb. The combined heating surface was 1,421 sq ft and the grate area 21·8 sq ft. It was not an imaginative engine, but there; it was Midland, and the Midland company had put into service only one imaginative design since the angry departure of Richard Deeley. Still, the class answered fairly enough on the expresses to Derry and Portrush.

With the completion of the Greenisland Loop and its consequent acceleration, there was need for a more powerful and more adaptable

---

[1] She acquired vermilion side-rod flutes from loving volunteer hands in the strike of 1933.
[2] In the English sense. In Ireland the "Midland" had been the MGWR.

design for main-line work. (There were no very advanced goods engines; one of them dated back to the end of the 1850s, though there cannot have been much, if anything left of the original.)

Anticipating the North Atlantic Express, H. P. Stewart produced in 1933 the first of a 2–6–0 design with 6ft coupled wheels and 19in by 26in cylinders having 9in piston valves (16⅜in travel), building it at York Road, Belfast. Restrictions on weight and size put a more powerful engine out of the question, even were it needed, but advantage was taken of the Irish gauge to make the firebox wider than it would have been with an English Mogul design. The boiler had an evaporative heating surface of 1,081 sq ft, which with 266 sq ft in the superheater gave a combined total of 1,347 sq ft. The grate area was 25 sq ft. The first of the class, No. 90, was named *Duke of Abercorn* for the opening ceremony of the Greenisland spur and bridges, and the rest of this initial series were numbered, and subsequently named thus:

NO.	NAME	NO.	NAME
91	*The Bush*	95	*The Braid*
92	*The Bann*	96	*Silver Jubilee*
93	*The Foyle*	97	*Earl of Ulster*
94	*The Maine*	98	*King Edward VIII*

Ulster rivers were the namesakes, and this particular Bann was the one flowing from Lough Neagh to the sea below Coleraine, not that on whose banks lived sweet Molly M'Cann in the ballad of County Down (Lower and Upper Bann respectively; the same loch fed both, though they flowed very different ways). To the Northern Counties mind, of course, the third Bann, down in County Wexford, simply did not exist in polite conversation. If anybody had heard of it, they probably thought its banks were peopled by Jesuits and witches. Of the other names, *Earl of Ulster* was almost inevitable, while its predecessor (bestowed in 1935) was necessary to the furtherance of Northern Loyalty. Let the Great Northern stick to its birds of prey! As for the unspeakable Great Southern with its pagan queens . . . !

In appearance, the new Mogul engines were not everybody's idea of a handsome locomotive.There seemed to be a lot of daylight ahead of the smokebox, as in a gawky girl with a very long lap. Initially, the Derby style of chimney was mounted, but by 1936 *The Braid* had a form which suggested those of Stanier and the later practice of Bowman Malcolm, an improvement on the Midland object.

In 1934, the North Atlantic Express left Portrush at 8.10 am to arrive at York Road, Belfast, at 9.30, making an average speed of 49 mph. It was lightly loaded with two 57ft coaches (brake-third and tricomposite respectively) and a 60ft buffet car. In the down direction it left York Road at 5.15 pm to reach Portrush at 6.35. It was indeed a plush commuters' train. On Saturdays it left the city at 12.40 midday. On June 1, 1937, the up train's time was reduced to 74 minutes including a stop at Ballymena, with 32 minutes for the 31 miles thence to Belfast where it arrived at 9.24. This made it the fastest booked run in Ireland, at 58·1 mph.

Stewart's Mogul engines were much liked. In 1938 there appeared No. 99 *King George VI* and No. 100 *Queen Elizabeth* with larger, Stanier-type tenders carrying 3,000 gallons and 7 tons of water and fuel. Four more were built during the war years: Nos. 101 and 102 in 1940, No. 103 (named *Thomas Somerset* for the Chairman) in 1942 and No. 104 in 1943. During the air attacks on Belfast, April 15–16 and May 4–5, 1941, all the Northern Counties Committee's locomotives escaped, although the Works, offices, station and hotel at York Road were all burnt, with most of the records and twenty carriages. Of wagons, 250 had been burnt or heavily damaged. For a while, Whitehouse became the Belfast terminus of the railway, with a special bus service into the city.

Lastly of the NCC locomotives, when Ivatt was in command in England, came a 2-6-4 tank engine version of the well-proven Moguls, numbered 5–8. They were equipped with self-cleaning smokeboxes, rocking grates and self-emptying ashpans. The pressure was the now standard one of 200lb/sq in. These relatively big tank engines were useful on the Larne line which had very heavy traffic. When the Moguls had appeared on the main line, they had been barred west of Coleraine on account of turntable limitations at Derry. On the much shorter Larne line, a modern tank engine had long been wanted. These could be used on fast traffic anywhere, subject to water-stops.

With the nationalisation of the LMS, its useful Irish railway passed, under Government, to the newly constituted Ulster Transport Authority. Northern Irish Government had little enthusiasm for the look of its gift-horse's mouth, though that government's more immediate concern was to kill the Great Northern Railway, a very admirable undertaking, by biting large pieces out of it wherever it encroached on the border to the advantage of persons living south thereof. One may sniff political malice here, but, to be sure, the ruling clique in Northern Ireland had long had an incendiary attitude towards railways in general.

Locomotive Shed Indications

LONG AFTER the passing of the London Midland & Scottish company, people like to know about sheds and shed allocations in steam days. On the LMS there were of course sheds galore, each group having its mother-shed, where certain heavy repairs could be efficiently carried out. In the last days of the LMS, this was the tally, based on final divisions and sub-divisions of May 1946:

WILLESDEN	1A	Hereford	4—
Camden	1B	Brecon	4—
Watford	1C	Gurnos	4—
RUGBY	2A	Trench	4—
Nuneaton	2D	Coalport	4—
Warwick	2E	Clee Hill	4—
Coventry	2F	CREWE NORTH	5A
Market Harborough	2—	Whitchurch	5—
Seaton	2—	Crewe South	5B
BLETCHLEY	2B	Stafford	5C
Northampton	2C	Stoke	5D
Leighton Buzzard	2—	Alsager	5E
Aylesbury	2—	Uttoxeter	5F
Newport Pagnell	2—	CHESTER	6A
Oxford	2—	Mold Junction	6B
Cambridge	2—	Birkenhead	6C
BESCOT	3A	LLANDUDNO	
Bushbury	3B	JUNCTION	7A
Walsall	3C	Bangor	7B
Aston	3D	Holyhead	7C
Monument Lane	3E	Rhyl	7D
Wednesbury	3—	Denbigh	7—
Tipton	3—	EDGE HILL	8A
Albion	3—	Warrington	8B
SHREWSBURY	4A	Speke Junction	8C
Swansea	4B	Widnes	8D
Upper Bank	4C	LONGSIGHT	9A
Abergavenny	4D	Stockport	9B
Tredegar	4E	Macclesfield	9C
Carmarthen	4—	Buxton	9D
Llandovery	4—	SPRING BRANCH	10A
Craven Arms	4—	Preston	10B
Ludlow	4—	Patricroft	10C
Knighton	4—	Pladder Lane	10D
Builth Road	4—	Sutton Oak	10E

CARNFORTH	11A	Normanton	20D
Barrow	11B	Manningham	20E
Oxenholme	11D	Ilkley	20—
Tebay	11E	SKIPTON	20F
Coniston	11—	Hellifield	20G
Lakeside	11—	Keighley	20—
CARLISLE KINGMOOR	12A	Lancaster	20—
Upperby	12B	SALTLEY	21A
Penrith	12C	Bournville	21B
Workington	12D	Bromsgrove	21C
Moor Row	12E	Stratford-on-Avon	21D
Beattock	12F	BRISTOL	22A
Dumfries	12G	Gloucester	22B
Stranraer	12H	Bath and Radstock	22C
Kirkcudbright	12—	Templecombe	22D
Newton Stewart	12—	Highbridge	22E
PLAISTOW	13A	Tewkesbury	22—
Devons Road	13B	Wells	22—
Tilbury	13C	BANK HALL	23A
Shoeburyness	13D	Aintree	23B
Upminster	13E	Southport	23C
CRICKLEWOOD	14A	Wigan	23D
Kentish Town	14B	ACCRINGTON	24A
St. Albans	14C	Rose Grove	24B
WELLINGBOROUGH	15A	Lostock Hall	24C
Kettering	15B	Lower Darwen	24D
Leicester	15C	BLACKPOOL	24E
Bedford	15D	Fleetwood	24F
NOTTINGHAM	16A	WAKEFIELD	25A
Peterborough	16B	Huddersfield	25B
Kirkby	16C	Goole	25C
Mansfield	16D	Mirfield	25D
DERBY	17A	Sowerby Bridge	25E
Burton	17B	Low Moor	25F
Coalville	17C	Farnley Junction	25E
Rowsley	17D	NEWTON HEATH	26A
Overseal	17—	Agecroft	26B
TOTON	18A	Bolton	26C
Westhouses	18B	Bury	26D
Hasland	18C	Bacup	26E
Staveley	18D	Lees	26F
SHEFFIELD	19A	POLMADIE	27A
Millhouses	19B	Greenock Ladyburn	27B
Canklow	19C	Greenock Princes Pier	27—
Heaton Mersey	19D	Hamilton	27C
Belle Vue	19E	MOTHERWELL	28A
Trafford Park	19F	Edinburgh	28B
Northwich	19—	Carstairs	28C
LEEDS	20A	PERTH	29A
Stourton	20B	Crieff	29—
Royston	20C	Aberfeldy	29—

Blair Atholl	29—	Grangemouth	31D
Aberdeen	29B	Dawsholm	31E
Dundee	29C	Dumbarton	31—
Forfar	29D	Yoker	31—
Arbroath	29—	INVERNESS	32A
Brechin	29—	Dingwall	32—
CORKERHILL	30A	Dornoch	32—
Hurlford	30B	Fort George	32—
Beith	30—	Fortrose	32—
Muirkirk	30—	Tain	32—
Ardrossan	30C	Wick	32—
Ayr	30D	Thurso	32—
ST. ROLLOX	31A	Helmsdale	32—
Stirling	31B	Kyle of Lochalsh	32—
Killin	31—	Aviemore	32B
Oban	31C	Forres	32C
Ballachulish	31—	Keith	32—

Well, there they are! Some are still important and others have no longer a railway of any sort. Apparent in the foregoing list is the old system of sub-shedding on more than one railway. Many of the unlettered sheds, and certainly in Scotland, were very small. From one's own recollection, that at Killin had reasonable room for one small Drummond tank engine. The post-LMS Brighton-built 2–6–4T which was its last occupant was a tight fit.

Summary of Named Stanier Locomotives

Princess Royal

NO.	NAME	NO.	NAME
6200	The Princess Royal	6207	Princess Arthur of Connaught
1	Princess Elizabeth	8	Princess Helena Victoria
2	Princess Anne (1952)	9	Princess Beatrice
3	Princess Margaret Rose	6210	Lady Patricia
4	Princess Louise	11	Queen Maud
5	Princess Victoria	12	Duchess of Kent
6	Princess Marie Louise		

Coronation

NO.	NAME	NO.	NAME
6220	Coronation	39	City of Chester
21	Queen Elizabeth	6240	City of Coventry
22	Queen Mary	41	City of Edinburgh
23	Princess Alice	42	City of Glasgow
24	Princess Alexandra	43	City of Lancaster
25	Duchess of Gloucester	44	King George VI
26	Duchess of Norfolk	45	City of London
27	Duchess of Devonshire	46	City of Manchester
28	Duchess of Rutland	47	City of Liverpool
29	Duchess of Hamilton	48	City of Leeds
6230	Duchess of Buccleuch	49	City of Sheffield
31	Duchess of Atholl	6250	City of Lichfield
32	Duchess of Montrose	51	City of Nottingham
33	Duchess of Sutherland	52	City of Leicester
34	Duchess of Abercorn	53	City of St. Albans
35	City of Birmingham	54	City of Stoke-on-Trent
36	City of Bradford	55	City of Hereford
37	City of Bristol	56	Sir William A. Stanier, FRS
38	City of Carlisle	57	City of Salford

Jubilee

NO.	NAME	NO.	NAME
5552	Silver Jubilee	92	Indore
53	Canada	93	Kolhapur
54	Ontario	94	Bhopal
55	Quebec	95	Southern Rhodesia
56	Novia Scotia	96	Bahamas
57	New Brunswick	97	Barbados
58	Manitoba	98	Basutoland
59	British Columbia	99	Bechuanaland
5560	Prince Edward Island	5600	Bermuda
61	Saskatchewan	01	British Guiana
62	Alberta	02	British Honduras
63	Australia	03	Solomon Islands
64	New South Wales	04	Ceylon
65	Victoria	05	Cyprus
66	Queensland	06	Falkland Islands
67	South Australia	07	Fiji
68	Western Australia	08	Gibraltar
69	Tasmania	09	Gilbert and Ellice Islands
5570	New Zealand	5610	Gold Coast/Ghana
71	South Africa	11	Hong Kong
72	Eire	12	Jamaica
73	Newfoundland	13	Kenya
74	India	14	Leeward Islands
75	Madras	15	Malay States
76	Bombay	16	Malta GC
77	Bengal	17	Mauritius
78	United Provinces	18	New Hebrides
79	Punjab	19	Nigeria
5580	Burma	5620	North Borneo
81	Bihar and Orissa	21	Northern Rhodesia
82	Central Provinces	22	Nyasaland
83	Assam	23	Palestine
84	North West Frontier	24	St. Helena
85	Hyderabad	25	Sarawak
86	Mysore	26	Seychelles
87	Baroda	27	Sierra Leone
88	Kashmir	28	Somaliland
89	Gwalior	29	Straits Settlements
5590	Travancore	5630	Swaziland
91	Udaipur	31	Tanganyika

NO.	NAME	NO.	NAME
32	Tonga	74	Duncan
33	Aden	75	Hardy
34	Trinidad	76	Codrington
35	Tobago	77	Beatty
36	Uganda	78	De Robeck
37	Windward Islands	79	Armada
38	Zanzibar	5680	Camperdown
39	Raleigh	81	Aboukir
5640	Frobisher	82	Trafalgar
41	Sandwich	83	Hogue
42	Boscawen	84	Jutland
43	Rodney	85	Barfleur
44	Howe	86	St. Vincent
45	Collingwood	87	Neptune
46	Napier	88	Polyphemus
47	Sturdee	89	Ajax
48	Wemyss	5690	Leander
49	Hawkins	91	Orion
5650	Blake	92	Cyclops
51	Shovell	93	Agamemnon
52	Hawke	94	Bellerophon
53	Barham	95	Minotaur
54	Hood	96	Arethusa
55	Keith	97	Achilles
5656	Cochrane	98	Mars
57	Tyrwhitt	99	Galatea
58	Keyes	5700	Britannia/Amethyst
59	Drake	1	Conqueror
5660	Rooke	2	Colossus
61	Vernon	3	Thunderer
62	Kempenfelt	4	Leviathan
63	Jervis	5	Seahorse
64	Nelson	6	Express
65	Lord Rutherford of Nelson	7	Valiant
66	Cornwallis	8	Resolution
67	Jellicoe	9	Implacable
68	Madden	5710	Irresistible
69	Fisher	11	Courageous
5670	Howard of Effingham	12	Victory
71	Prince Rupert	13	Renown
72	Anson	14	Revenge
73	Keppel	15	Invincible

NO.	NAME	NO.	NAME
16	*Swiftsure*	5730	*Ocean*
17	*Dauntless*	31	*Perseverance*
18	*Dreadnought*	32	*Sanspareil*
19	*Glorious*	33	*Novelty*
5720	*Indomitable*	34	*Meteor*
21	*Impregnable*	35	*Comet*
22	*Defence*	36	*Phoenix*
23	*Fearless*	37	*Atlas*
24	*Warspite*	38	*Samson*
25	*Repulse*	39	*Ulster*
26	*Vindictive*	5740	*Munster*
27	*Inflexible*	41	*Leinster*
28	*Defiance*	42	*Connaught*
29	*Furious*		

Class 5

NO.	NAME
5154	*Lanarkshire Yeomanry*
56	*Ayrshire Yeomanry*
5157	*The Glasgow Highlander*
58	*Glasgow Yeomanry*

Index

Abercorn, Duke of, 207
Aberdeen, a bleak arrival, 151
Abergavenny-Brynmawr Line, 65 *et seq*
Accidents
    Diggle, July 5, 1923, 34
    Euston, April 26, 1924, 35
    Lytham, November 3, 1924, 36
    Wellingborough, MR, 1898, *ff*. 36
    Birmingham, LNWR and MR, 1892, 37
    Munich East, Whit-Monday, 1926: 37, 191
    Darlington, LNER, 1928, 37
    Hope, September 3, 1925, 51
    Llandudno, October 12, 1925, 52
    Fenny Stratford (train and bus),
    December 8, 1925, 52
    Parkgate and Rawmarsh, November 19,
    1926, 53
    Cofton, May 11, 1927, 53
    Charfield, October 13, 1928, 53, 88
    Dinwoodie, October 25, 1928, 53
    Ashchurch, January 8, 1929, 54
    Doe Hill, February 12, 1929, 54
    Explosion of the *Fury*, 78
    Tragi-comedy at Stanmore, *ff*. 83
    Leighton Buzzard, March 22, 1931, 118
    Fleet, SR, 119
    Dagenham Dock, December 18, 1931, 119
    Great Bridgeford, July 17, 1932, 120
    Port Eglinton Junction, September,
    1934, 120
    Winwick Junction, September 28, 1934,
    120
    Kings Langley, March 13, 1935, 122
    Castle Douglas, December 30, 1935, 124
    Oakley, January 21, 1938, 125
    Rutherglen, April 8, 1938, 125
    Indian epidemic, 141, 147
    Harrow, BR, October 8, 1952, 144
    Bihta, EIR, July 17, 1937, 147
    Preston, LNWR, 159
    Slough, GWR, July 2, 1941, 162
    Bletchley, October 13, 1939, 184
    Achterneed, January 13, 1940, 184
    Carr-Bridge, March 5, 1940, 185
    Cleghorn explosion, September 10, 1940,
    186
    Gretna Junction, November 5, 1940, 186
    Wembley, October 14, 1940, 188
    Blackpool (fallen aircraft) August 27,
    1941, 188
    Holmes Chapel, September 14, 1941, 189
    Eccles, December 30, 1941, 189
    Kirkby, April 19, 1945, 189
    Bourne End, September 30, 1945, 190
    Weedon, 1915 and 1951, 191
    Norton Fitzwarren, GWR, 1890 and 1940,
    191

Salisbury, LSWR, 1906, 191
Lichfield, January 1, 1946, 201
Balmuckety Crossing (train and bus)
    July 25, 1946, 201
Pass of Brander, August 8, 1946, 202
Polesworth, July 21, 1947, 202
Manchester Victoria, December 10, 1947,
    202
Adams, J. H., 25
Air Attacks, 174 *et seq*, 212
Aircraft, early, 10, 147 *et seq;* Leonardo da
    Vinci's helicopter, 85; production in
    LMS shops, 178; Mosquito, 183
Alcock, George, 16
Allen, Cecil J., 149
Allen, G. H. Loftus, 47, 51, 130
Anderson, J. E., 136
Announcement, Public, 116
Architectural Review, 165
Argile, T. E., 117
Ashover Light Railway, 137
Aspinall, Sir John, 15; internment of, 17

Bain, David, 40
Baldwin, Stanley, Earl, 42
Ballantyne, J., 116
Barrie, Derek S. M., 47, 149
Beames, H. P. M., Late Crewe designs,
    64 *et seq;* decency in disappointment,
    135; retirement, 141
Beeching, Lord, 31
Beeston, Diesel trials at, 105
Belfast and Northern Counties Railway,
    (NCC), 19, Greenisland Loop, 55, 206;
    general survey, 205-212; signalling, 206 *et*
    seq; North Atlantic Express, 208, 211;
    Leyland rail-car, 208; locomotives, 209 *et*
    seq; air attack on Belfast, 212
Belpaire, Alfred de, 139
Bennett, Enoch Arnold, *The Grim Smile of*
    the Five Towns, 32
Birmingham Railway Carriage and Wagon
    Company, 89
Bishop, J., 17
Boileau, Ethel, *Hippy Buchan*, *ff*. 44
Bond, R. C., 136, 141; looking for spare
    parts by matchlight, 145, 166
Bowen, Cooke, C. J., 67
Braddock, Mrs Bessie, M.P., (the lady
    dances), 193
Brangwyn, Sir Frank, 46
Brennan, Louis, monorail, 32
British Smoke Eliminator Company, 137
British Transport Commission, 193
Buchan, John, (Lord Tweedsmuir), "The
    Gorbals Diehards", 159

Buckley, Driver William, (who died well), 123
Bulleid, Oliver V. S., 136; 147; 197
Burgess, H. G., 37; 39; 73
Burrows, Sir Robert, 196
Burton and Ashby Light Railway, 18
Bussey Coal Distillation Company, "The Glenboig outing", 54
Butterworth, Sir A. Kaye, 31
Byrom, C. R., 40; 105; 108 *et seq*

Camden Town, bridge rebuilt, 34
Cameron, Sir Donald Young, poster design, 47
Cammell Laird, carriages, 89
Canada, Royal Scot tour, 127 *et seq;* Coronation Scot tour, 153 *et seq*
Caprotti, valve gear, 67; 160
Carriages, Follows's travelling office, 39; Stamp's travelling office, 40; "Ro-railer" bus, 84; Pullman cars, 86; Derby methods, 87 *et seq;* last clerestory, 88; first all-steel, 89; sleeping cars, 90, 180; new Royal Scot, 91; Coronation Scot, 148; royal saloons, 164, 181; for war service, 181; Irish, 208
"Cauld Kail", 32
Cawkwell, Sir William, 17
Cellini, Benvenuto, 130
Centenary Celebrations, Stockton and Darlington, 44, 59; Liverpool and Manchester, 44 *et seq*
Chalmers, Walter, 137
Chamberlain, Neville, 177
Chambers, H., 136; 141
Chapelon, André, 146; 197
Cheshire Lines, 18
Claughton, Sir Gilbert, 15
Churchill, Viscount, 135
Churchill, (Sir) Winston, special train, 182
Clarke, Driver, T. J., 149
Closures, an early run of, 55
Clower, W., 51
Coleman, F. C., Editor of *Modern Transport*, 99
Coleman, T. F., 136; 141; 145 *et seq*
Collett, C. B., 134
Constituent Companies, 9 *et seq*
Control, C. T. C. on the Midland, 19; extension of, 115 *et seq*
Corbett, S. P. W., 149
"Coronation Scot", 144 *et seq*
Cortez-Leigh, Colonel F. A., 84
Cox, E. S., 7
Cravens of Sheffield, "Ro-Railer", 85
Cromwell, Oliver, 7; 107
Crova, Cav. Carlo, Italian reforms, 100
Curzon, Lord, of Kedleston, 42

Darbyshire, G. L., 50; 184; 203
Dautry, Raoul, French reforms, 100
Davies, Ashton, 17; 41; 112
Dawes Plan, 39
De Glehn, Alfred-George, 146
Deeley, E. M., 20

Deeley, R. M., 20; 51
Depression, World Trade, 1930, 87 *et seq*
Design, Definitions of, 96
Diesel Traction, converted Bury electric train, 84; see also under Locomotives
Directors, first LMS Board, 33
Dorpmuller, Dr Julius, G. M., German State Railway, 39
Doyle, Sir Arthur Conan, *The Poison Belt*, 16
Du Pont–de Nemours Chemical Group, 38
Dublin and South Eastern Railway, LNWR subsidy, 205
Dublin Port and Docks Board, 37
Dundalk, Newry and Greenore Railway, 19
Drummond, Dugald, 136, anger at "blowing-off", 140
Dunn, J. M., on Beames 0-8-4 tank engines, *ff.* 66

Edge, Selwin F., motor pioneer, 85
Edinburgh, London to, non-stop, 48
Eliot, T. S., paraphrased, 203
Elliot, Sir John, 7; 76; 173
Ellis, Christopher, Canadian broadcaster, *ff.* 127
English Electric Company, Diesel shunting locomotive, 105
Euston Station, London, in 1923; proposed demolition, 101

Fairburn, C. E., 156; 2-6-4T engines, 163
Findlay, Sir George, 17
Follows, J. H., 19; 39; 98
Forbes, Stanhope, 47
Ford, G. N., 41
Foreign railway instances, 10, 39
Fowler, Sir Henry, 51; 60 *et seq;* succession as C.M.E., 69; compound express engines, 70 *et seq;* "Royal Scots", 75; "Baby Scots", 80; 2-6-4T, 81; 2-6-2T, 82; 0-6-0 goods, 83; "Jinties", 83; 0-8-0 goods, 83; dock shunters, 84; diesel train, 84; humiliating order to, 133; vice-presidency, 134
Freight Traffic, Lemon's methods, 98 *et seq;* "fitted freights", 114 *et seq*
Fröhlich rail-brakes, 103

Gairns, J. F., *The Railway Gazette*, 138
Geddes, Sir Auckland, 33
Geddes, Sir Eric, 11
Gee, J. F., 50
George, V., R.I., 157
George, Fireman H., 158
Georgian Group, 101
German State Railway, 10; accident on, 37, 191; 39; Hamm yards, 102
Giesl-Geislingen, 197
Glasgow Orpheus Choir, narrow escape of, 118
Gooch, Sir Daniel, 209
Gore-Browne, Colonel Eric, Chairman, Southern Railway, 196
Granet, Sir William Guy, 9; 20; 4; 38
Grängesberg–Oxelösund Railway, turbine

propulsion, 142
Great Northern Railway (Ireland),
   assassination by Government, 19, 212
Grasete, E. D., 41
Gresley, Sir Nigel, 147
Guy, Sir Henry, 142

Hamel, Gustav, aviator, 10
Harrison, C. S., 184
Hartley, Sir Harold, 51; 134; 184
Hichens, W. L., 89
Hookham, J. A., 26; 68
Horace, an Ode quoted, 204
Horne, L. W., 17
Hotels, "Best" and others, 21
Howard-Williams, see Williams
Hughes, George, C.M.E., 17; Retirement, 69
Hughes, Capt W. H., ship *Scotia*, 172
Hunt, S. H., 39
Hutton, J. W., 203

Illinois Central Railroad, Markham Yards,
   102
Imperial Chemical Industries, 38
India, Pacific Locomotive Committee, 141;
   Wedgwood Committee, 145
Irwin, R. C., 17
Isle of Man Railway, in clover, 10
Ivatt, H. G., 136, 196 *et seq*

Jackson, Sir Herbert, 167
Jackson, Sir Hugh, 7
Johnson, Harry O., Swedish CME, 142
Joint Railways, 18; County Donegal, 29

Karrier Motors, "Ro-Railer", 84
Kay, John A., Editor, *The Railway Gazette*,
   ff. 139
Kipling, Rudyard, "Miss Sichliffe", 82;
   "Ties of Common Funk", 116; "What the
   Mess intended", 148; *In the Presence*, 173
Knox, E. V. ("Evoe"), 47
Knutsford, Lord, public announcement
   suggestion, 116

Lawrence, Lord, 15; 33
Leathers, Lord, Minister of Transport, 178
Leeds Forge Company, carriages, 89
Lemon, Sir Ernest, 7; 84; 96 *et seq;*
   locomotive running reform, 107; war
   service, 183
Lemon, F. A., 136
Lemon, Maj. R. M. L., 7; 183
Lewis, Fireman J., 149
Lincoln, President Abraham, *ff*. 98
Ljungström, turbines, 142
Lloyd George, Earl, sometime
   Prime Minister, 42
Lloyd, Harold, American actor, 106
Locomotives, Midland, 20; Hookham's
   experimental, 26, 68; from 1923 to 1930,
   57 *et seq;* Hughes 4-6-0, 57; painting of,
   58; renaming of *Malta*, 59; compound,

60, 70; Hughes 4-6-4T, 61; Hughes
2-6-0, 61; late Scottish designs, 62;
"Tishies", 64; Beames 0-8-4T, 65;
Caprotti valve-gear, 67, 160; Bowen
Cooke's, 67; Hughes 0-8-0, 69; Somerset
and Dorset, 72, 160; Fowler's class 2
passenger, 72; Beyer–Garratt, 73; crisis,
74; Royal Scot, 75 *et seq; Fury*, 77;
Baby Scots-Patriots, 80, 198; Fowler's
2-6-4T, 81; Fowler's 2-6-2T, 82;
Fowler's 0-6-0, 83; "Jinties" 83; 0-6-0
dock shunters, 84; first diesel shunters,
105; massacre of Glasgow & South
Western, 135; Kitson dock shunters, 137;
chimney designs, 137; 0-4-4T, 138;
Stanier's 2-6-0, 138; first Pacifics, 138; a
whistle recital, 139; Timken bearings, 140;
Great Western Kings, 140; turbine, 142;
Princess Coronation-Duchess, 144 *et seq;*
the *Princess Elizabeth* adventure, 145;
bogies, 146; French, on GWR, 147;
streamlining of, 147, 152; rebuilding the
Royal Scots, 155 *et seq;* Stanier's, for
general service, 156 *et seq;* Great Western
Halls, 159; for war service, 161 *et seq;*
Stanier's tank engines, 163; Armstrong-
Whitworth diesel, 165; English Electric
diesel, 165; some immigrants, 179; last
steam, 197 *et seq;* main-line diesel, 199 *et
seq;* Northern Counties Committee,
Ireland, 209 *et seq*
London & North Eastern Railway, passenger
   accelerations, 110; streamlined
   locomotives, 147
London & South Western Railway,
   "demountable flats", 99
London, Chatham & Dover Railway,
   bankruptcy, 10; "Cramptons", 147

McCormick, Colonel, *Chicago Tribune*, a
   memorable Anglophobe,130
Mais, S. P. B., 76
Malcolm, Bowman, a lifelong C.M.E., 209
"Manifold": *The North Staffordshire Railway*,
   ff. 32
Marshall, C. F. Dendy, *Resistance of Express
   Trains*, 148
Marshalling Yards, mechanisation of, 102
   et seq
Mauldin, Colonel H. H., 103
Metropolitan Carriage, Wagon and Finance
   Company, 89
Metropolitan-Vickers, turbines, 144
Milne, Sir James, G.M. of Great Western,
   135
Ministry of Transport, 11,178
Mitchell, Joseph, Engineer of Highland
   Railway, 41
Moon, Sir Richard, 7
Moore-Brabazon, Colonel J. T. C., sometime
   Minister of Transport, 178
Motors, Rise of, 44; a Press row, 99;
   "Mechanical Horse", 99; some respectable
   bus companies, 131
Mount, Lt. Colonel Sir Alan, 52, 119, 123, 188

NCC, see Belfast and Northern Counties Railway
Named Trains, blossoming of, 47
Nash, George C., *The LMS at War*, 158, 170
Nationalisation (State Ownership), first rumblings, 191; Transport Act, 1947, 193
New Statesman and Nation, 148
Newlands, Alexander, 41
Newns, Fireman Edward, 123
Nobel Industries, Limited, 38
Nock, Oswald S; on Sir William Stanier, 133, ff. 136; on Coronation Scot trial, 149; 160
North, Driver W., 158

Ord, Lewis, Inquiry on freight handling, 98 et seq
Orpen, Sir William: *The Driver*, 47

Paget, Cecil, 19
Pape, F. A., 203
Parke, John F., *Modern Transport*, 170
Passengers, curious types of, 152
Paterson, Murdoch, Engineer of Highland Railway, 14
Pepys, Samuel, sometime Secretary to the Admiralty, 107
Perkins, Thomas R., a dedicated passenger, 160
Pettigrew, W. F., 25
Pickersgill, William; engines for the Oban line, 62
Posters: Apotheosis of, 45
Potter, Stephen, 46
Pringle, Colonel Sir John, 35, 36
Public Announcement, 56
Pullar, Albert, 23

Quirey, J., 39

Railway and Canal Commission, ruling on unremunerative lines, 56
Railway Executive Committee, set up, 169; end of, 193
Railways Act, 1921, 7; 9 et seq; 31 et seq 195
Ramsden Family, on the Furness Railway, 26
Ree, Sir Frank, 47
Reid, Robert W., 39; 51; appointed Vice-President, 96
Reith, Sir John, sometime Minister of Transport, 178
Renard & Krebs, historic aeronauts, 1885, 147
Riddles, R. A., 136; 141; 145; 204
Roberton, Sir Hugh S., eminent conductor, 118
Roosevelt, President Franklin D., "New Deal", 97
"Ro-Railer", 84
"Royal Scot", long non-stop runs, 49; North American tour, 127
Royden, Lord, 194 et seq
Royle, T. W., 7; 41; 117; 203
Rudy, Charles, 85; 130

Rugby, Joint locomotive testing station, 166
Ruskin, John, *Seven Lamps of Architecture*, 200
Russell, Fred V., ff. 103
Rutherford, David, 26

Sabotage, on the LNER, 1926, 43
"Sapper", *Bulldog Drummond*, ff. 44
Schmidt Superheated Steam Company, 77
Shearman, John, 7, 85
"Small Engine Policy", 20
Smith, F. G., 133
Snowblocks, 171
"Soapy Sam", see Wilberforce, the Rt Rev S.
South Eastern & Chatham Railway, Excellence of second class, 208
Speeds, Accelerations of the '30s, 109 et seq, 145 et seq
"Square Deal", 131
Stamp, Lord, 31; origin and rise of, 38; a rude remark from Caithness, 50; habits, 98; reverse side of his economics, 126; exasperation with Locomotive Department, 134; sad end of, 175
"Standard Railroad of the World" (New York Central), 10
Stanier, Sir William, 78, 117; locomotive designs, 132 et seq; loan of GW locomotive, 133; two diplomatic luncheons, 134; C.M.E. of the LMS, 135; first new designs, 138; first Pacific, 138 et seq; Indian missions, 141, 145; turbine locomotive, 142 et seq; "Duchess" Pacifics, 144 et seq; P.Inst.Loco.E, ff. 146; Government appointment, 155; bogies, 156; 4-6-0 and 2-8-0 locomotives, 156; tank locomotives, 163 et seq; P.Inst.Mech.E, 166; F.R.S., 167
Statistics, a recipe for cooking, ff. 196
Steinbeck, John: *The Grapes of Wrath*, ff. 100
Stephenson, George, 166
Stewart, H. P., 210 et seq
Streamlining, 147, 152
Strikes: "Scotch Strike", 12; T.U.C. general strike, 1926, 42; A.S.L.E.F., 1924, 42; Irish, 1933, 210
Sutherland Family, deeds and misdeeds, 24
Sweden, turbine locomotives, 142
Symes, S. J., 136, 145

Taylor, Ernest, 50
Taylor, J. Kenneth, *The Railway Gazette*, 138
Thornton, Sir Henry, ff. 103
Torrens, Major J. A. W., Chairman, NCC, 207
Toton, mechanised marshalling, 103 et seq
Towle, A. E., Controller of Hotels, 111
Tunnels, Chevet replacement, 34
Trams: Burton and Ashby, 18, 43; Wolverton and Stony Stratford, 43
Transport Act, 1947, 193
Trench, Colonel A. C., 187
Trench, Ernest F. C., 17, 202

Urie, David C., 72, 136

Urie, J. C., *ff.* 136

Urie, Robert Wallace, 136

United States of America: New York Central Railroad, 10; mechanised marshalling yards, 102 *et seq*; "Royal Scot" tour, 126 *et seq;* sex-appeal in technical advertising, 140; "Coronation Scot" tour, 153

Vale, Edmund, 76

Van Sant, Robert M., V.P., Baltimore and Ohio Railroad, 154

Victorian Society, 101

Vinci, Leonardo da: mediaeval helicopter design, 85

Wagons, freight; laughing-stock of Europe, 40; transformer carriers, 92

Walker, Sir Herbert, 92

Wallace, Captain Euan, sometime Minister of Transport, 178

Wallace, W. K., Northern Irish locomotives, 209

War, 1939-1945, 169 *et seq;* end of, and aftermath, 193 *et seq*

Watson, Sir Arthur, 16

Watts, Arthur, 47

Webb, F. W., 7

Wedgwood Family, 33

Wells, Herbert G., railway references in books, 32

Wembley, British Empire Exhibitions, 64

Whitelegg, Robert, 27; engine *Lord Glenarthur*, 63; G.M. of Beyer, Peacock and Company, 73

Wilberforce, Rt. Rev. Samuel, 7

Wilde, Oscar, *The Ballad of Reading Gaol*, 157

Wilkinson, Norman, eminent marine painter, 46

Williams, Chief Officer N., ship *Duke of York*, 172

Williams, Sir Thomas, 16

Williams, Howard, G.M., Central Argentine Railway, 16

Wood, Sir William V., 176 *et seq*, 203

Work study, origins, 100

Young Plan, *ff.* 39

Zeppelin, Count Ferdinand von, aircraft designer, 148